Introducing Microsoft® Silverlight™ 2, Second Edition

Laurence Moroney

PUBLISHED BY
Microsoft Press
A Division of Microsoft Corporation
One Microsoft Way
Redmond, Washington 98052-6399

Library of Congress Control Number: 2008920565

Printed and bound in the United States of America.

3 4 5 6 7 8 9   QWT   3 2 1 0 9 8

Distributed in Canada by H.B. Fenn and Company Ltd.

A CIP catalogue record for this book is available from the British Library.

Microsoft Press books are available through booksellers and distributors worldwide. For further information about international editions, contact your local Microsoft Corporation office or contact Microsoft Press International directly at fax (425) 936-7329. Visit our Web site at www.microsoft.com/mspress. Send comments to mspinput@microsoft.com.

Microsoft, Microsoft Press, Access, DirectShow, Expression, Expression Blend, InfoPath, IntelliSense, Internet Explorer, MSDN, Outlook, Silverlight, SQL Server, Visio, Visual Basic, Visual C#, Visual Studio, Win32, Windows, Windows Media, Windows NT, Windows Server, and Windows Vista are either registered trademarks or trademarks of the Microsoft group of companies. Other product and company names mentioned herein may be the trademarks of their respective owners.

The example companies, organizations, products, domain names, e-mail addresses, logos, people, places, and events depicted herein are fictitious. No association with any real company, organization, product, domain name, e-mail address, logo, person, place, or event is intended or should be inferred.

Acquisitions Editor: Ben Ryan
Developmental Editor: Devon Musgrave
Project Editor: Victoria Thulman
Editorial Production: Custom Editorial Productions, Inc.
Technical Reviewer: Umesh Patel; Technical Review services provided by Content Master,
                        a member of CM Group, Ltd
Cover: Tom Draper Design

Body Part No. X14-55515

It isn't easy being the wife or child of a writer. I dedicate this book to my wife Rebecca and my children Claudia and Christopher. I'm sorry for all those just-one-more-minute-until-I-finish-this-part conversations while making you wait for dinner or playing. Thanks, guys; you're the best!

I also want to thank the One who makes it all possible, the God of Abraham, Isaac, Jacob, and Jesus, for giving us life, love, happiness, and hope.

Table of Contents

What do you think of this book? We want to hear from you!

Microsoft is interested in hearing your feedback so we can continually improve our books and learning resources for you. To participate in a brief online survey, please visit:

www.microsoft.com/learning/booksurvey/

Acknowledgments

Thanks to the entire staff at Microsoft Press and Microsoft Learning for putting this book together. Thank you to Victoria Thulman in particular who had to project manage me through this process and to whom I owe a huge debt of gratitude for keeping me honest and on pace.

Introduction

Why Silverlight?

As the Web grows and evolves, so do the expectations of the Web user. When the first Web browser was developed, it was created to provide a relatively simple way to allow hyperlinking between documents. Then these early browsers were coupled with the cross-machine protocols encompassing the Internet, and suddenly documents stored on computer servers anywhere in the world could be hyperlinked to each other.

Over time, the people who were using the Internet changed—the user base expanded from a small group of people associated with universities and computational research to encompass the general population. And what had been an acceptable user interface for experts in the field was greatly lacking for commercial applications. People now want high-quality user interfaces that are simple to use—and as more types of information, including many kinds of media files, are available on the Internet, it becomes more difficult to satisfy users' expectations about how easy it should be to access the information they want.

The need to supply users with sophisticated methods of accessing Internet resources that were easy to use led to advanced application technologies. One type of technology, for example, created "plug-in" browser tools that allowed the browser to use some of the user's local computational horsepower.

ActiveX controls, Java Applets, and Flash applications are examples of plug-in technology. Asynchronous JavaScript and XML (AJAX) is another tool that has been introduced to develop new and exciting user interfaces that benefit from immediate partial updates. Using AJAX, the browser's screen area doesn't flash or lock up since the need for full-page refreshes is reduced.

Although AJAX provides technology to enable developers to build Web sites that contain more complex content and are more dynamic than HTML alone could provide, AJAX does have its limitations. For example, it allows asynchronous communication with the server, which means that applications can update themselves using background threads, eliminating the screen flicker so often seen with complex Web user interfaces. But AJAX is strictly a browser-to-server communications mechanism. It lacks graphics, animation, video, and other capabilities that are necessary to provide for truly multimedia user interfaces.

Microsoft has built a Web user experience (UX) strategy to address these limitations by identifying three levels of desired user experience—"good," "great," and "ultimate," which are mapped to development and run-time technologies. These are combined in this book with a term you may find that I use a lot—"rich" or "richness." When I say "rich," I'm trying to describe a concept that's hard to put into words. It's the feeling you get when you use a traditional Web application, with the limitations built into the browser and HTML, versus a desktop application that has the entire operating system to call on for services and capability. The Web applications of today just don't have the same feeling and capability as desktop applications, and the user generally realizes that they are limited by the technology. With Silverlight (and AJAX), the goal is to create Web applications that are much more like desktop applications, and ultimately, to create applications that are indistinguishable from desktop applications.

The lowest level of user experience, the "good" level, can be achieved with the browser enhanced by AJAX. This level identifies the baseline UX expectation moving forward from today—the type of asynchronous, dynamic, browser application empowered by AJAX.

The top or "ultimate" level is the rich client desktop running Windows Vista and using the Windows Presentation Foundation (WPF) and the .NET Framework. These offer a run time that allows developers to create extremely rich applications that are easily deployed and maintained. Broadcast quality graphics, video, and animation are available at this level, as well as application services such as file-based persistence and integration with other desktop applications. In addition, WPF separates design and development technologies so that user interfaces are designed and expressed in a new language called XML Application Markup Language (XAML). Design tools such as the Microsoft Expression series were aimed at designers who are now able to produce their work as XAML documents. Developers then use the resulting XAML to bring the designers' dreams to reality more easily by activating the XAML with code.

I mentioned that there are three levels in the UX strategy because as AJAX and .NET/WPF evolved, it became obvious that there was room in the middle for a new technology that effectively combines the best of both worlds—the global scalability of the Internet application coupled with the richness of the desktop application. This level was named the "great" experience and represents the browser enhanced by AJAX with a new technology: Silverlight.

Silverlight is a plug-in for the browser that renders XAML and exposes a programming interface. Thus, it allows designers and developers to collaborate when building Internet applications that provide the richness of desktop applications.

The first release of Silverlight exposed a JavaScript-oriented programming model that provided powerful scripting of XAML elements within the browser. Silverlight 2 adds to this greatly by including a .NET runtime that allows you to use .NET programming languages to go beyond this, manipulating XAML, providing a control base, networking support, powerful data libraries, extensibility and greatly improved performance.

In this book, you'll be looking at Silverlight and how to use it to enhance Web user experience.

Silverlight can change the way you think about building applications for the Web. Instead of Web sites, you will build Web experiences. At the heart of a great experience is great design, and with Silverlight, designers and developers can come together like never before through XAML and the Microsoft Expression line of tools.

In this book, my goal is to help you understand the technologies that work together to develop and deploy Silverlight Web applications, from writing basic code that uses Silverlight to using advanced tools to create and deliver Silverlight content. When you have finished reading this book and have worked the examples, you should be ready to use what you've learned to enhance the Web applications you're developing right now. Imagine what you'll be able to do tomorrow!

Who This Book Is For

This book is written for developers who are already working every day to bring new and better Web applications to Internet users and who are interested in adding this cutting-edge Microsoft technology to their store of knowledge—to find out how it can be applied as a tool to bring users more interesting, more capable, and more effective user interfaces. Development managers may also find the easy-to-read style useful for understanding how Silverlight fits into the bigger Microsoft Web technology picture. With luck, this book will provide managers with the technological background they need so that when their developers come to them to talk about Silverlight—with excited looks on their faces—they will understand what the excitement is about!

What This Book Is About

This book is broken into two parts. Part I, *Introducing Silverlight 2*, takes you through the basics of Silverlight. It looks at what Silverlight is and what tools are used to create and maintain Silverlight experiences, including Microsoft Expression Blend and Microsoft Visual Studio.

Part I also looks into the XAML technology and how it uses XML to define your entire user experience, from layout to controls to animation and more. Finally, this part delves into the Silverlight plug-in itself and how it can be used to interface with the browser so that your applications become first-class browser citizens.

Part II, *Programming Silverlight 2*, takes you into some more detail on the high-level concepts of Silverlight 2. It's not an exhaustive reference by any means, but it is designed as a straightforward, no-nonsense introduction to the major things that you'll be doing as a Silverlight developer. You'll take a two-chapter tour of the built-in controls before looking at how easy it is to build your own controls. You'll then look at data, communications, programming for animation, the ASP.NET controls for Silverlight as well as some of the advanced controls for managing media, ink, and the new *DeepZoom* component that provides eye-popping presentation of images. The book wraps up with a look at the exciting new Dynamic Languages support in Silverlight.

System Requirements

To develop Silverlight applications as used in this book, you will need the following (again, available at *http://silverlight.net/GetStarted/*):

- Microsoft Visual Studio 2008
- Microsoft Expression Design
- Microsoft Expression Blend
- Microsoft Silverlight Software Development Kit

For Microsoft Silverlight, the recommended system configuration is 128 MB of RAM and 450 MHz or faster processor on Windows and 1 GB of RAM on Intel 1.83 GHz or faster processor on Mac OSX.

For Microsoft Visual Studio 2008, the recommended configuration is 2.2 GHz or higher CPU, 1024 MB or more RAM, 1280 x 1024 display, 7200 RPM or higher hard disk. (The minimum requirements are 1.6 GHz CPU, 384 MB RAM, 1024 x 768 display, 5400 RPM hard disk.) For Windows Vista, the following is recommended: 2.4 GHz CPU, 768 MB RAM.

The Companion Web Site

This book features a companion Web site that makes available to you all the code used in the book. This code is organized by chapter, and you can download it from the companion site at this address:

http://www.microsoft.com/mspress/companion/9780735625280

Support for This Book

Microsoft Press provides support for books and companion content at the following Web site:

http://www.microsoft.com/learning/support/books/

Find Additional Content Online As new or updated material becomes available that complements your book, it will be posted online on the Microsoft Press Online Developer Tools Web site. The type of material you might find includes updates to book content, articles, links to companion content, errata, sample chapters, and more. This Web site will be available soon at *www.microsoft.com/learning/books/online/developer* and will be updated periodically.

Questions and Comments

If you have comments, questions, or ideas regarding the book or the companion content, or questions that are not answered by visiting the sites just listed, please send them to Microsoft Press via e-mail to:

mspinput@microsoft.com

Or via postal mail to:

Microsoft Press
Attn: Introducing Microsoft Silverlight 2 Editor
One Microsoft Way
Redmond, WA 98052-6399

Please note that Microsoft software product support is not offered through the above addresses.

About the Author

 Laurence Moroney is a Senior Technology Evangelist at Microsoft, focusing on Silverlight and User Experience. He has more than a decade of experience in software design and implementation and has authored about a dozen books on topics as varied as the Windows Presentation Foundation, Web Development, Security, and Interoperability. In addition to this, he has written over 150 articles for various print and online media and has spoken on these topics in conferences around the world. When not working on Silverlight or writing, he also works as a sports journalist covering Major League Soccer, the United States National Men's and Women's teams and the new Seattle Sounders FC. Laurence lives in Sammamish, Washington, with his wife Rebecca and his two children.

Part I
Introducing Silverlight 2

Chapter 1
Introducing Silverlight 2

Silverlight represents the next step toward enriching the user's experience through the technology of the Web. The goal of Silverlight is to bring the same fidelity and quality found in the user interfaces (UIs) associated with desktop applications to Web applications, allowing Web developers and designers to build applications for their clients' specific needs. It is designed to bridge the technology gap between designers and developers by giving them a common format in which to work. This format will be rendered by the browser and will be based on XML, making it easy to template and to generate automatically. The format is XAML—Extensible Application Markup Language.

Before XAML, a Web experience designer would use one set of tools to express a design using familiar technology. The developer would then take what the designer provided and would interpret it using the technology of his or her choice. The design would not necessarily transfer properly or problem-free into development, and the developer would need to make many alterations that could compromise the design. With Silverlight, the designer can use tools that express a design as XAML, and the developer can pick up this XAML, activate it with code, and deploy it.

Microsoft Silverlight is a cross-browser, cross-platform plug-in that was developed to deliver rich media experience and rich interactive Internet applications via the Web. It offers a full programming model that supports AJAX, .NET, and dynamic languages such as Python and Ruby. Silverlight 1.0 is programmable by using actual Web technologies including AJAX, JavaScript, and DHTML. Silverlight 2 adds dynamic and .NET language support, as well as a host of new features that are only possible when using the .NET Framework, such as Isolated Storage, Networking, a rich control set, and more.

The first part of this book will introduce you to the fundamentals of Silverlight 2 by looking at the design and development tools that are available to you, and the second part will examine the programming model more closely.

Silverlight and User Experience

Silverlight is designed to be part of a much larger ecosystem that is used to deliver the best possible end-user experience. There are a number of typical scenarios for accessing information via the Internet:

- Mobile devices
- Digital home products

- Unenhanced browsers (no plug-ins)

- Enhanced browsers (using plug-ins such as Flash, Java, or Silverlight)

- Desktop applications

- Office productivity software

Over the years, users' expectations about how these applications should work have evolved. For example, the *expectation* is that the experience of using an application on a desktop computer should provide more to the user than the same type of application on a mobile device because, as users, we are accustomed to having much more power on the desktop than we do on a mobile device. In addition, many users assume that "because this application is on the Web," it may not have the same capacity level as a similar desktop application. For example, a user may have lower expectations about a Web-based e-mail application because they don't believe it can offer the same e-mail capability that office productivity software such as Microsoft Office Outlook provides.

However, as these platforms are converging, the user's expectations are also increasing—and the term *rich* is now commonly used to describe an experience above the current baseline level of expectation. For example, the term "rich Internet application" was coined in response to the increased level of sophistication that Web users were seeing in applications powered by AJAX to provide a more dynamic experience in scenarios, such as e-mail and mapping. This evolution in expectations has led to customers who now demand ever richer experiences that not only meet the needs of the application in terms of functionality and effectiveness but also address the perception of satisfaction that the user has with a company's products and services. This can lead to a lasting relationship between the user and the company.

As a result, Microsoft has committed to the User Experience (UX) and is shipping the tools and technologies that you as a developer can use to implement rich UX applications. Additionally, they are designed to be coherent—that is, skills in developing UX-focused applications will transfer across the domains of desktop and Web application development. So, if you are building a rich desktop application but need a Web version, then you will have a lot of cross-pollination between the two. Similarly, if you are building a mobile application and need an Internet version, you won't need two sets of skills, two sets of tools, and two sets of developers.

Concentrating on the Web, Figure 1-1 shows the presentation and programming models that are available today. As you can see, the typical browser-based development technologies are CSS/DHTML in the presentation model and JavaScript/AJAX/ASP.NET in the development model. On the desktop, with the .NET Framework 3.x, XAML provides the presentation model, and the framework itself provides the development model. There is an overlap between these, and this is where the Silverlight-enhanced browser provides a "best of both worlds" approach.

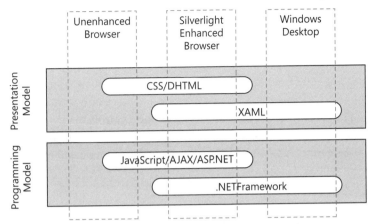

FIGURE 1-1 Programming and presentation models for the Web.

The typical rich interactive application is based on technologies that exist in the unenhanced browser category. The typical desktop application is at the other end of the spectrum, using unrelated technologies. The opportunity to bring these together into a rich application that is lightweight and runs in the browser is realized through the Silverlight-enhanced browser that provides the CSS/DHTML and XAML design model and the JavaScript/AJAX/.NET Framework programming model.

Silverlight achieves this by providing a browser plug-in that enhances the functionality of the browser with the typical technologies that provide rich UIs, such as timeline-based animation, vector graphics, and audiovisual media. These are enabled by the Silverlight browser-based XAML rendering engine. The rich UI may be designed as XAML, and because XAML is an XML-based language and because XML is just text, the application is firewall-compatible and (potentially) search-engine friendly. The browser receives the XAML and renders it.

When combined with technology such as AJAX and JavaScript, this can be a dynamic process—you can download snippets of XAML and add them into your UI, or you can edit, rearrange, or remove XAML that is currently in the render tree using simple JavaScript programming.

Silverlight Architecture

As I mentioned, the core functionality of Silverlight is provided by a browser plug-in that renders XAML and provides a programming model that can be either JavaScript and browser-based or the .NET Framework and CLR-based. The architecture that supports this is shown in Figure 1-2. When scripting the control in the browser, the main programming interface that is exposed in Silverlight 1.0 is via the JavaScript DOM API. This allows you to catch user events that are raised within the application (such as mouse moves or clicks over a specific element) and have code to execute in response to them. You can call methods on the JavaScript DOM for XAML elements in order to manipulate them—allowing, for example, control of media playback or animations to be triggered.

For a richer and more powerful experience, you can also program an application that is rendered by the control using the new .NET Framework CLR. In addition to what you can do in JavaScript, this capability offers many of the namespaces and controls that come as part of the .NET Framework, allowing you to do things that are either very difficult—or not possible—in JavaScript, such as accessing data with ADO.NET and LINQ, communicating with Web Services, building and using custom controls, and so on.

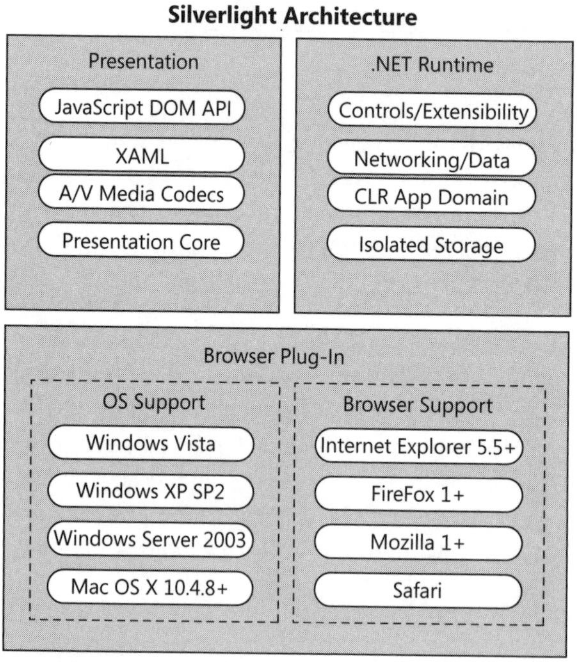

Silverlight Architecture

Presentation	.NET Runtime
JavaScript DOM API	Controls/Extensibility
XAML	Networking/Data
A/V Media Codecs	CLR App Domain
Presentation Core	Isolated Storage

Browser Plug-In

OS Support	Browser Support
Windows Vista	Internet Explorer 5.5+
Windows XP SP2	FireFox 1+
Windows Server 2003	Mozilla 1+
Mac OS X 10.4.8+	Safari

FIGURE 1-2 Silverlight architecture.

Additionally, the presentation runtime ships with the software necessary to allow technologies such as WMV, WMA, and MP3 to be played back in the browser *without* any external dependencies. So, for example, Macintosh users do not need Windows Media Player to play back WMV content—Silverlight is enough. Underpinning the entire presentation runtime is the presentation code, and this manages the overall rendering process. This is all built into the browser plug-in that is designed to support the major browsers available for both Windows and the Macintosh.

The architecture of a simple application running in the browser using Silverlight is shown in Figure 1-3.

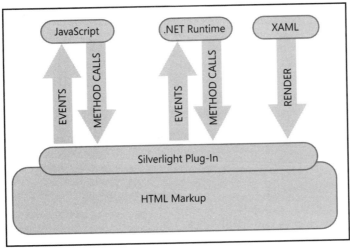

FIGURE 1-3 Application architecture with Silverlight.

As the application runs within the browser, it is typically made up of HTML. This markup contains the calls to instantiate the Silverlight plug-in. As users interact with the Silverlight application, they raise events that can be captured by either JavaScript or .NET Framework functions. In turn, program code can make method calls against the elements within the Silverlight content to manipulate it, add new content, or remove existing content. Finally, XAML can be read by the plug-in and rendered. The XAML itself can exist inline in the page, externally as a static file, or as dynamic XAML returned from a server.

Silverlight and XAML

Now that we've taken a high-level look at the architecture of Silverlight and how a typical application will look, let's examine the base technology that holds the UX together: XAML.

XAML is an XML-based language that is used to define the visual assets of your application. This includes UIs, graphical assets, animations, media, controls, and more. It was introduced by Microsoft for the Windows Presentation Foundation (WPF), formerly Avalon, which is a desktop-oriented technology and part of the .NET Framework 3.0 and beyond. It's designed, as discussed earlier, to bridge the gap between designers and developers when creating applications.

The XAML used in Silverlight differs from that in the WPF in that it is a *subset* that is focused on Web-oriented features. So, if you're familiar with XAML from the WPF, you'll notice some missing tags and functionality, such as the *<Window>* element.

XAML uses XML to define the UI using XML elements. At the root of every Silverlight XAML document is a container element, such as a *Canvas*, that defines the space on which your UI will be drawn. When building a Silverlight Web application, you'll have a root *Canvas* that contains the XML namespace declarations that Silverlight requires.

Here's an example:

```
<Canvas
  xmlns="http://schemas.microsoft.com/client/2007"
  xmlns:x="http://schemas.microsoft.com/winfx/2006/xaml"
  Width="640" Height="480"
  Background="White"
  >
</Canvas>
```

You will notice that two namespaces are declared. The typical XAML document contains a base set of elements and attributes as well as an extended set, which typically uses the *x:* prefix. An example of an extended namespace attribute is the commonly used *x:Name*, which is used to provide a name for a XAML element, allowing you to reference it in your code. The root *Canvas* element declares the namespace location for each of these.

The *Canvas* element is a container. This means that it can contain other elements as children. These elements can themselves be containers for other elements, defining a UI as an XML document tree. So, for example, the following is a simple XAML document containing a *Canvas* that contains a number of children, some of which are *Canvas* containers themselves:

```
<Canvas
  xmlns="http://schemas.microsoft.com/client/2007"
  xmlns:x="http://schemas.microsoft.com/winfx/2006/xaml"
  Width="640" Height="480"
  Background="Black"
  >
    <Rectangle Fill="#FFFFFFFF" Stroke="#FF000000"
        Width="136" Height="80"
        Canvas.Left="120" Canvas.Top="240"/>
    <Canvas>
        <Rectangle Fill="#FFFFFFFF" Stroke="#FF000000"
            Width="104" Height="96"
            Canvas.Left="400" Canvas.Top="320"/>
        <Canvas Width="320" Height="104"
            Canvas.Left="96" Canvas.Top="64">
          <Rectangle Fill="#FFFFFFFF" Stroke="#FF000000"
              Width="120" Height="96"/>
          <Rectangle Fill="#FFFFFFFF" Stroke="#FF000000"
              Width="168" Height="96"
              Canvas.Left="152" Canvas.Top="8"/>
        </Canvas>
    </Canvas>
</Canvas>
```

Here you can see that the root *Canvas* has two children, a *Rectangle* and another *Canvas*. This second *Canvas* also contains a *Rectangle* and a *Canvas*, and the final *Canvas* contains two more *Rectangle*s. This hierarchical structure allows for controls to be grouped together logically and to share common layout and other behaviors.

Silverlight XAML supports a number of shapes that can be combined together to form more complex objects. You'll find a lot more details about using XAML in Chapter 4, "XAML Basics," but a few of the basic shapes available include the following:

- *Rectangle*   Allows you to define a rectangular shape on the screen
- *Ellipse*   Allows you to define an ellipse or circle
- *Line*   Draws a line connecting two points
- *Polygon*   Draws a many-sided shape
- *Polyline*   Draws many line segments
- *Path*   Allows you to create a nonlinear path (like a scribble)

In addition, XAML supports *brushes*, which define how an object is painted on the screen. The inside area of an object is painted using a *fill* brush, and the outline of an object is drawn using a *stroke*. Brushes come in many types, including solid color, gradient, image, and video.

Following is an example using a *SolidColorBrush* to fill an ellipse:

```
<Ellipse Canvas.Top="10" Canvas.Left="24"
        Width="200" Height="150">
    <Ellipse.Fill>
       <SolidColorBrush Color="Black" />
    </Ellipse.Fill>
</Ellipse>
```

In this case, the brush uses one of the 141 Silverlight-supported named colors, *Black*. You also can use standard hexadecimal RGB color notation for custom colors.

Fills and strokes also may have a gradient fill, using a gradient brush. The gradient is defined by using a number of *gradient stops* across a *normalized space*. So, for example, if you want a linear gradient to move from left to right—phasing from black to white through shades of gray—you would define stops according to a normalized line. In this case, consider the beginning of the normalized line as the 0 point and the end as the 1 point. So, a gradient from left to right in a one-dimensional space has a stop at 0 and another at 1. Should you want a gradient that transitions through more than two colors—from black to red to white, for example—you would define a third stop somewhere between 0 and 1. Keep in mind that when you create a fill, however, you are working in a two-dimensional space, so (0,0) represents the upper-left corner, and (1,1) represents the lower-right corner. Thus, to fill a rectangle with a gradient brush, you would use a *LinearGradientBrush* like this:

```
<Rectangle Width="200" Height="150" >
  <Rectangle.Fill>
```

```
<LinearGradientBrush StartPoint="0,0" EndPoint="1,1">
  <LinearGradientBrush.GradientStops>
    <GradientStop Color="Red" Offset="0" />
    <GradientStop Color="Black" Offset="1" />
  </LinearGradientBrush.GradientStops>
</LinearGradientBrush>
  </Rectangle.Fill>
</Rectangle>
```

XAML also supports text through the *TextBlock* element. Control over typical text properties such as content, font type, font size, wrapping, and more are available through attributes. Following is a simple example:

```
<TextBlock TextWrapping="Wrap" Width="100">
  Hello there, how are you?
</TextBlock>
```

Objects can be transformed in XAML using a number of transformations. Some of these include the following:

- ***RotationTransform***   Rotates the element through a defined number of degrees

- ***ScaleTransform***   Used to stretch or shrink an object

- ***SkewTransform***   Skews the object in a defined direction by a defined amount

- ***TranslateTransform***   Moves the object in a direction according to a defined vector

- ***MatrixTransform***   Used to create a mathematical transform that can combine all of the above

Transformations may be grouped so that you can provide a complex transformation by grouping existing ones. That is, you could move an object by translating it, change its size by scaling it, and rotate it simultaneously by grouping the individual transformations together. Here's a transformation example that rotates and scales the canvas:

```
<Canvas.RenderTransform>
  <TransformGroup>
    <RotateTransform Angle="-45" CenterX="50" CenterY="50"/>
    <ScaleTransform ScaleX="1.5" ScaleY="2" />
  </TransformGroup>
</Canvas.RenderTransform>
```

XAML supports animations through defining how their properties are changed over time using a timeline. These timelines are contained within a *storyboard*. Different types of animation include:

- ***DoubleAnimation***   Allows numeric properties, such as those used to determine location, to be animated

- ***ColorAnimation***   Allows colored properties, such as fills, to be transformed

- *PointAnimation* Allows points that define a two-dimensional space to be animated

As you change properties, you can do it in a linear manner, so that the property is phased between values over a timeline, or in a "key frame" manner, in which you would define a number of milestones along which the animation occurs. We'll examine all of this in a lot more detail in Chapter 5, "XAML: Transformation and Animation."

Beyond this basic XAML, you will define your full UIs using controls and layout using XAML, too. These will be explored in more detail in Chapter 7, "Silverlight Controls: Presentation and Layout," and in the rest of the chapters in Part 2 "Programming Silverlight 2."

Silverlight and the Expression Suite

Microsoft has introduced the Expression Suite of tools to provide a robust, modern set of tools for designers to express their work using artifacts that developers can include while developing using the Microsoft Visual Studio tool suite.

There are several tools in the Expression Suite:

- *Expression Web* This is a Web design tool that allows you to use HTML, DHTML, CSS, and other Web standard technologies to design, build, and manage Web applications.

- *Expression Media* This is a media asset management tool that permits you to catalog and organize these assets, including the facility to encode and change encoding between different formats.

- *Expression Encoder* This application is designed to allow you to manage encoding of media assets. It can also be used to bundle media with the relevant code to have a Silverlight media player for it.

- *Expression Design* This is an illustration and graphic design tool that you can use to build graphical elements and assets for Web and desktop application UIs.

- *Expression Blend* This tool is designed to let you build XAML-based UIs and applications for the desktop with WPF or for the Web with Silverlight.

When using Silverlight, you'll use some or all of these applications. In the rest of this chapter, we'll take a look at how Design, Blend, and Encoder enhance your toolkit in designing and building Silverlight applications.

Silverlight and Expression Design

Expression Design is a graphical design tool that allows you to build graphical assets for use in your applications. It's a huge and sophisticated tool, so we will just provide an overview of how it can be used for Silverlight XAML here. Expression Design allows you to blend vector-based and raster-based (bitmap) images for complete flexibility.

It supports many graphical file formats for import, such as:

- Adobe Illustrator—PDF Compatible (*.ai)

- Adobe Photoshop (*.psd)

- Graphical Interchange Format (.gif)

- Portable Network Graphics format (.png)

- Bitmaps (.bmp, .dib, .rle)

- JPEG formats (.jpeg, .jpg, .jpe, .jfif, .exif)

- Windows Media Photos (.wdp, .hdp)

- Tagged Image File Format (.tiff, .tif)

- Icons (.ico)

It supports export of the following image types:

- XAML Silverlight Canvas

- XAML WPF Resource Dictionary

- XAML WPF Canvas

- Adobe Illustrator (.ai)

- Portable Document Format (.pdf)

- Adobe Photoshop (.psd)

- Tagged Image File Format (.tif, .tiff)

- JPEG formats (.jpeg, .jpg)

- Windows Bitmap (.bmp)

- Portable Network Graphics format (.png)

- Graphical Interchange Format (.gif)

- Windows Media Photos (.wdp)

As you can see, Expression Design supports export of graphical assets as XAML files. Later in this chapter, you'll see how to use Expression Design to design the graphical elements of a simple application, and you'll export these as XAML, which you can use in Expression Blend and Visual Studio to create an application.

Figure 1-4 shows the Export XAML dialog box in Expression Design. There are several format options, one of which is XAML Silverlight Canvas (shown selected). This option will format your drawing using the subset of XAML elements that are usable by Silverlight, allowing you to import the resulting XAML into Visual Studio or Expression Blend to build your Silverlight application.

FIGURE 1-4 Exporting XAML from Expression Design.

This will export the content as an XML document containing a *Canvas* element that contains the elements of your design. Here's a (truncated) example:

```
<?xml version="1.0" encoding="utf-8"?>
<Canvas xmlns="http://schemas.microsoft.com/winfx/2006/xaml/presentation"
xmlns:x="http://schemas.microsoft.com/winfx/2006/xaml" x:Name="Document">

  <Canvas x:Name="Layer_1" Width="640.219" Height="480.202" Canvas.Left="0" Canvas.Top="0">
    <Ellipse x:Name="Ellipse" Width="135" Height="161" Canvas.Left="0.546544"
      Canvas.Top="20.3998" Stretch="Fill" StrokeLineJoin="Round" Stroke="#FF000000"
      Fill="#FFFFC800"/>
    <Path x:Name="Path" Width="135.103" Height="66.444" Canvas.Left="-0.555986"
      Canvas.Top="-0.389065" Stretch="Fill" StrokeLineJoin="Round" Stroke="#FF000000"
      Fill="#FF000000" Data="..."/>
    <Path x:Name="Path_0" Width="19.4583" Height="23.9019" Canvas.Left="75.8927"
      Canvas.Top="76.1198" Stretch="Fill" StrokeLineJoin="Round" Stroke="#FF000000"
      Fill="#FF000000" Data="..."/>
    <Path x:Name="Path_1" Width="11.0735" Height="24.0564" Canvas.Left="60.473"
      Canvas.Top="106.4" Stretch="Fill" StrokeLineJoin="Round" Stroke="#FF000000"
      Fill="#FF000000" Data="..."/>
    <Path x:Name="Path_2" Width="76" Height="29.8274" Canvas.Left="31.5465"
      Canvas.Top="127.4" Stretch="Fill" StrokeThickness="7" StrokeLineJoin="Round"
      Stroke="#FF000000" Data="..."/>
    <Path x:Name="Path_3" Width="20.3803" Height="27.1204" Canvas.Left="31.2028"
      Canvas.Top="75.306" Stretch="Fill" StrokeLineJoin="Round" Stroke="#FF000000"
      Fill="#FF000000" Data="..."/>
  </Canvas>
</Canvas>
```

You can then cut and paste this XAML into Expression Blend or Visual Studio, and you will be able to use the graphical element in your application.

Silverlight and Expression Blend

Expression Blend has native support for the creation of Silverlight applications. When you launch Expression Blend and create a new project, you have two options for creating Silverlight projects, as you can see from Figure 1-5.

FIGURE 1-5 Silverlight support in Expression Blend.

The two options for Silverlight projects are:

- **Silverlight 1 Site**   This creates a Silverlight JavaScript project, giving you a folder that contains a simple Web application containing an HTML page that has the requisite scripts to embed a Silverlight object as well as a default XAML document containing a single canvas. It does not contain any of the implementation details for .NET programming, so the descriptive term 1 Site is used, even though the Silverlight control is still version 2. This will likely change in future versions of Expression Blend to Silverlight JavaScript Site. Chapter 6, "The Silverlight Browser Control," will look at programming JavaScript applications in a little more detail.

- **Silverlight 2 Application**   This creates a Silverlight project with everything necessary to program against it using the .NET Framework. There will be more on Silverlight 2 in Chapter 3, "Using Visual Studio with Silverlight 2," and then Part 2 of this book (Chapters 7–14) will cover it in much more detail.

Exploring the Silverlight 1 Site Project

When you create a new Silverlight Script application using Blend, your project will contain a default HTML file that contains all the requisite JavaScript to instantiate the Silverlight control.

In addition, Blend also creates a basic XAML page called Page.xaml and an associated Java-Script file called Page.xaml.js. Expression Blend treats this as a "code-behind" JavaScript file in a manner that is similar to how Visual Studio treats the C# code-behind file associated with an ASPX page. Finally, Blend gives you a copy of the Silverlight.js file that is part of the Silverlight software development kit (SDK). This file manages the instantiation and downloading of the Silverlight plug-in for your users. You can see the project structure in Figure 1-6.

FIGURE 1-6 Project structure for a Silverlight Script application.

The Default Web Page

Listing 1-1 shows the code for the basic Web page that is created for you by Blend for Silver-light projects.

LISTING 1-1 Default.html from Silverlight Template

```
<!DOCTYPE html PUBLIC "-//W3C//DTD XHTML 1.0 Transitional//EN"
"http://www.w3.org/TR/xhtml1/DTD/xhtml1-transitional.dtd">
<!-- saved from url=(0014)about:internet -->
<html xmlns="http://www.w3.org/1999/xhtml">
<head>
  <title>SilverlightSite1</title>

  <script type="text/javascript" src="Silverlight.js"></script>
  <script type="text/javascript" src="Page.xaml.js"></script>
  <style type="text/css">
    #silverlightControlHost {
      height: 480px;
      width: 640px;
    }
    #errorLocation {
      font-size: small;
      color: Gray;
    }
  </style>
  <script type="text/javascript">
  function createSilverlight()
  {
    var scene = new SilverlightSite1.Page();
    Silverlight.createObjectEx({
```

```
        source: "Page.xaml",
        parentElement: document.getElementById("silverlightControlHost"),
          id: "SilverlightControl",
          properties: {
            width: "100%",
            height: "100%",
            version: "1.0"
          },
        events: {
          onLoad: Silverlight.createDelegate(scene, scene.handleLoad),
          onError: function(sender, args) {
            var errorDiv = document.getElementById("errorLocation");
            if (errorDiv != null) {
              var errorText = args.errorType + "- " + args.errorMessage;
              if (args.ErrorType == "ParserError") {
                errorText += "<br>File: " + args.xamlFile;
                errorText += ", line " + args.lineNumber;
                errorText += " character " + args.charPosition;
              }
              else if (args.ErrorType == "RuntimeError") {
                errorText += "<br>line " + args.lineNumber;
                errorText += " character " + args.charPosition;
              }
              errorDiv.innerHTML = errorText;
            }
          }
        });
      }

  if (!window.Silverlight)
    Silverlight = {};
  Silverlight.createDelegate = function(instance, method) {
    return function() {
      return method.apply(instance, arguments);
    }
  }
</script>
</head>

<body>
  <div id="silverlightControlHost">
  <script type="text/javascript">
    createSilverlight();
  </script>
  </div>

  <div id='errorLocation'></div>
</body>
</html>
```

As you can see, it imports two JavaScript files: Silverlight.js and Page.xaml.js. You'll be looking at each of these files shortly.

The Silverlight control instantiation takes place in the *<div>* at the bottom of the page. This contains a call to the *createSilverlight* function, which is implemented at the top of the page. This creates a new Silverlight object using either the *createObjectEx* function (which, in turn, resides in Silverlight.js) or the *createObject* function. When using the *createObjectEx* function, the syntax for specifying the parameters uses the JavaScript Object Notation (JSON) syntax, as shown in this example. You can alternatively use the *createObject* function, which uses standard parameters.

The first parameter is the source XAML. This can be a reference to a static external file (which is used in this case as Page.xaml), a reference to the URL of a service that can generate XAML, or a reference to a named script block on the page that contains XAML.

The second parameter is the parent element. This is the name of the *<div>* that contains the Silverlight control. As you can see in Listing 1-1, this is called *SilverlightControlHost*.

The third parameter is the ID that you want to use for this control. If you have multiple Silverlight controls on a page, you need to have a different ID for each.

The fourth parameter is the property settings for the control properties. These can include simple properties such as width, height, and background color, as well as complex ones. More complex property settings include:

- ***inplaceInstallPrompt***   Determines the install type for Silverlight. If this is set to *true*, the user implicitly accepts the license and directly downloads and installs the plug-in. If it is set to *false*, the user is directed to *http://www.silverlight.net* and, from that site, can accept the license and download the plug-in.

- ***isWindowless***   If set to *true*, the control is considered *windowless*, meaning that you can overlay non-Silverlight content on top of it.

- ***framerate***   Determines the maximum frame rate for animations.

- ***version***   Determines the minimum Silverlight version your application will accept. As you can see in Listing 1-1, the version is listed as 1.0—this isn't a bug, but simply an instruction that this application is backward compatible and should work on 1.0. If this was instead 2.0, and Silverlight 2 was not installed, then the user would be taken to the install experience for Silverlight 2.

The fifth parameter is used to map events to event handlers. The events are implemented in a JavaScript class called *scene,* which was declared at the top of the function:

```
var scene = new SilverlightSite1.Page();
```

The *createSilverlight* function declares that the *onLoad* event should be handled by a member function of the *scene* class called *scene.handleLoad*. It does this by creating a delegate using this syntax:

```
onLoad: Silverlight.createDelegate(scene, scene.handleLoad)
```

This class is implemented in the JavaScript code-behind for Page.xaml called Page.xaml.js. You can see this in Listing 1-2.

LISTING 1-2 JavaScript Code-Behind Page.xaml

```
if (!window.SilverlightSite1)
  SilverlightSite1 = {};

SilverlightSite1.Page = function()
{
}

SilverlightSite1.Page.prototype =
{
  handleLoad: function(control, userContext, rootElement)
  {
    this.control = control;

    // Sample event hookup:
    rootElement.addEventListener("MouseLeftButtonDown",
        Silverlight.createDelegate(this, this.handleMouseDown));
  },

  // Sample event handler
  handleMouseDown: function(sender, eventArgs)
  {
    // The following line of code shows how to find an element by name
this.control.content.findName("Storyboard1").Begin();
  }
}
```

Here you can see JavaScript code to create a class called *SilverlightSite1.Page*. It contains two member functions, *handleLoad* and *handleMouseDown*.

The function *handleLoad* adds another event listener for the *MouseLeftButtonDown* event by creating a delegate associating this event and the *handleMouseDown* function, which is also defined within this JavaScript.

Thus, the template application creates a default HTML file that contains an instance of Silverlight with a single canvas that fires an event when it loads. The load event wires up the mouse down event, demonstrating that event declaration, delegation, and handling are available at both design time and run time.

Silverlight and Expression Encoder

Expression Encoder is an application that allows you to encode, enhance, and publish your video content using Silverlight. It comes with a UI that is consistent with the rest of the Expression suite or with a command-line interface that can be used for batch work. You can see Expression Encoder in Figure 1-7.

FIGURE 1-7 Expression Encoder.

Expression Encoder allows you to import video from any format for which a DirectShow filter is available and installed in your system. It will then re-encode the video into a VC-1–capable WMV using one of a number of preset profiles optimized for the delivery client. These include settings for devices, as well as for streaming or on-demand content delivered over the Internet.

You aren't limited to what the preset profiles give you—you can override any of the video and audio encoding settings. Figure 1-8 (on page 20) shows an example of how a video encoding may be tweaked.

Media Encoder includes a number of preset media player applications for Silverlight. These will "wrap up" your video with a Silverlight JavaScript-based application that can be used on any Web server to provide a complete Silverlight-based viewing experience.

In addition to encoding, metadata can be added to your video. A classic metadata experience is when tags are encoded into the video and the application then reacts to these tags. Inserting tags with Expression Encoder is very simple. Simply drag the playhead to the desired point, select Add Marker, and enter the appropriate information for the marker.

FIGURE 1-8 Configuring a video encoding profile.

You can see this in Figure 1-9 on the right side of the screen, where the marker time and type of ball that is shown on the screen at that time has been configured.

FIGURE 1-9 Adding Markers to a stream.

The Output tab allows you to select the template player that you want to use.

Figure 1-10 shows where the template that matches the Expression product line has been selected. To create a video player with this template, simply import a video, and press the Encode Button with this template selected.

FIGURE 1-10 Using Encoder to build a Silverlight media player.

After you've done this, you'll get a full-featured media player in Silverlight for your video content. You can see an example of a Silverlight media player in Figure 1-11.

This section just scratches the surface of what is possible with Expression Encoder and how it can be used with Silverlight. For more details, please refer to *http://www.microsoft.com/expression*.

FIGURE 1-11 Media player generated by Expression Encoder.

Summary

In this chapter, you were introduced to Silverlight 2 and learned how it fits into the overall Web and UX landscape. You discovered how technology from Microsoft is applied to current UX scenarios, and you were introduced to an overview of the Silverlight architecture, including XAML and how it is used to implement rich UIs.

Additionally, you saw how the Microsoft Expression Suite is designed to complement traditional development tools such as Visual Studio for creating Silverlight applications. You specifically learned how Expression Design is used to build graphical assets and how Expression Blend is used to link these together into an interactive application as well as using Expression Encoder to manage your video assets.

Now it's time to go deeper. In the next few chapters, you'll learn more about the Silverlight API, starting with a more detailed examination of Expression Blend and how it is used by Silverlight in the next chapter.

Chapter 2
Using Expression Blend with Silverlight 2

Expression Blend is a professional design tool intended to create engaging experiences for Windows and the Web. It allows you to blend all the necessary design elements for your Web experiences, including video, vector art, text, animation, images, and other content such as controls, with one set of tools. Expression Blend is designed to aid you in the building of Windows-based as well as Web-based applications. This chapter will introduce you to this tool, giving you a tour of what is possible with it. Expression Blend has far too many aspects to cover in one chapter, but by the end of this chapter, you'll have a good grasp of the basics and will be ready to delve further into the features of this wonderful tool on your own!

Getting Started with Expression Blend

Expression Blend is available as part of the Microsoft Expression suite. Details are available at *http://www.microsoft.com/expression*.

After you've downloaded and installed Expression Blend, launch it from the Start menu. You'll see the Blend integrated development environment (IDE), as shown in Figure 2-1.

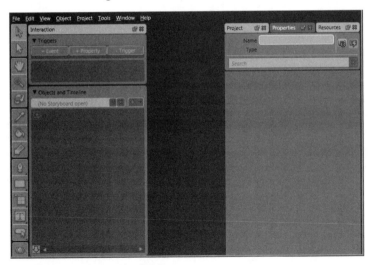

FIGURE 2-1 Expression Blend IDE.

To create a new application, select New Project from the File menu to open the New Project dialog box, as shown in Figure 2-2.

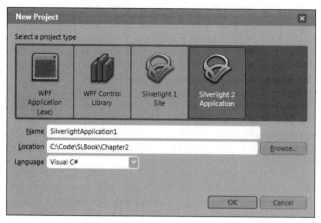

FIGURE 2-2 New Project dialog box options in Expression Blend.

The options that you are given are:

- **WPF Application (.exe)**   This option creates a client-executable application built on the Windows Presentation Foundation (WPF); this type of project is a *Windows Only* application.

- **WPF Control Library**   This option creates a DLL file that may be used for shared controls across WPF applications; this type of project is a *Windows Only* application.

- **Silverlight 1 Site**   This option creates a Web site that uses the Silverlight control. It contains the basic JavaScript components to instantiate a Silverlight control as well as a sample XAML document with JavaScript-based event handlers, and it was covered in Chapter 1, "Introducing Silverlight 2." This option creates a *Web*-based and therefore *multiplatform* application.

- **Silverlight 2 Application**   This option creates a Silverlight application based on the Silverlight 2 runtime. This application includes the .NET Framework runtime that supports your .NET-based applications, allowing them to run in a browser. When you select this type of project, you'll be able to pick your preferred programming language (either Microsoft Visual Basic or Microsoft Visual C#). This option also creates a *Web*-based and therefore *multiplatform* application.

Chapter 1 gave you some details about the Silverlight 1 Site template, and you can refer back to that chapter for more information about this option. For the rest of this chapter, we'll be focusing on the Silverlight 2 Application template.

Creating a Silverlight 2 Application

Open the New Project dialog box to create a Silverlight 2 application, and name your new project TestApp. Expression Blend will create a new project for you that contains everything you need for a Silverlight 2 .NET application.

You can see the project structure that it creates in Figure 2-3. This is identical to the product structure that is built by Visual Studio, which will be discussed in much more detail in Chapter 3, "Using Visual Studio with Silverlight 2."

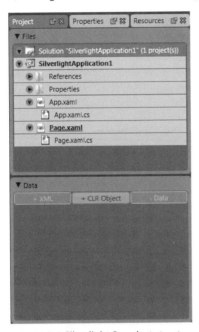

FIGURE 2-3 Silverlight 2 project structure.

What's important to note about the structure is that there are two XAML files in this application, and neither of them are a Silverlight XAML page, as in Silverlight 1. This is one way in which a Silverlight 2 Application project differs fundamentally from a Silverlight 1 Site project.

The Default *Page*

Silverlight 2 deals with your XAML as a *Page*. Thus, the template creates your default application XAML content as a file named Page.xaml. You'll see that the root of this, not surprisingly, is a *UserControl* and not a *Canvas*, as you may have been familiar with from Silverlight 1.

Following is the XAML for the default Page.xaml:

```
<UserControl
        xmlns="http://schemas.microsoft.com/client/2007"
        xmlns:x="http://schemas.microsoft.com/winfx/2006/xaml"
        xmlns:d="http://schemas.microsoft.com/expression/blend/2008"
        xmlns:mc="http://schemas.openxmlformats.org/markup-compatibility/2006"
        mc:Ignorable="d"
        x:Class="TestApp.UserControl1"
        d:DesignWidth="640" d:DesignHeight="480">

        <Grid x:Name="LayoutRoot" Background="White" />
</UserControl>
```

Note the use of *<UserControl>* to host the content.

You'll see a small difference between this XAML and that created by Microsoft Visual Studio (in Chapter 3). For example, this XAML has a few extra namespace declarations. Blend uses these for parsing the XAML to render in the designer. They don't affect your design beyond that, and you can safely ignore these.

You'll see that UserControl1 has a code-behind file that is generated for you. This will be named UserControl1.xaml.cs or UserControl1.xaml.vb, depending on which language you selected when creating the project. The file contains the basic code required to construct the *UserControl*. You can see it here:

```
using System;
using System.Windows;
using System.Windows.Controls;
using System.Windows.Documents;
using System.Windows.Ink;
using System.Windows.Input;
using System.Windows.Media;
using System.Windows.Media.Animation;
using System.Windows.Shapes;

namespace TestApp
{
  public partial class UserControl1 : UserControl
  {
    public UserControl1()
    {
      // Required to initialize variables
      InitializeComponent();
    }
  }
}
```

You aren't *restricted* to using this file for your application logic. You can, of course, create other .cs (or .vb) files that can contain shared logic, but this one will be launched whenever the control is instantiated by the Silverlight runtime.

The Default App.xaml and Code-Behind Files

App.xaml and App.xaml.cs define the startup conditions for your application. These will be the first things loaded and executed by Silverlight on startup and the last things closed when the application is shut down.

This is accomplished using the *OnStartup* and *OnExit* events. These are set up for you by the project template. Note that UserControl1 does not render by default—it has to be instructed to render as part of the applications startup. This is accomplished in the *OnStartup* event handler, where the *RootVisual* for the application is set to an instance of *UserControl1:*

```
public App()
{
  this.Startup += this.OnStartup;
  this.Exit += this.OnExit;
  InitializeComponent();
}

private void OnStartup(object sender, StartupEventArgs e)
{
  // Load the main control here
  this.RootVisual = new Page();
}

private void OnExit(object sender, EventArgs e)
{
}
```

App.xaml does not support visual elements directly, so you cannot add controls or other visual elements directly. Just because it is XAML, don't think of it as a design surface. In this case, XAML is used for definition purposes only. For example, you can define application-specific resources for your application using it.

App.xaml.cs is useful for initialization of data that you want to use across several user controls. Keep this in mind as you design your application. For example, you could store some text that could be used across your application by declaring it as a resource in your App.xaml:

```
<Application
  xmlns="http://schemas.microsoft.com/client/2007"
  xmlns:x="http://schemas.microsoft.com/winfx/2006/xaml"
  x:Class="TestApp.App">
    <Application.Resources>
        <TextBlock x:Key="txtResource" Text="Hello"></TextBlock>
    </Application.Resources>
</Application>
```

You can now easily access this content from any control in your application as follows:

```
TextBlock t = (TextBlock)Application.Current.Resources["txtResource"];
string strTest = t.Text;
```

Executing the Application

One thing that you may see is *missing* if you are sharp-eyed is a page to host the Silverlight control. Don't worry! Blend will automatically generate one for you. You'll see this when you launch the application.

Before going any further, add a simple *TextBlock* to your *UserControl* to render some text. Here's an example:

```
<UserControl
  xmlns="http://schemas.microsoft.com/client/2007"
  xmlns:x="http://schemas.microsoft.com/winfx/2006/xaml"
  xmlns:d="http://schemas.microsoft.com/expression/blend/2008"
  xmlns:mc="http://schemas.openxmlformats.org/markup-compatibility/2006"
  mc:Ignorable="d"
  x:Class="TestApp.UserControl1"
  d:DesignWidth="640" d:DesignHeight="480">

  <Grid x:Name="LayoutRoot" Background="White" >
    <TextBlock Text="Hello"/>
  </Grid>
</UserControl>
```

Now if you execute the application, you'll see something like the output shown in Figure 2-4.

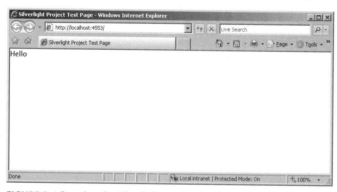

FIGURE 2-4 Running the Silverlight application from Blend.

This simple application runs using the Cassini Web server (hence the random port number, 55924, that you can see in the address box in Figure 2-4) by generating an HTML page to host the Silverlight content.

Let's take a look at the source code for this page by using the browser command View Source. You can see the source code here:

```
<!DOCTYPE html PUBLIC "-//W3C//DTD XHTML 1.0 Transitional//EN"
"http://www.w3.org/TR/xhtml1/DTD/xhtml1-transitional.dtd">
<html xmlns="http://www.w3.org/1999/xhtml" >
<head>
```

```
<title>Silverlight Project Test Page </title>

<style type="text/css">
html, body {
 height: 100%;
 overflow: auto;
}
body {
 padding: 0;
 margin: 0;
}
#silverlightControlHost {
 height: 100%;
}
</style>

<script type="text/javascript">
  function onSilverlightError(sender, args) {
    if (args.errorType == "InitializeError")  {
      var errorDiv = document.getElementById("errorLocation");
      if (errorDiv != null)
        errorDiv.innerHTML = args.errorType + "- " + args.errorMessage;
    }
  }
</script>
</head>

<body>
    <div id='errorLocation' style="font-size: small;color: Gray;"></div>

    <div id="silverlightControlHost">
    <object data="data:application/x-silverlight,"
    type="application/x-silverlight-2-b1" width="100%" height="100%">
      <param name="source" value="TestApp.xap"/>
      <param name="onerror" value="onSilverlightError" />
      <param name="background" value="white" />

      <a href="…"
        style="text-decoration: none;">
      <img src="…"
        alt="Get Microsoft Silverlight" style="border-style: none"/>
      </a>
    </object>
    <iframe style='visibility:hidden;height:0;width:0;border:0px'></iframe>
    </div>
</body>
</html>
```

Do take note of the *<object>* tag. This attempts to instantiate Silverlight, and should it fail, it renders an image with a hypertext reference (HREF) to the Silverlight download in its place. You'll see more about this and other ways of instantiating the Silverlight object in Chapter 6, "The Silverlight Browser Control."

The Expression Blend IDE

Expression Blend offers a flexible IDE that is designed to maximize the amount of information on the screen while keeping it easy for the user to understand what is going on and not be overwhelmed.

The IDE has two main application workspace layouts: the Design workspace, which is used primarily for constructing and customizing your user interface (UI), and the Application workspace, which is used primarily for designing your timeline-based animations. You can switch between the workspaces using the F6 key or by selecting the workspace you want from the Active Workspace options on the Window menu.

The screen is divided into *panes* in the Expression Blend IDE, and each of the panes has a fixed purpose, as you'll discover when we tour them now.

The Tools Pane

The tools pane is on the far left side of the screen. It contains *tools*, such as Paint or Clip, that can be used to manipulate any object; *visual elements*, such as a *Rectangle* or *Ellipse*; *layout elements*, such as the *StackPanel* or *Canvas;* and *controls*, such as *Button* or *TextBox*). You can see the tools pane in Figure 2-5.

FIGURE 2-5 Expression Blend tools pane.

In Blend, similar tools can be collected together into a single icon on this tool pane. If you look at Figure 2-5, you can see how to view a set of similar tools by finding the white triangle in the lower-right corner of the tool. When this triangle is present, you can hold down the mouse button on that tool to find more members in the same "family" as the selected object. So, for example, if you hold down the mouse on the Rectangle tool, you'll see a pop-up box that shows you the other available shapes, as you can see in Figure 2-6.

FIGURE 2-6 Grouped tools.

One nice shortcut that Blend provides is the way it creates a default tool on the toolbar when you have used a tool from the family of tools. That is, the tool that you just used will be displayed on the toolbar, so you don't need to hold down the mouse, wait for the menu, and then select the tool again to use it the next time.

So, for example, in Figure 2-6, the *Rectangle* is displayed on the toolbar, and when you hold down the mouse, you will see a box displaying the other visual element tools of this type that are available. If you then select the *Ellipse* and draw with it on the design surface, the toolbar will change to display the *Ellipse* instead of the *Rectangle*.

The Interaction Pane

The interaction pane, shown in Figure 2-7 and usually located just to the right of the tools pane, is designed to help you with the following tasks:

- View all of the objects on your design surface, including their hierarchy when you are using container objects.

- Select objects so you can modify them. This isn't always possible on the design surface because objects can be placed off screen or behind other objects.

- Create and modify animation timelines. You'll learn more about how to do this in the section titled "Using Blend to Design Animations" later in this chapter.

The interaction pane is designed to have two separate highlights. The currently selected object is highlighted in grey—in Figure 2-7, you can see that the *Border* control is highlighted in grey. This is the object that you can currently amend with the properties window or by dragging it around the design surface.

Although it appears grey in the figure, you can see on your screen that the *LayoutRoot* control has a yellow border around it. On the design surface, you'll also see this yellow border. This indicates that this is the currently selected container.

In addition to manipulating objects, you also use the interaction pane to create animations and storyboards. You do this by clicking on the plus sign (+) button at the top of the interaction pane. You'll explore the ways you can use this to create animations in the section titled "Using Blend to Design Animations" later in this chapter.

FIGURE 2-7 Interaction pane.

The Design Surface

The design surface is the main pane in the Expression Blend IDE screen, and this is where you can manipulate all the objects visually or by amending their underlying XAML code directly.

On the right side of the design pane, you will see three tabs:

- The Design tab gives you the pure design surface.

- The XAML tab gives you the XAML editing Window.

- The Split tab provides you with a split window—one half in design view and the other half in XAML view.

You can see the design pane in split view in Figure 2-8.

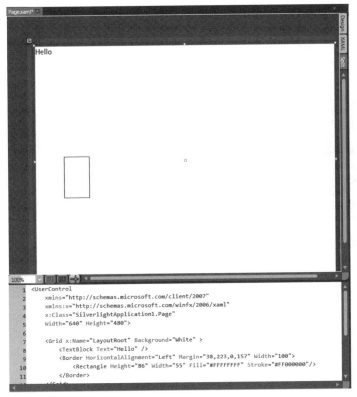

```
1  <UserControl
2      xmlns="http://schemas.microsoft.com/client/2007"
3      xmlns:x="http://schemas.microsoft.com/winfx/2006/xaml"
4      x:Class="SilverlightApplication1.Page"
5      Width="640" Height="480">
6
7      <Grid x:Name="LayoutRoot" Background="White" >
8          <TextBlock Text="Hello" />
9          <Border HorizontalAlignment="Left" Margin="38,223,0,157" Width="100">
10             <Rectangle Height="86" Width="55" Fill="#FFFFFFFF" Stroke="#FF000000"/>
11         </Border>
```

FIGURE 2-8 Design pane in split view.

Note that you can use the Zoom feature in design view, so when you are working on sophisti-cated interfaces, you can zoom in for a detailed view and zoom out for an overview. You do this using the Zoom tool at the lower-left corner of the design pane. You can drop it down to select preset zoom settings, type the specific value you want in the box provided, or drag the mouse within it to set the desired zoom level.

The Project Pane

The project pane (shown in Figure 2-9) is used to manage the files in your project. The impor-tant thing to note in this pane is the use of context menus. Depending on *where* you right-click in this pane, you'll get a different (and appropriate) context menu. You might be familiar with context menus that provide commands for a specific pane, but in this case, you'll get dif-ferent menus when you right-click the solution, the project, the References folder, and so on in the project pane.

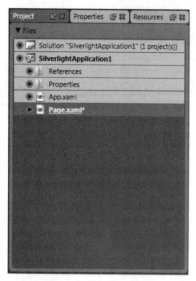

FIGURE 2-9 Project pane.

A *solution* is a collection of one or more projects. When you edit a solution, you can manage everything to do with the solution itself, including building, debugging, cleaning, and managing individual projects. In Figure 2-9, you can see the solution TestApp listed at the top of the project pane, and the pane indicates that there is one project within the solution.

A *project* is a collection of items that, when combined, make up an application that contains one or more Silverlight *Pages*. The project definition contains all the references to external components that this application needs within the References folder. When you right-click the project, the context menu that displays for the project allows you to manipulate the contents of the project, with options such as adding new items based on a template, adding existing items from other projects, or deleting items from the project.

The *References* folder within the project is used to manage references to precompiled assemblies that contain information that you want to use in your project. For example, if you want to use a custom control, it will be compiled into an assembly, so if you reference that assembly in your references, you can then use it within your application.

The *Properties* folder contains the application manifest file that describes all the properties of the project, including the list of references, so that the application can understand from where they are loaded at run time. The Properties folder should not be confused with the properties pane, indicated by the Properties tab at the top of the window shown in Figure 2-9 and explained in more detail in the following section.

The Properties Pane

The properties pane is used to manage all the visual aspects of a particular element. Since XAML elements have many configurable properties, this pane gives you two very useful shortcuts.

The first shortcut is provided by the division of the properties pane into several classifications, typically providing access to the following visual aspects of elements:

- **Brushes**   Allow you to set fill and stroke options as well as use an opacity mask on your element. You'll see a lot more detail about how brushes are used in Chapter 4, "XAML Basics."

- **Appearance**   Allows you to set extended appearance properties for your object. Note that the available appearance properties will change drastically based on the object that you are currently editing. So, for example, if you are editing a *Rectangle* element, the Appearance section of the properties pane will allow you to set things like the corner radii, but if you are editing a *Button* element that doesn't have corner radii, you will not have this option available.

- **Layout**   Allows you to edit the various layout options for your object, such as Width, Height, and Alignment options. You can also use layout options to change the position of an object within a grid—if the layout is on a grid.

- **Common Properties**   Effectively the properties that are common across a *type* of object. So, for example, the common properties for controls that are distinct from shapes are typically edited here. These options can be very difficult to use, depending on the object that you are editing. For example, if you are editing a control, a common property will be its tab index, but if you are editing a shape, the tab index will not be available.

- **Transform**   Provides you with the ability to edit the *RenderTransform* of your object. This defines how the object can be manipulated by the rendering system. Transformations are covered in detail in Chapter 5, "XAML: Transformation and Animation."

- **Miscellaneous**   The catch-all location for properties that aren't available on any of the other classifications.

Do take note that these classification panes are further subdivided. You'll notice that many of them have an arrow at the bottom of the pane that can be used to expand and contract the properties view. This allows you to hide lesser-used properties until you need them.

The second shortcut in the properties pane is its Search feature, which allows you to search for a particular property. For example, if you know you want to edit some features of a font but don't know the name of the property itself, you can type **font** into the search engine, and the classifications and available properties will be filtered so that only those that have to do with fonts are displayed. This is done immediately upon a keystroke, so if you are searching for a font property—in our example, as soon as you type **fo**—you will see available properties displayed such as **fo**_reground_ and _rendertrans**form**_ as well as the font properties, as shown in the list of properties displayed at the bottom of Figure 2-10.

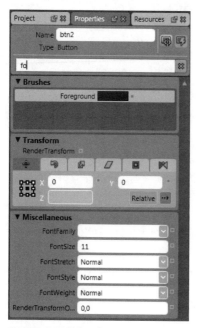

FIGURE 2-10 Using the properties pane.

Now let's take a look at how you can use all these tools we've introduced to build Silverlight applications.

Using Blend to Build Silverlight Applications

The main design-oriented functions that you can use Blend to accomplish as you put together your application include the following:

- Organizing the layout
- Placing and customizing visual elements
- Placing and customizing controls
- Designing animations

You'll explore each of these functions of Blend in the rest of this chapter.

Layout

In Silverlight, you use special tools to create and organize the layout of your application. There are several options available to you, and we will look at each of them in turn.

Using a Grid

The Grid layout element allows you to lay elements out in a structure that looks like a table. (Do not confuse the Grid layout element with a *Grid* control that gives you functionality similar to a spreadsheet.) When using a Grid layout tool, you can specify how your elements are placed by indicating their coordinates with virtual row and column designations within the Grid layout. For example, consider the following XAML:

```
<Grid x:Name="LayoutRoot" Background="White" >
  <Button Height="38" Margin="104,72,0,0" Width="58" Content="Button"/>
  <Button Height="24" Margin="210,72,0,0" Width="54" Content="Button"/>
  <Button Height="49" Margin="0,96,158,0" Width="80" Content="Button"/>
  <Button Height="54" Margin="297,185,270,0" Width="67" Content="Button"/>
  <Button Height="33" Margin="104,217,0,213" Width="87" Content="Button"/>
</Grid>
```

When rendered, this will appear as shown in Figure 2-11.

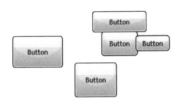

FIGURE 2-11 Random buttons.

Now, if you wanted to organize these buttons, you could carefully set their positions by dragging them around the design surface to place them at roughly the positions where you want them, but if you position them this way, you will need to zoom in to make sure pixels are aligned.

Alternatively, you could use the Grid layout, where you can use the layout properties of the button to determine its location in the grid. If you start with a new Silverlight project, you'll see that it has a Grid layout element on it called *LayoutRoot*. Select this element in your project, and look at the Layout properties associated with it. Expand the properties viewer until you see the settings for the ColumnDefinitions and RowDefinitions, as shown in Figure 2-12.

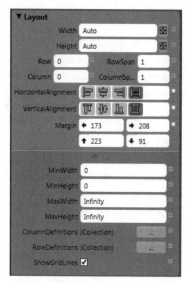

FIGURE 2-12 Layout editor for a grid.

Because ColumnDefinitions and RowDefinitions are collections, each one has an ellipsis (...) button to the right of the setting name. This indicates that another dialog box will open when you click it. Select the button next to the ColumnDefinitions property setting, and the ColumnDefinition collection editor will display, as shown in Figure 2-13.

FIGURE 2-13 ColumnDefinition collection editor.

Use this dialog box to add, remove, and manage columns. Click the Add Another Item button three times to add three columns. Repeat this for the RowDefinitions property setting so that you have a grid that is comprised of three rows and three columns. After you have made these changes to ColumnDefinitions and RowDefinitions, you will see that the designer pane displays a 3 × 3 layout grid, as you can see in Figure 2-14.

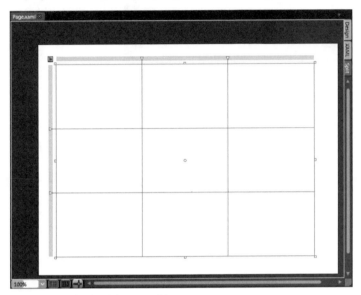

FIGURE 2-14 The 3 × 3 Layout grid.

Now, whenever you are placing an element on the screen, you'll see pink guidelines that show you how you can snap to a particular grid element, as shown in Figure 2-15. (They appear as wider grey lines in the figure.) Snapping the button to the grid and column layout like this will ensure that the button is always at that relative position and size in the grid.

Place another button in the central square on the grid, as shown in Figure 2-15. This time, do not snap it to the grid. Then run the application and experiment with resizing the window. You'll see that the first button will always remain at the same relative position and the same size, but the second button will change its width and/or height to stay relative to the size of the screen.

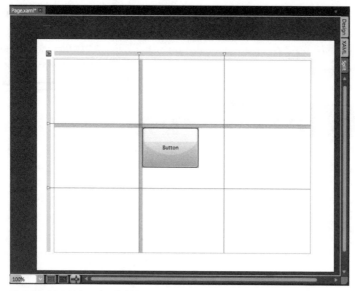

FIGURE 2-15 Using the Grid layout.

Using *Canvas*

The *Canvas* layout is a completely free-format drawing surface. You can specify the desired location for a control by setting its *Canvas.Top* and *Canvas.Left* properties or by using its *Margin* property.

So, for example, consider the following XAML:

```
<Canvas Height="261" Width="439">
  <Button Height="101" Width="110" Canvas.Left="101" Canvas.Top="82.5" Content="Button"/>
</Canvas>
```

You will see that the *Canvas.Top* and *Canvas.Left* properties for the button have been set. These indicate that the button will always be at those values *relative* to the parent *Canvas*, so as the *Canvas* moves, the button will move also. The *Canvas* layout is covered in more detail in Chapter 4.

Using *StackPanel*

The *StackPanel* layout will always orient its child controls either horizontally or vertically, stacking them (hence the name) based on the *Orientation* property. Note that the panel will override the positioning of the controls. For example, look at the following XAML:

```
<StackPanel Height="337" Width="224">
  <Button Canvas.Top="100" Height="64" Width="98"

    Orientation="Vertical" Content="Button"/>
  <Button Height="85" Width="92" Content="Button"/>
```

```
    <Button Height="48" Width="205" Content="Button"/>
</StackPanel>
```

You can see that the first button has its *Canvas.Top* property set to 100. You would expect that this would mean that the control would then be drawn at that position, but as Figure 2-16 shows, this is not the case, and it is stacked by the *StackPanel* layout at the top of the *StackPanel* (because the *StackPanel* has its *Orientation* property set to *Vertical*).

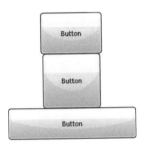

FIGURE 2-16 Buttons in a *StackPanel*.

When you have many controls in a *StackPanel*, you may go beyond the bounds of the Panel control itself, in which case the controls will be clipped to the bounds of the *StackPanel*. To get around this problem, you can use a ScrollViewer, which is explained in the next section.

Using the ScrollViewer

The ScrollViewer provides scroll bars that allow the user to pan around the contents of a layout if the contents exceed the bounds of the ScrollViewer. It can only contain one child control, so unless you are using a control that needs a large view area (such as an *Image*), it is typically only used to contain other containers.

For example, following is a *StackPanel* in which the contents exceed the vertical space available to it:

```
<StackPanel Height="300" Width="199">
  <Button Height="44" Width="86" Content="Button"/>
  <Button Height="57" Width="75" Content="Button"/>
  <Button Height="70" Width="59" Content="Button"/>
  <Button Height="109" Width="95" Content="Button"/>
  <Button Height="104" Width="88" Content="Button"/>
</StackPanel>
```

The *StackPanel* in this example is 300 pixels high, but the total height of all the buttons is 384 pixels, and so the bottom button will be cropped, as you can see in Figure 2-17.

FIGURE 2-17 Cropped elements in a *StackPanel*.

Now, if you contain this within a ScrollViewer, you'll get better results. Note that the *Stack-Panel* will still crop the buttons if you do not change its height, so if you need to have an area of height 300, you can set the ScrollViewer to have this height and then set the *StackPanel* to have a different height. Here's the XAML to do this:

```
<ScrollViewer Height="300" Width="300">
  <StackPanel Height="400" Width="199">
    <Button Height="44" Width="86" Content="Button"/>
    <Button Height="57" Width="75" Content="Button"/>
    <Button Height="70" Width="59" Content="Button"/>
    <Button Height="109" Width="95" Content="Button"/>
    <Button Height="104" Width="88" Content="Button"/>
  </StackPanel>
</ScrollViewer>
```

You can see how the ScrollViewer created here appears in Figure 2-18.

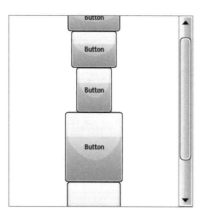

FIGURE 2-18 Using the ScrollViewer.

Now you can scroll up and down the button list, and the buttons will all be available; none are unavailable because of cropping if you use the ScrollViewer. Note that the button at the bottom in Figure 2-18 can be revealed by dragging the scroll bar down.

The Border Control

Not to be confused with the Border Patrol—part of the Department of Homeland Security— the Border Control is simply used to draw a border, background, or both around another element. For example, consider the following XAML:

```
<Border Height="318" Width="405" Background="#FFFF0000">
  <Button Height="234"
    HorizontalAlignment="Center"
    VerticalAlignment="Center"
    Width="239"
    RenderTransformOrigin="0.5,0.5"
    Content="Button">
  </Button>
</Border>
```

This will create a red background behind the button.

Placing and Customizing Visual Elements

The visual elements available are defined in the XAML specification, and you will learn about each of them in detail in Chapter 4. Right now, let's take a look at the basic shapes and tools that are available on the toolbar. These include the following shapes:

- *Rectangle* Select this shape to draw a straight-sided quadrilateral with 90-degree angles at each corner. You can make a square by creating a *Rectangle* with equal width and height properties.

- *Ellipse* Use this shape to draw an elliptical figure, an oval. You can make it a *Circle* by making the width and height properties equal.

- *Line* This shape simply draws a straight line between two end points.

There are also tools available on the toolbar that you can use to create free-form shapes:

- **Pen** Use this tool to draw a set of connected line segments represented by an underlying *Path* element.

- **Pencil** Use this tool to draw a set of connected elements, which can be lines or curves. Blend will take the strokes that the user draws and represent them with an underlying *Path* element.

Each of these visual elements, including those created with the Pen and Pencil tools, are represented by a single element, and this element can then be treated as any other object; that is, you can modify it in many ways, including setting its properties or animating it. For example, consider Figure 2-19, in which the Pencil tool has been used to draw a set of con-nected curves to create a representation of the word *Hello* in script. Look on the Objects And Timeline view, and you'll see the object represented as a *Path*.

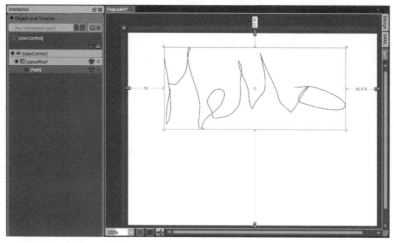

FIGURE 2-19 Editing a *Path* object.

Now, this pencil "drawing" of the word *Hello* is treated as a single object, so you can edit its properties, including *Fill*, *Brush*, and so forth, simply by selecting it from the Objects And Timeline view and then editing the properties in the property pane, as with any other object.

Placing and Customizing Controls

Controls are treated by Blend in exactly the same way as visual elements. You simply select them from the toolbar and draw them on the design surface. After you've created them on the design surface, then you can edit their properties. Controls are discussed in detail in Chap-ter 7, "Silverlight Controls: Presentation and Layout."

One thing to note is that Blend gives you two families of controls on the toolbar. The first in-cludes the Text controls: *TextBlock* and *TextBox*. The second includes the set of basic user in-terface controls: *Button*, *CheckBox*, *ListBox*, *RadioButton*, *ScrollBar*, *Slider*, and *GridSplitter*.

Finally, the toolbar gives you the option to add controls that aren't part of this set. You can do this by selecting the Asset Library link at the bottom of the toolbar. This will display the Asset Library dialog box, as shown in Figure 2-20.

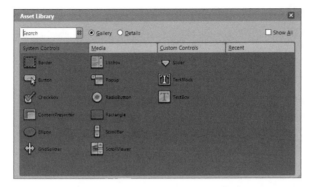

FIGURE 2-20 Asset Library dialog box.

You can select controls in the Asset Library dialog box to add them to the toolbar. You also can search for specific controls by entering the term in the search box. So, for example, if you want to use a *MediaElement* control, start typing the letters of the control's name. When you see the control you want (in this case, the *MediaElement*), you can select it, and it will then be available to you on the toolbar.

Then you can draw the control on the design surface and manipulate its properties with the properties editor, as you have done with the visual elements and layout controls.

Using Blend to Design Animations

We will examine how to create animations in detail in Chapter 5, but to put it succinctly, animations occur in Silverlight whenever a property of an object changes its value over time. You can design these kinds of animations visually in a very straightforward manner by using Blend and the timeline editor.

One form of animation that Silverlight supports is the *DoubleAnimation*, which is used to change numeric properties, such as the width of an *Ellipse* visual element. Another is the *ColorAnimation*, which is used to change the color of the *Brush* property.

For example, consider the *Ellipse* shown in Figure 2-21 (which appears as a circle because its height and width properties are equal). To visually design an animation that changes the width of this *Ellipse* element, you'll add a new *Storyboard* that contains the animation.

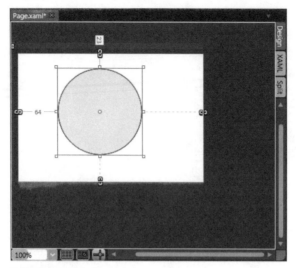

FIGURE 2-21 Drawing a circle.

On the Objects And Timeline view, select the *Ellipse* and then press the + button next to the *Storyboard* list at the top of the pane. Accept the defaults in the Create Storyboard dialog box that display, and then the Timeline editor will appear. You'll also see the message Timeline Recording Is On at the top of the Blend window. Press the F6 key to rearrange the workspace so that the timeline is displayed to make it easier to work on an animation. Your screen should look something like the one shown in Figure 2-22.

Look for the yellow line in the timeline view. This denotes the *current* position on the timeline. Drag it to the 2-second mark, and then click the Record Keyframe tool at the top of the time-line. It looks like a blob with a little green plus sign (+) at its lower-right side. You'll see a little oval that appears in the timeline at the 2-second mark, as shown in Figure 2-23.

Now that you have defined a keyframe, any changes that you make to the properties of the object will be recorded at that key frame, so go ahead and change the width of the *Ellipse* while the yellow line is still at the 2-second mark, indicating the current position of the time-line. For example, change the width to **200** and the *Fill* color to **Red**.

Now drag the playhead (the top of the vertical yellow line on the timeline) left and right, and you'll see a preview of the animation previewed, with the width and color of the circle shape changing over time.

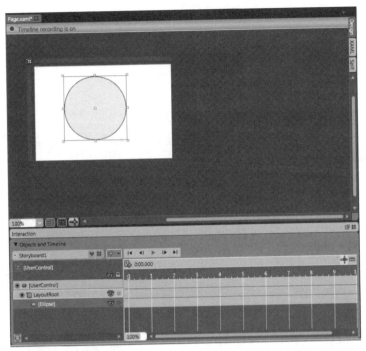

FIGURE 2-22 Editing the timeline.

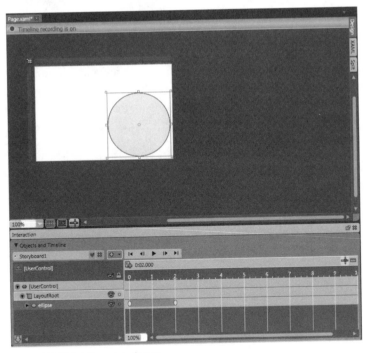

FIGURE 2-23 Adding a key frame.

You can see the XAML that is generated by your visual creation of the animation here:

```
<UserControl.Resources>
  <Storyboard x:Name="Storyboard1">
    <DoubleAnimationUsingKeyFrames Storyboard.TargetName="ellipse"
      Storyboard.TargetProperty="(FrameworkElement.Width)"
      BeginTime="00:00:00">
      <SplineDoubleKeyFrame KeyTime="00:00:02" Value="200"/>
    </DoubleAnimationUsingKeyFrames>
    <ColorAnimationUsingKeyFrames Storyboard.TargetName="ellipse"
      Storyboard.TargetProperty="(Shape.Fill).(SolidColorBrush.Color)"
      BeginTime="00:00:00">
      <SplineColorKeyFrame KeyTime="00:00:02" Value="#FFFF2200"/>
    </ColorAnimationUsingKeyFrames>
  </Storyboard>
</UserControl.Resources>
<Ellipse Height="100" Width="100" Fill="#FFFFF500" Stroke="#FF000000" x:Name="ellipse"/>
```

You'll delve into the structure of this XAML in much more detail in Chapter 5, but the important elements to note here are the *Storyboard.TargetName* instances that indicate which element the animation is being defined for, and the *Storyboard.TargetProperty* that indicates the property that is going to be changed. As you can see in this XAML, there are two animations, one that changes the width of the target and the other that changes its color. Silverlight then takes this definition and uses it to calculate the values required for each frame at the time the animation is rendered.

Summary

In this chapter, you learned the basics of working with Expression Blend, taking a quick tour of what it offers you as a designer or developer creating and implementing your own Silverlight applications. You saw how Blend can be used to create Silverlight solutions and projects, and then you saw what tools the Blend IDE offers you to add and manage visual elements, layout, controls, and animations in your application.

We've just begun to investigate what you can do with Blend in this chapter, but your introduction to Blend here may well inspire you to want to learn more about it.

The other half of the designer/developer workflow tool package is found in Visual Studio. In Chapter 3, you'll take a look at how you can use this tool, what it has in common with Blend, and what powerful features it provides for developers. You will have the chance to use Visual Studio to build your first Silverlight application—a sliding picture puzzle game.

Chapter 3
Using Visual Studio with Silverlight 2

In Chapter 1, "Introducing Silverlight 2," you were introduced to Silverlight 2 and saw the architecture that allows Silverlight and the .NET Framework to work together. You saw how XAML is used as a model for representing your user interface (UI) elements, interactions, and animations. In addition, you saw how the programming model for Silverlight can be hosted within the browser and programmed with JavaScript, or it can be hosted within a .NET Runtime for the browser and programmed using C# or other .NET languages.

Then, in Chapter 2, "Using Expression Blend with Silverlight 2," you took a closer look at Expression Blend, learning more about the design tool that is used to build Silverlight experiences.

In this chapter, you'll be taking a developer's view of this process, getting some hands-on experience as you use Microsoft Visual Studio 2008 to build a simple sliding picture puzzle game. You'll build on this example in later chapters. By the end of this chapter, you'll have a good understanding of how to use C# and Visual Studio 2008 to build .NET-based applications.

Installing the Visual Studio Tools for Silverlight

The Visual Studio tools for Silverlight include a "chained" installer that takes care of installing the runtime (for Windows), the Silverlight 2 Software Development Kit (SDK), and the Visual Studio tools themselves. It can be downloaded from *http://www.silverlight.net*.

Please note that there are some prerequisites for installing the tools:

- You must be using a release version of Visual Studio 2008. The tools will not work with a beta version. You can use any edition of Visual Studio 2008.

- The Web Authoring feature of Visual Studio must be installed.

- You must uninstall any previous versions of the Silverlight runtime before continuing.

- You must uninstall any previous versions of the Silverlight SDK before continuing.

- You must uninstall any previous versions of the Visual Studio Tools for Silverlight before continuing.

- Uninstall the Visual Studio update KB947520 before continuing.

If you haven't met these criteria, the installer will fail, and you will see the dialog box shown in Figure 3-1.

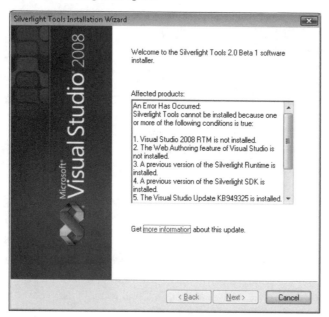

FIGURE 3-1 Failed installation of the Visual Studio Tools.

If you have the correct prerequisites, you'll see the dialog box shown in Figure 3-2.

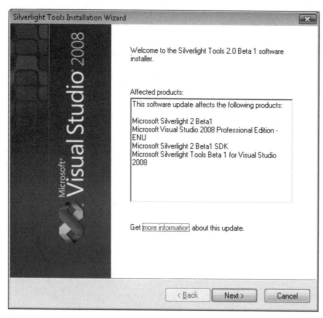

FIGURE 3-2 Dialog box indicating that you are ready to install Visual Studio Tools for Silverlight.

Click Next, and you'll see a screen where you can read and accept the license agreement. After you do so, the installation will begin immediately. You can see what the installation process should look like in Figure 3-3.

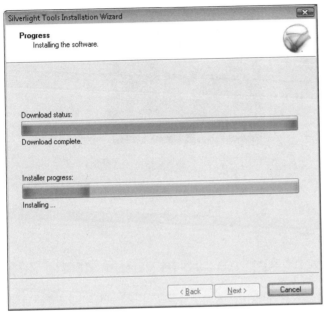

FIGURE 3-3 Installing the Silverlight Tools.

When the installer finishes downloading and installing, you'll have the Silverlight runtime, the SDK, and the Visual Studio tools all ready to go. Note that early versions of the SDK do not integrate the Help feature directly into Visual Studio. However, there is a Readme file located at \Program Files\Microsoft SDKs\Silverlight\v2.0\Documentation\VS-Help that will give you instructions on how to integrate it manually.

Using Visual Studio to Build a Silverlight Application

Now that you have installed the Visual Studio Tools for Silverlight, you are ready to learn how to use them to design and build an application. Figure 3-4 shows the Silverlight sliding picture puzzle game in action. This application has been written entirely in C# and XAML and is hosted in the browser.

FIGURE 3-4 Sliding picture puzzle game.

In the following sections, you'll see how to use Visual Studio 2008 and Silverlight to build this application in the C# language.

Creating a Silverlight Application in Visual Studio 2008

After you've installed Visual Studio and all of the necessary tools and templates for Silverlight, you will be able to create Silverlight applications. To do this, select New Project from the File menu. This will open the New Project dialog box (see Figure 3-5).

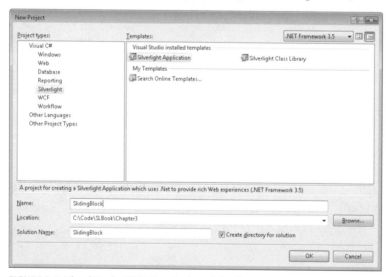

FIGURE 3-5 Visual Studio 2008 New Project dialog box.

Make sure that the .NET Framework 3.5 filter is selected from the drop-down list at the upper right in this dialog box (see Figure 3-5), and select Silverlight from the Project Type list. You'll see that the Silverlight Application and Silverlight Class Library templates are available.

Select the Silverlight Application template type, and give your project a name and location. Click OK, and Visual Studio will launch the Silverlight Application Wizard (see Figure 3-6).

This wizard gives you several options for how you can create and manage your Silverlight application. All Silverlight applications in 2.0 are built as user controls that can then be instantiated and hosted on a page. Thus, this discussion concentrates on how you will do this.

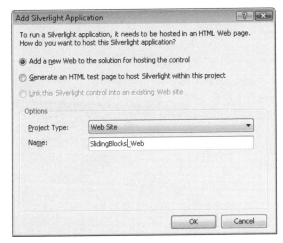

FIGURE 3-6 Silverlight Application Wizard.

The available options are:

- **Add A New Web To The Solution For Hosting The Control**   This option is the default option, and it will create a new Web site or Web application project that is configured to host and run your Silverlight application. It's a useful shortcut for building new Silverlight applications (as you are doing in this book!) because it handles the coding details required to host the Silverlight control on a page, leaving you to focus on Silverlight itself. Use the options pane to select the type of project for the Web (it can be Web site or Web Application) and to name it.

- **Generate An HTML Test Page To Host Silverlight Within This Project**   This will create a new page at run time each time you try to debug and test your application. This is particularly useful if you want to concentrate solely on the Silverlight application and don't want to worry about the overhead of having a separate Web project. Your final control can then be deployed to a server and instantiated on a Web page.

- **Link This Silverlight Control Into An Existing Web Site**   This option will allow you to link the Silverlight control to an existing Web site in your solution. If you are creating a new project, the option will not be available. If you are adding a Silverlight application to an existing solution that has a Web project, you will be able to select this option.

Accept the defaults, as shown in Figure 3-6, and a new Visual Studio solution, containing a Silverlight control and a Web Site that hosts the control, will be created for you. You can see the project structure for this in Figure 3-7.

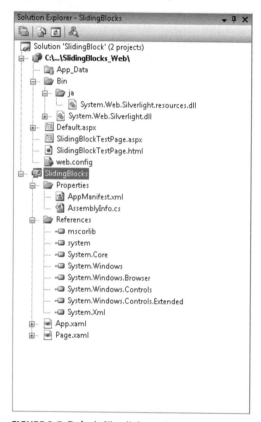

FIGURE 3-7 Default Silverlight project setup.

As you can see in Figure 3-7, two solutions have been created for you: the basic Silverlight control (*SlidingBlocks*) and a Web site. In the next section, you will examine these projects and learn what each one contains. Following that, you'll start building the application.

The Silverlight Control Project

The basic project that is created for you by the template contains a number of files, including the application manifest, the application XAML file with its code-behind, a sample page with its code-behind, the assembly information file, and some references. We'll look at each of these files in turn. This section introduces some of the complexities of a Silverlight project, which you might want to skip over if you just want to start coding, but I would recommend that you come back and read this information so that you can understand how everything hangs together.

Understanding the Silverlight Project Properties

The best way to get started is to look at the project properties. To do this, right-click the SlidingBlocks project in the solution explorer and select Properties. The Project Properties dialog box will appear (see Figure 3-8).

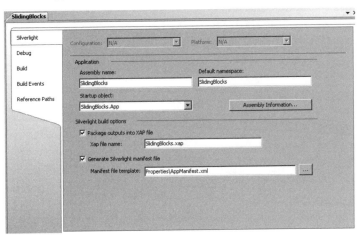

FIGURE 3-8 Silverlight Project Properties dialog box.

If you are familiar with this dialog box, you'll notice that there is an extra tab for Silverlight. This is selected in Figure 3-8, showing the Silverlight options.

The Assembly Name defaults to the project name. When the application is compiled into a DLL, this is the name that will be used.

The Default Namespace also defaults to the project name. If you reference classes within the project, they will be prefixed by this namespace.

The Startup Object defaults to the name of the project followed by .App (i.e., SilverlightBlocks.App). This is a class in your application that will execute first. The template defines this class in App.xaml and its associated code-behind App.xaml.cs that you'll be looking at in a later section.

Clicking the Assembly Information button will call up the Assembly Information dialog box (see Figure 3-9). This allows you to define the metadata for your assembly, including Title, Description, Copyright, and Trademark information. This is stored in the AssemblyInfo.cs file and compiled into your Silverlight application.

The Package Outputs Into XAP File option allows you to specify an .xap file (new to Silverlight 2) that contains all of the outputs of your project compilation. Typically this is the DLL containing your Silverlight component and its application manifest. This is convenient for Web-based applications, as the Silverlight component only needs to be pointed at one file (the XAP file) to download and use multiple components.

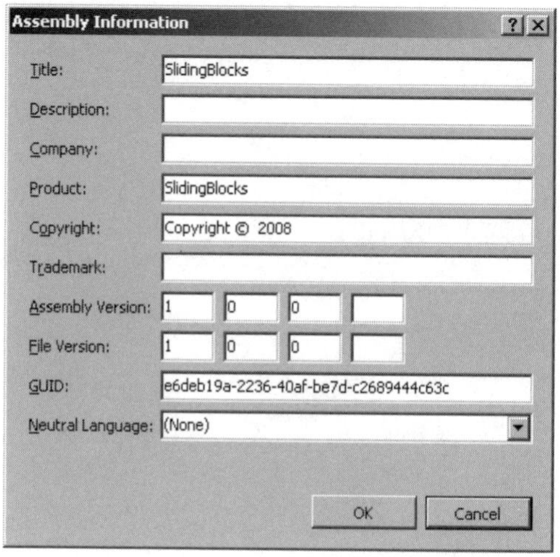

FIGURE 3-9 Defining the Assembly Information.

> **Tip**   The XAP file is just a ZIP file with a different extension. If you want to investigate its contents, just rename it with a .zip extension and open it with your favorite ZIP utility. Don't forget to change the file extension back to .xap when you're finished!

Finally, you are given the option to generate the Silverlight manifest file itself. This file contains details on everything within the package that the Silverlight application will use, such as additional components or controls that are necessary for your application to execute. You'll be seeing more of this as you progress through this book.

The Properties Files

The first folder within your project is the Properties folder that contains the properties files: AppManifest.xml and Assemblyinfo.cs.

AppManifest.xml is generated for you as you compile your project. If your project has any dependencies at run time, such as external controls, references to them are placed here.

Assemblyinfo.cs contains the metadata to be compiled into your DLL that was configured in the Assembly Information dialog box (see Figure 3-9). You can manually change the information by editing this code file if you wish, but the recommended approach is to use the dialog box.

References

The References folder contains references to a number of assemblies. These are the core Silverlight assemblies that are needed to make your application run:

- ***mscorlib***   This contains the basic core types that are used by Silverlight applications.

- ***system***   This contains many of the high-level types used for developing and debugging Silverlight applications, such as the compiler and the debugging and diagnostics classes.

- ***System.core***   This contains the LINQ data functionality.

- ***System.Xml***   This contains the Silverlight XML processing libraries.

- ***System.Windows***   This contains the core Windows and Silverlight functionality, including the Silverlight controls.

- ***System.Windows.Browser***   This contains the libraries used for interacting with the browser.

- ***System.Windows.Controls***   This contains the core set of Silverlight controls. It includes all the basic UI elements.

- ***System.Windows.Controls.Extended***   This contains the extended set of Silverlight controls. It includes complex additional controls such as the *Calendar* and *Watermarked-TextBox* controls.

Silverlight also has a number of nondefault assemblies that can be added to provide plug-in functionality, some of which you'll be looking at through the course of this book. An example of this is the Dynamic Language Runtime functionality.

The App.xaml and App.xaml.cs Files

App.xaml is created for you by the integrated development environment (IDE) when you create a Silverlight project using the template. It is generally used to store application-global information.

App.xaml contains the declarations for the application's behavior. Here's an example of the default App.xaml that is created by the template:

```
<Application xmlns="http://schemas.microsoft.com/client/2007"
             xmlns:x="http://schemas.microsoft.com/winfx/2006/xaml"
             x:Class="SlidingBlocks.App">
  <Application.Resources>
  </Application.Resources>
</Application>
```

The first thing to take note of is the *x:Class* attribute, which specifies the name of the class into which this XAML and its associated code-behind will be compiled. As you can see, in this case it is SlidingBlocks.App, which you may remember from the Project Properties dialog box back in Figure 3-8 is defined as the startup object for this application. Thus, when the Silverlight project is run, this class will contain the startup functionality.

You can specify a function to execute upon application startup using the *Startup* attribute. This simply contains the name of the code function within the code-behind that will execute when the application starts. You can also specify the function to execute when the application finishes using the *Exit* attribute, which contains the name of the function within the code-behind that will execute when the application closes.

The code for the default code-behind that is generated by the template is shown here:

```
using System.Windows;
using System;

namespace SlidingBlocks
{
    public partial class App : Application
    {

        public App()
        {
            this.Startup += this.Application_Startup;
            this.Exit += this.Application_Exit;

            this.UnhandledException += this.Application_UnhandledException;
            InitializeComponent();
        }

        private void Application_Startup(object sender, EventArgs e)
        {
            // Load the main control
            this.RootVisual = new Page();
        }

        private void Application_Exit(object sender, EventArgs e)
        {

        }
        private void Application_UnhandledException(
            object sender, ApplicationUnhandledExceptionEventArgs e)
        {

        }

    }
}
```

First take a look at the constructor (which is the function with the same name as the code module, in this case *App()*). It uses the code method to wire up the *Startup* and *Exit* functions. This was already done in the XAML file, so it isn't necessary to do this in code—but it does show some of the nice flexibility of the XAML/code-behind model that allows you to wire up events at design time (by specifying them in the XAML) or at run time (by declaring them in code).

Next, you can inspect the *Application_Startup* and *Application_Exit* functions. Notice that they take two parameters—the object that raised the event and an arguments object. You'll be seeing this function signature often as you program your Silverlight applications.

The *Application_Startup* function contains code that sets the *RootVisual* property of the application to a new *Page* object, declaring that the UI of the *Page* object is the first UI screen that this application should render. If you are going to use other UI screens declared in XAML, these will be launched from within the *Page* object.

The *Page* object is the default XAML object that is created to host your application UI by the template, which you'll be looking at in the next section.

The Page.xaml and Page.xaml.cs Files

The Page.xaml file provides the default UI for your application. When compiled along with its associated code-behind, it will form the *Page* class, from which a *Page* object can be created. If you recall from the previous section, the *RootVisual* property of the application was set to a new instance of a *Page* object, thus allowing this class to provide the default UI.

You can see the default XAML for Page.xaml here:

```
<UserControl x:Class="SlidingBlocks.Page"
        xmlns="http://schemas.microsoft.com/client/2007"
        xmlns:x="http://schemas.microsoft.com/winfx/2006/xaml"
        Width="400"
        Height="300">

    <Grid x:Name="LayoutRoot" Background="White" >

    </Grid>
</UserControl>
```

First, you'll notice that the container for the XAML is a *UserControl*, which is something you may not be familiar with from Silverlight 1.0. As mentioned earlier, when building Silverlight 2 applications in Visual Studio, you actually build controls that compile into a DLL within an XAP that Silverlight opens and renders.

In this case, you'll see that this *UserControl* instance is called *SlidingBlocks.Page*. *SlidingBlocks* is the namespace (take a look back at the project properties to see this), and *Page* is the name of the class within that namespace.

The *xmlns* and *xmlns:x* declarations configure the default namespace and the extended namespace, respectively, to be used to validate the XAML. Earlier you saw the *x:Class* attribute used to define the class for this control, and this is an example of using the extended namespace, which is prefixed by *x:*.

Finally, the width and height are set to the default 640 × 480.

Next comes the root *Grid*. In Silverlight 2, your root element must be a *Container*, which in this case is a *Grid* called *LayoutRoot*. All elements of your UI design will ultimately be children of this node.

The code-behind for this XAML is shown here:

```
using System;
using System.Windows;
using System.Windows.Controls;
using System.Windows.Documents;
using System.Windows.Ink;
using System.Windows.Input;
using System.Windows.Media;
using System.Windows.Media.Animation;
using System.Windows.Shapes;

namespace SlidingBlocks
{
    public partial class Page : UserControl
    {
        public Page()
        {
            // Required to initialize variables
            InitializeComponent();
        }
    }
}
```

If you are familiar with C#, this will look very similar to code you may have used before. Basically, it is a boilerplate class file named *Page* that inherits from the *UserControl* type. In the class constructor, the special *InitializeComponent()* call is used to set everything up. You add your page-specific code to this module, as you'll see in the section titled "Building a Silverlight 2 Game" later in this chapter, where you will create the sliding picture puzzle.

The Web Project

In addition to the control project, the template also created a Web project that hosts your Silverlight application. This Web project contains two ASPX files: Default.aspx, which is an empty Web Form on which you can build an application; and a test page called *<ApplicationName>*TestPage.aspx (e.g., SlidingBlocksTestPage.aspx), which contains everything necessary to run Silverlight from ASP.NET.

Although Silverlight does not have any server-side dependencies, ASP.NET offers some controls that allow the generation of the client-side JavaScript and HTML necessary to host Silverlight in the browser.

The TestPage file includes references to these controls. Following is the full markup for the ASPX file:

```
<%@ Page Language="C#" AutoEventWireup="true" %>

<%@ Register Assembly="System.Web.Silverlight"
    Namespace="System.Web.UI.SilverlightControls" TagPrefix="asp" %>

<!DOCTYPE html PUBLIC "-//W3C//DTD XHTML 1.0 Transitional//EN"
  "http://www.w3.org/TR/xhtml1/DTD/xhtml1-transitional.dtd">

<html xmlns="http://www.w3.org/1999/xhtml" >
<head runat="server">
    <title>Test Page For SlidingBlocks</title>
</head>
<body style="height:100%;margin:0;">
    <form id="form1" runat="server" style="height:100%;">
    <div>
        <asp:ScriptManager ID="ScriptManager1" runat="server">
        </asp:ScriptManager>
        <asp:Silverlight ID="Xaml1" runat="server"
          Source="~/ClientBin/SlidingBlocks.xap"
          Version="2.0" Width="100%" Height="100%" />
    </div>
    </form>
</body>
</html>
```

Note that this is an evolving technology, so your version number attributes and public key attributes may differ slightly. Don't worry—if your code was generated by the template, you should be in good shape.

You'll notice that there are two ASP.NET controls referenced on this page. The first is the *ScriptManager* control, which is an artifact of ASP.NET AJAX and is a terrific control that is used to manage the downloading and referencing of all necessary JavaScript libraries at the correct time and in the correct place.

The second is the *Silverlight* control. Notice that it takes the XAP that we discussed earlier as its parameter. This control will generate the correct HTML code to create the *DIV* and *CreateSilverlight* functions.

When you run this page, you'll see that a lot of HTML and JavaScript is generated. Toward the bottom of the code, shown in bold here, you'll see where Silverlight is created and pointed at the XAP file. Here's a snippet:

```
<script type="text/javascript">
//<![CDATA[
Sys.Application.initialize();
Sys.Application.add_init(function() {
    $create(Sys.UI.Silverlight.Control,
        {"source":"ClientBin/SlidingBlocks.xap"},
         null, null, $get("Xaml1"));
        });
//]]>
</script>
```

This script is interpreted by the browser to instantiate the *Silverlight* control. Please note that this code relies on ASP.NET and the ASP.NET Silverlight controls to work properly. If you are instantiating from something other than ASP.NET, you can still use the SDK-based JavaScript tools to instantiate Silverlight. This is covered in depth in Chapter 6, "The Silverlight Browser Control."

Building a Silverlight 2 Game

Silverlight follows the model of separating the design from the development by having the design in XAML technology and the code for the development in code-behind technology, typically (though not exclusively) programmed with C#.

In this example, you'll use very little XAML—just enough to contain the *Canvas* in which the puzzle pieces will be kept and the image that shows the completed image. If you refer back to Figure 3-4, you will see these on the left and right, respectively. Note that although the default page has a *Grid* as its main container, we'll use a *Canvas* in this game for simplicity.

Creating the UI in XAML

As you saw in Figure 3-4, the UI for this game is very simple, consisting of an area of the screen (contained within a *Canvas*) where the sliding blocks reside and another area that renders the finished image.

Here's an example of the XAML that provides the *Canvas* and the completed image:

```
<UserControl x:Class="SlidingBlocks.Page"
        xmlns="http://schemas.microsoft.com/client/2007"
        xmlns:x="http://schemas.microsoft.com/winfx/2006/xaml"
        Width="640"
        Height="480"
        >

    <Canvas x:Name="LayoutRoot" >
        <Canvas x:Name="GameContainer" />
        <Image Source="s1.JPG" Canvas.Left="500"
            Height="400" Width="400" Stretch="UniformToFill">
        </Image>
    </Canvas>
</UserControl>
```

As you can see, it is very straightforward. The *Canvas* that will contain the pieces of the puzzle is called *GameContainer*, and the image that renders the completed puzzle image is static and thus does not need to be named. It is prefilled with the image sl.jpg that exists within the same Web project. That's everything you need for your design, so in the next section, you'll start looking at the code.

Writing the Game Code

The game code in this example is written using C#. You could easily translate it into VB.NET, IronPython, or any other supported language that you want to use, but in most cases, this book will use C#.

Initializing the Data Structures

The first step in writing the code for this game is in initializing the data structures that will be used by the application. In this case, we are going to break the image up into 16 tiles, 15 of which will be shuffled across the board. One tile is not used; instead, there is a blank space that is used by the player to slide the blocks around.

In Silverlight, you cannot create a subimage from an existing image, but you can clip an image according to a clipping path. Clipping shouldn't be confused with cropping. In the former, you dictate which parts of the image to draw; in the latter, you remove all but the desired part of the image. Silverlight does not support cropping, so you have to clip an image.

The problem with clipping is that the rest of the image dimensions are still available and clickable. So, for example, if you have a 400 × 400 image and you clip a 100 × 100 square at position (100,100), you will still have a 400 × 400 object that will be blank (but still clickable) except for a 100 × 100 square at position (100,100). This doesn't suit our needs to create a sliding picture puzzle, so what can we do?

The answer comes by containing the image within a *Canvas* that is the same dimensions as the clip and then using a translate transform on it so that the clipped part of the image is at the upper-left corner of this *Canvas*, and thus the *Canvas* only renders the clipped region.

So, for a 4 × 4 puzzle made up of 16 blocks, you need 16 images and 16 *Canvas* objects. You'll also need something to represent the board so that you know which image is in which square. Here's the code to declare these:

```
Canvas[] cI = new Canvas[16];
Image[] i = new Image[16];
int[] board = new int[16];
```

Creating the Puzzle Pieces

To create the puzzle pieces, you will have to load the sl.jpg image into each element in the array of images. This is achieved by using a uniform resource identifier (URI) to point to the image and the *BitmapImage* class (from *System.Windows.Media.Imaging*) to read the data from that URI and point it at the image control:

```
i[nx].Source = new BitmapImage(uri);
```

From your constructor, you can call a function (*InitBoard*) that will be used to instantiate the pieces:

```
public Page()
{
    // Required to initialize variables
    InitializeComponent();
    InitBoard();
}
```

You can see this function here:

```
void InitBoard()
{
  Uri uri = new Uri("sl.jpg", UriKind.Relative);
  int nx = 0;
  for (int ix = 0; ix < 4; ix++)
    for (int iy = 0; iy < 4; iy++)
    {
      nx = (ix * 4) + iy;
      i[nx] = new Image();
      i[nx].Height = 400;
      i[nx].Width = 400;
      i[nx].Stretch = Stretch.UniformToFill;
      RectangleGeometry r = new RectangleGeometry();
      r.Rect = new Rect((ix * 100), (iy * 100), 100, 100);
      i[nx].Clip = r;
      i[nx].Source = new BitmapImage(uri);
      i[nx].SetValue(Canvas.TopProperty, Convert.toDouble(iy * 100 * -1));
      i[nx].SetValue(Canvas.LeftProperty, Convert.toDouble(ix * 100 * -1));

      cI[nx] = new Canvas();
      cI[nx].Width = 100;
      cI[nx].Height = 100;
      cI[nx].Children.Add(i[nx]);
      cI[nx].SetValue(Canvas.NameProperty, "C" + nx.ToString());
      cI[nx].MouseLeftButtonDown += new
        MouseButtonEventHandler(Page_MouseLeftButtonDown);
      if (nx < 15)
        GameContainer.Children.Add(cI[nx]);
    }

  // Mix up the pieces
  shuffle();
```

```
// Draw the board
drawBoard();
```

}

Be sure to add a reference to *System.Windows.Media.Imaging* at the top of your code page:

```
using System.Windows.Media.Imaging;
```

At first, this may look a little complex, but on closer inspection, it is actually quite straightforward. A nested loop from 0–3 on the x- and y-axes is set up. This, as you may have guessed, is used to manage the 4 × 4 array for the images themselves.

The *Image* and *Canvas* arrays used to store the blocks are one-dimensional arrays with 16 elements each (as less memory and code are used to store them this way), so to figure out how to map a two-dimensional *ix, iy* coordinate to a one-dimensional array, the following calculation is needed:

```
nx = (ix * 4) + iy;
```

Each *Image* element is then set up with a 400 × 400 dimension with *UniformToFill* stretch. You can find more about how to use images in Chapter 4, "XAML Basics."

Next, the clip region is calculated. This is done using a *RectangleGeometry*:

```
RectangleGeometry r = new RectangleGeometry();
r.Rect=new Rect((ix*100), (iy*100) ,100,100);
i[nx].Clip = r;
```

This defines a Rectangle at the appropriate coordinates (derived by multiplying *ix* and *iy* by 100) with the appropriate size (100 × 100) and then assigns it to be the clipping region for the current image (*i[nx]*).

Next, the image is loaded by setting it to the value of the *BitmapImage*, which is initialized from the URI of the image, and it is translated into position. An image that is clipped at position (100,100) has to be moved by (−100,−100) for the clipped area to appear in the upper-left corner. Thus, the *Top* and *Left* properties have to be set to −100 multiplied by the current *iy* and *ix* values, respectively.

```
i[nx].Source = new BitmapImage(uri);
i[nx].SetValue(Canvas.TopProperty, Convert.toDouble(iy * 100 * -1));
i[nx].SetValue(Canvas.LeftProperty, Convert.toDouble(ix * 100 * -1));
```

The images have not yet been added to a parent *Canvas*, so this is the next step. The *Canvas* needs to be initialized, sized, and the respective image added to it as a child. Here's the code:

```
cI[nx] = new Canvas();
cI[nx].Width = 100;
```

```
cI[nx].Height = 100;
cI[nx].Children.Add(i[nx]);
```

Now that we have our *Canvas* and it contains our clipped image, we complete our initialization by naming our *Canvas* (so that we can track it later when we click it), defining an event handler to manage what happens when the user clicks it, and finally adding it to the parent *Canvas*. We don't need to position the block yet. That will happen after the board is shuffled. Note that we don't add the final image to the board because we want to have an empty space.

```
cI[nx].SetValue(Canvas.NameProperty, "C" + nx.ToString());
cI[nx].MouseLeftButtonDown += new
    MouseButtonEventHandler(Page_MouseLeftButtonDown);
if(nx<15)
    GameContainer.Children.Add(cI[nx]);
```

Finally, we want to shuffle the pieces and draw the game board. You'll see the code for this in the next section.

Shuffling the Pieces

The puzzle pieces are shuffled using a fairly simple shuffle algorithm that goes through the array 100 times, picking out two random elements on each occasion; if the two elements are different, it swaps their contents. At the end, it loads the value −1 into the last element to recognize that it is the empty square.

You can see the shuffle algorithm here:

```
void shuffle()
{
  // Initialize Board
  for (int n = 0; n < 15; n++)
  {
    board[n] = n;
  }
  Random rand = new Random(System.DateTime.Now.Second);
  for (int n = 0; n < 100; n++)
  {
    int n1 = rand.Next(15);
    int n2 = rand.Next(15);
    if (n1 != n2)
    {
      int tmp = board[n1];
      board[n1] = board[n2];
      board[n2] = tmp;
    }
  }
  board[15] = -1;

}
```

Now that the pieces are shuffled, our next step will be to draw the board.

Drawing the Board

At this point, you have all of the blocks defined as *Image* elements within *Canvas* elements, and you have an array of integers, where the value at index *n* is going to be the tile to display at that position. You've also shuffled this array of integers, so now it's time to draw the game board. This is achieved simply by using this code:

```
void drawBoard()
{
  int nx = 0;
  int ny = 0;
  for (int n = 0; n < 15; n++)
  {
    nx = n / 4;
    ny = n % 4;
    if(board[n]>=0)
    {
      cI[board[n]].SetValue(Canvas.TopProperty, Convert.toDouble(ny * 100));
      cI[board[n]].SetValue(Canvas.LeftProperty, Convert.toDouble(nx * 100));

    }
  }
}
```

This will loop from 0 to 14 (there are 15 blocks in the puzzle) and calculate an *x,y* coordinate for each block in a 4 × 4 grid. The *x* value is simply the integer division of the loop index by 4, and the *y* value is simply the modulus of the loop index by 4. If we multiply these by 100, we then get the right position to draw the *Canvas* element.

At this point, we have fully initialized the game. The image is positioned on the right, and our shuffled board of image blocks is on the left.

Handling User Control

The next thing to do is to start handling the user interaction. In a game such as this, the expected behavior is that the user clicks an image block, and if this block is next to the empty space, the block that the user clicked will slide into the space, leaving a new empty space behind. So, we need to handle the clicking of the *Canvas* containing the Image block. If you remember all the way back to the initialization of the blocks, you saw this line:

```
cI[nx].MouseLeftButtonDown
        += new MouseButtonEventHandler(Page_MouseLeftButtonDown);
```

This defined that the *Page_MouseLeftButtonDown* event handler will fire when the *Canvas* is clicked. This event handler has been wired up for each of the *Canvas* blocks.

The code for this event handler has two sections. The first section identifies which *Canvas* raised the event and where that *Canvas* is in the board:

```
void Page_MouseLeftButtonDown(object sender, MouseButtonEventArgs e)
{
  Canvas c = sender as Canvas;
  int nCanvasID = -1;
  int nBoardLoc = -1;
  int nEmptyLoc = -1;
  for (int i = 0; i < 16; i++)
  {
    if (c == cI[i])
    {
      nCanvasID = i;
      break;
    }
  }
  for (int i = 0; i < 16; i++)
  {
    if (board[i] == nCanvasID)
    {
      nBoardLoc = i;
    }
    else if (board[i] == -1)
    {
      nEmptyLoc = i;
    }
  }
}
```

So, for example, you may have clicked on the block that represents the upper-left corner of the finished image (block 0), but it is currently in the lower-left corner of the board (position 12). When the click event is raised, you would look through the array of *Canvas* elements that represent the blocks until you find one that matches the *Canvas* that was actually clicked, and from here you could get its index in the array, loading it into the *nCanvasID* variable (which in our previous hypothetical case would be 0). You can then scan through the board to find where item 0 is and, when you find it, assign this value to the *nBoardLoc* variable (which in our hypothetical case is 12) and, while you are at it, find the location of the empty space on the board and load that into *nEmptyLoc*.

The second section of code then needs to check to see if we can move, and if we can, it moves the block into the space and updates the board accordingly.

```
// Check if we can move
if ((nBoardLoc == nEmptyLoc + 1) ||
    (nBoardLoc == nEmptyLoc - 1) ||
    (nBoardLoc == nEmptyLoc + 4) ||
    (nBoardLoc == nEmptyLoc - 4))
{
    int nx = nEmptyLoc/4;
    int ny = nEmptyLoc%4;

    cI[nCanvasID].SetValue(
```

```
            Convert.toDouble(Canvas.TopProperty, ny * 100));
        cI[nCanvasID].SetValue(

            Convert.toDouble(Canvas.LeftProperty, nx * 100));

        board[nEmptyLoc] = nCanvasID;
        board[nBoardLoc] = -1;

        checkWinner();
    }
    else
    {
        // do nothing
    }


}
```

To do this, you first check the position of the empty location relative to the position of the location of the block that you clicked. If it is immediately above, below, to the left, or to the
right of the current block, you can move it. Because the board is a one-dimensional array representing a 4 × 4 board, this is easy to do. Items to the left and to the right of the current item
are off by −1 and +1, respectively, and items above and below are off by −4 and +4, respectively, so if you seek the blocks at these indices for the empty block, you know that you can
move.

To move, you then need to get the x and y coordinates relative to the position of the empty
block and assign them to the position of the clicked block. Then assign the board location
that previously contained the empty block to contain the value of the *Canvas* that you just
clicked, and the board location that previously contained the *Canvas* that you just clicked to
−1, indicating that it is now empty.

Finally, you'll call the *checkWinner()* function to see if the board has been successfully
unscrambled.

Checking Winning Condition

The *checkWinner* function checks to see if the board has been successfully unscrambled. This,
again, is very straightforward. The board is unscrambled if every item at index n in the board
array is equal to n—that is, *Canvas* 0 is at index 0, *Canvas* 1 is at index 1, and so on.

The most efficient way to do this is to assume that you have a winning board and scan
through it until *board[n]* is not equal to n, at which point you have a losing board and you
break the loop. If you make it all the way through the board, you have a winner.

```
void checkWinner()
    {
        bool bCompleted = true;
        for (int n = 0; n < 15; n++)
```

```
        {
            if (n != board[n])
            {
                bCompleted = false;
                break;
            }
        }
        if (bCompleted)
        {
            // The Player has won the game....do something nice for them.
        }
    }
```

At this point, you have all the elements for a basic image sliding picture puzzle game written in C# for Silverlight 2, and it was done in just over 100 lines of code. You can build on this sample as you progress through this book—adding animation to the sliding of the blocks, saving high scores, allowing images to be uploaded to the application, and so forth. The sky is the limit to the enhancements you can add!

Summary

In this chapter, you took a look at Visual Studio 2008 and the various tools and templates that it offers you to develop Silverlight applications using .NET languages. You took a tour of a project based on the default Silverlight templates, inspecting each of the files and how it is used to develop and deploy a Silverlight application. You then put the theory into practice by using XAML and C# to build a fully featured sliding picture puzzle game. This gives you a taste of what you can do with Silverlight 2, but it barely scratches the surface of what is possible. In Part 2 of this book, "Programming Silverlight 2," you'll start looking in more depth at some of the major areas of functionality that are available from the .NET Framework, including building your own controls, networking and communication, data and XML, dynamic languages, and the ASP.NET server controls.

Chapter 4
XAML Basics

XAML is at the core of your Silverlight application. You use it to define your graphical assets, your interactions, your animations, and your timelines. It's based on XML, so everything is defined in text markup using attributes to declare properties, methods, and events.

In this chapter, we'll look at the common XAML components used to define the visual elements of your application. First, we'll examine how to make a layout, including how elements can be drawn on the screen relative to their containers and each other. We'll also look at the various brushes that can be used to fill shapes and controls, as well as the strokes that can be used to draw their outlines. Then you will learn about paths and geometries and how they can help you generate complex shapes and groups of shapes as well as how to use them to clip other objects or fills. Finally, we'll look at the controls that use these XAML components, including the *Canvas* that is at the heart of Silverlight layout, and we'll examine how to render text using the *Glyphs* and *TextBlock* controls.

XAML Layout Properties

Briefly, you use the *Canvas.Left* and *Canvas.Top* properties to lay out controls in XAML. These properties are referred to as *attached* properties, which simply means that they are available globally in your XAML code or they modify a property that's really exhibited by their parent. In addition to this, the *Canvas.ZIndex* attached property may be used to determine the Z-order position of the item, which defines the topmost object to be rendered if two or more overlap. The default Z-order behavior in XAML is that the last item drawn (farthest down in the XAML document) is topmost, but this can be overridden using *Canvas.ZIndex*.

So, consider the following XAML. It shows the code for a *Canvas* containing two rectangles. These use *Canvas.Left* and *Canvas.Top* to determine their upper-left corners relative to the canvas that contains them.

```
<Canvas>
    <Rectangle Fill="Red" Width="200" Height="128"
            Canvas.Left="8" Canvas.Top="8"/>
    <Rectangle Fill="Black" Width="280" Height="80"
            Canvas.Left="40" Canvas.Top="32"/>
</Canvas>
```

The black rectangle is drawn on top of the red one, as shown in Figure 4-1.

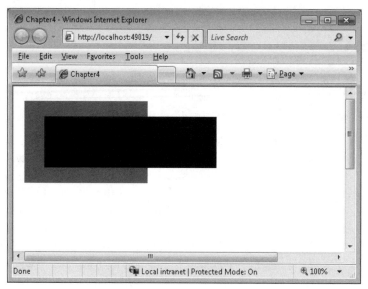

FIGURE 4-1 Rectangle layouts.

The red rectangle is positioned 8 pixels from the left and 8 pixels from the top of the parent canvas. The black one is positioned 40 pixels from the left and 32 pixels from the top. The black rectangle appears on top because it was the last one rendered.

You can use *ZIndex* to override this behavior. You can specify *ZIndex* to be a numeric value, and the highest numbered *ZIndex* will appear on top of lower numbered ones, as you see in the following code:

```
<Canvas>
    <Rectangle Canvas.ZIndex="2"
               Fill="Red" Width="200" Height="128"
               Canvas.Left="8" Canvas.Top="8"/>
    <Rectangle Canvas.ZIndex="1"
               Fill="Black" Width="280" Height="80"
               Canvas.Left="40" Canvas.Top="32"/>
</Canvas>
```

As shown in Figure 4-2, the red rectangle now appears on top of the black one, as you would expect, because the *ZIndex* value for the red rectangle is higher than the *ZIndex* value for the black rectangle.

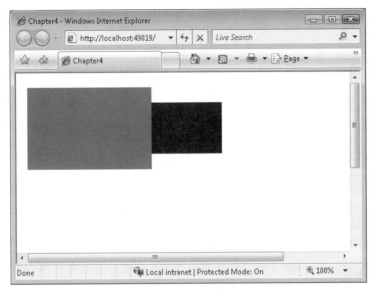

FIGURE 4-2 Changing the Z-order of elements.

XAML Brushes

You use *brushes* in XAML to determine how shapes are drawn and filled. In the earlier example, you saw that the two rectangles were filled using the known colors *Red* and *Black,* respectively. These are simple examples of using brushes. The next sections describe the more complex set of *Brush* types that XAML supports.

SolidColorBrush

The *SolidColorBrush* fills an area with a solid color. The color can be a named value, such as *Red* or *Black*, or it can be described in hexadecimal values indicating the alpha, red, green, and blue channel intensities. For example, the color white is described as *#FFFFFFFF* in hexadecimal notation, and the color red would be *#FFFF0000*.

LinearGradientBrush

The *LinearGradientBrush* fills an area with a linear gradient defined in two-dimensional space. The default gradient is defined using a normalized rectangle—a rectangle with its upper-left corner at (0,0) and its lower-right corner at (1,1). This defines the gradient as extending from the upper-left corner to the lower-right corner. If you define a color at each of these points, Silverlight will draw the gradient between them.

As an example, consider the following rectangle definition:

```
<Canvas>
    <Rectangle Width="200" Height="128" Canvas.Left="8" Canvas.Top="8">
        <Rectangle.Fill>
            <LinearGradientBrush>
                <GradientStop Color="#FF000000" Offset="0"/>
                <GradientStop Color="#FFFFFFFF" Offset="1"/>
            </LinearGradientBrush>
        </Rectangle.Fill>
    </Rectangle>
</Canvas>
```

This XAML snippet defines a *LinearGradientBrush* that extends from the upper-left corner to the lower-right corner of the rectangle. The first gradient stop, at the beginning of the gradient, is black (#FF000000), and the second gradient stop, at the end of the gradient, is white (#FFFFFFFF). You can see this rectangle rendered in Figure 4-3.

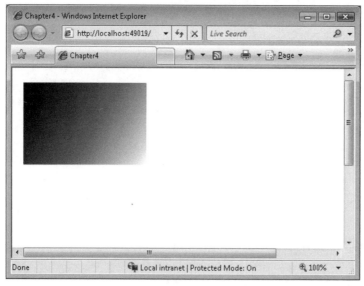

FIGURE 4-3 Using the *LinearGradientBrush*.

Changing the Gradient Direction

You can change the direction of the brush by setting the *StartPoint* and *EndPoint* properties of the *LinearGradientBrush*. To change the gradient fill direction to lower left to upper right, you can set these to (0,1) and (1,0), respectively, as shown:

```
<Rectangle Width="200" Height="128" Canvas.Left="8" Canvas.Top="8">
    <Rectangle.Fill>
        <LinearGradientBrush StartPoint="0,1" EndPoint="1,0">
            <GradientStop Color="#FF000000" Offset="0"/>
            <GradientStop Color="#FFFFFFFF" Offset="1"/>
```

```
        </LinearGradientBrush>
     </Rectangle.Fill>
  </Rectangle>
```

Figure 4-4 shows how this rectangle is rendered.

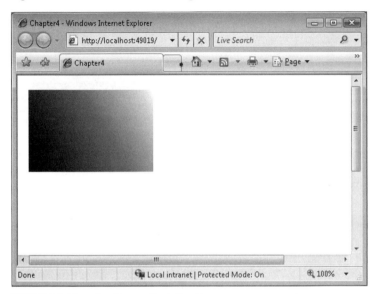

FIGURE 4-4 Changing the gradient direction.

Adding Gradient Stops

The previous examples show the minimum number of gradient stops, which is two. You can create other gradient stops containing colors and locations to control the gradient. For example, if you want your gradient to range from black to white to black again, you can define three stops like this:

```
<Rectangle Width="200" Height="128" Canvas.Left="8" Canvas.Top="8">
   <Rectangle.Fill>
      <LinearGradientBrush>
         <GradientStop Color="#FF000000" Offset="0"/>
         <GradientStop Color="#FFFFFFFF" Offset="0.5"/>
         <GradientStop Color="#FF000000" Offset="1"/>
      </LinearGradientBrush>
   </Rectangle.Fill>
</Rectangle>
```

The first stop, at position 0, is black; the second, half way along the gradient at position 0.5, is white; and the third stop, at the end of the gradient at position 1, is black again. If you render this, you will see something like the rectangle shown in Figure 4-5.

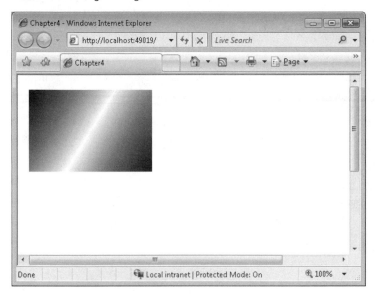

FIGURE 4-5 Using gradient stops.

The gradient stops are positioned using the *Offset* parameter; therefore, to move the white section of this gradient closer to the upper-left corner, you simply change its *Offset* so that it is closer to zero, as shown in this XAML snippet:

```
<Rectangle Width="200" Height="128" Canvas.Left="8" Canvas.Top="8">
    <Rectangle.Fill>
        <LinearGradientBrush>
            <GradientStop Color="#FF000000" Offset="0"/>
            <GradientStop Color="#FFFFFFFF" Offset="0.1"/>
            <GradientStop Color="#FF000000" Offset="1"/>
        </LinearGradientBrush>
    </Rectangle.Fill>
</Rectangle>
```

You can see how this changes the appearance of the rendered rectangle in Figure 4-6.

You can achieve some nice effects by experimenting with how you position and direct gradients. These properties can be used to fill shapes or to define strokes, as you will see later in this chapter.

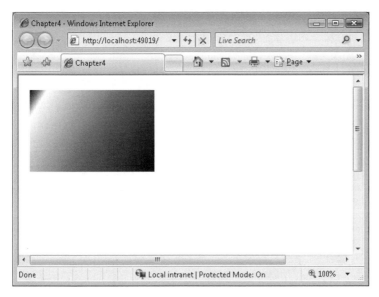

FIGURE 4-6 Positioning the gradient stop.

RadialGradientBrush

The *RadialGradientBrush* is similar to the *LinearGradientBrush* from a definition point of view, but it defines a circular gradient, with 0 marking the center of the circle of the gradient and 1 marking its outer edge. It's easier to show this by example, so consider this XAML:

```
<Rectangle Width="200" Height="128" Canvas.Left="8" Canvas.Top="8">
   <Rectangle.Fill>
      <RadialGradientBrush>
         <GradientStop Color="#FF000000" Offset="0"/>
         <GradientStop Color="#FFFFFFFF" Offset="1"/>
      </RadialGradientBrush>
   </Rectangle.Fill>
</Rectangle>
```

This fills the rectangle with a gradient brush with black at its center and white at its outer edge, as shown in Figure 4-7. Notice that because the outer edge of the rectangle is white, you see an ellipse. This is because the background color of the rectangle is the same as the outer gradient stop color for the brush.

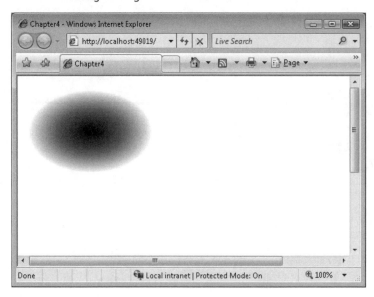

FIGURE 4-7 Filling a rectangle with the *RadialGradientBrush*.

Gradient stops for the *RadialGradientBrush* are defined using similar methods to those used for gradient stops for the *LinearGradientBrush*.

Setting the Focal Point

When you apply a fill with the *RadialGradientBrush*, you can set the focal point for the radial by using the *GradientOrigin* property. You use this to set the point from which the gradient emanates, normally at the center of the circle. Despite the circular nature of the *RadialGradientBrush*, the focal point is set in a rectangular normalized space. So, if you want the focal point to be at the upper-left corner, set the *GradientOrigin* to (0,0); if you want it at the lower-right corner, set the *GradientOrigin* to (1,1). The following example shows the gradient with the focal point set toward the lower right of the object, at (0.7,0.7):

```
<Rectangle Width="200" Height="128" Canvas.Left="8" Canvas.Top="8">
   <Rectangle.Fill>
      <RadialGradientBrush GradientOrigin="0.7, 0.7">
         <GradientStop Color="#FF000000" Offset="0"/>
         <GradientStop Color="#FFFFFFFF" Offset="1"/>
      </RadialGradientBrush>
   </Rectangle.Fill>
</Rectangle>
```

Figure 4-8 shows how it is rendered.

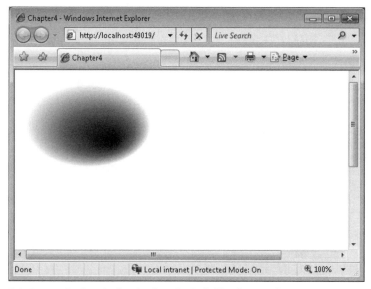

FIGURE 4-8 Setting the focal point of a *RadialGradientBrush*.

Changing the *SpreadMethod*

You can use the *SpreadMethod* property to determine how the gradient repeats. There are three possible values for *SpreadMethod*: *Pad*, *Reflect*, and *Repeat*. *Pad* fills the circle with the gradient as specified and is the default value. Figures 4-7 and 4-8 show a basic *RadialGradientBrush* with a spread set to *Pad*.

Following is the XAML for a rectangle filled with a gradient brush with its *SpreadMethod* set to *Reflect*. You can see the results in Figure 4-9.

```
<Rectangle Width="200" Height="128" Canvas.Left="8" Canvas.Top="8">
    <Rectangle.Fill>
        <RadialGradientBrush SpreadMethod="Reflect">
            <GradientStop Color="#FF000000" Offset="0"/>
            <GradientStop Color="#FFFFFFFF" Offset="1"/>
        </RadialGradientBrush>
    </Rectangle.Fill>
</Rectangle>
```

This causes the gradient to reflect, as you can see in Figure 4-9. The gradient is defined to range from black to white, but then it starts phasing from white to black again as a reflection.

Similarly, you can use the *Repeat* method to repeat the gradient from black to white. Figure 4-10 shows the result of this. Where the gradient would normally stop, the gradient pattern is instead repeated, repeating the phasing from black to white to the outside edges of the rectangle.

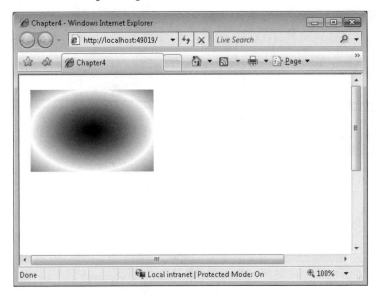

FIGURE 4-9 Using the *Reflect SpreadMethod*.

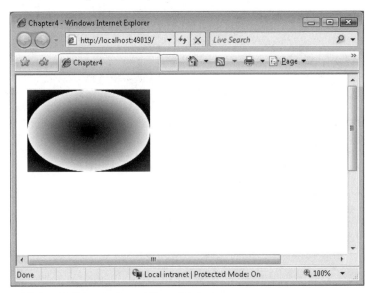

FIGURE 4-10 Using the *Repeat SpreadMethod*.

Setting the Radius of the *RadialGradientBrush*

You use the *RadiusX* and *RadiusY* properties to specify the desired radius for the gradient. The default value for each is 0.5. If you specify a value less than this, you will paint more than one circle with the *SpreadMethod* defining the rendering behavior. If you specify a value greater than 0.5, you effectively "zoom" the gradient.

For example, following is a XAML snippet that defines a *RadialGradientBrush* with *RadiusX* and *RadiusY* set to 0.1 and *SpreadMethod* not set (so it defaults to *Pad*).

```
<Rectangle Width="200" Height="128" Canvas.Left="8" Canvas.Top="8">
    <Rectangle.Fill>
        <RadialGradientBrush RadiusX="0.1" RadiusY="0.1">
            <GradientStop Color="#FF000000" Offset="0"/>
            <GradientStop Color="#FFFFFFFF" Offset="1"/>
        </RadialGradientBrush>
    </Rectangle.Fill>
</Rectangle>
```

This renders the rectangle with a *RadialGradientBrush* using a 0.1 radius, so it is effectively one-fifth the size of the objects we saw earlier. You can see this in Figure 4-11.

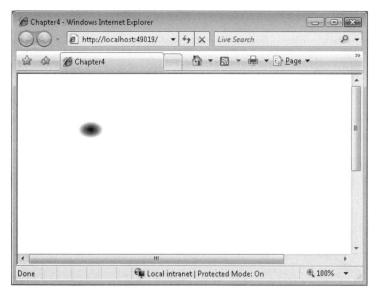

FIGURE 4-11 Setting the radius of the *RadialGradientBrush*.

When combined with the *SpreadMethod*, you can get some interesting effects. You can see an example with a *SpreadMethod* set to *Reflect* in Figure 4-12.

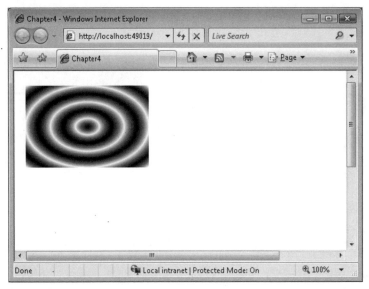

FIGURE 4-12 Combining a change in the radius setting and *SpreadMethod*.

Using *ImageBrush*

To fill a space with an image, you use the XAML *ImageBrush*. The default behavior will stretch the brush to fit the image to maintain the image's aspect ratio. The following XAML fills the contents of a rectangle with an *ImageBrush* (You can see the results of this in Figure 4-13.):

```
<Rectangle Width="200" Height="128" Canvas.Left="8" Canvas.Top="8">
    <Rectangle.Fill>
        <ImageBrush ImageSource="smily.jpg" />
    </Rectangle.Fill>
</Rectangle>
```

Stretching the Image

You can specify how the image fills the area that it is painting with the *Stretch* property. You can specify this using one of several different stretch modes: *None*, *Uniform*, *UniformToFill*, and *Fill*.

None renders the image untouched—no stretching takes place. *Uniform* scales the image to fit the rectangle dimensions but leaves the aspect ratio untouched. *UniformToFill* scales the image to completely fill the output area but preserves its aspect ratio (clipping the image as necessary). *Fill* will scale the image to fit the output dimensions using independent scaling on the x- and y-axes. This will distort the image to completely fill the available space.

You can see these options in action in Figure 4-14, which shows four rectangles that have been filled with the same image but use different stretch modes.

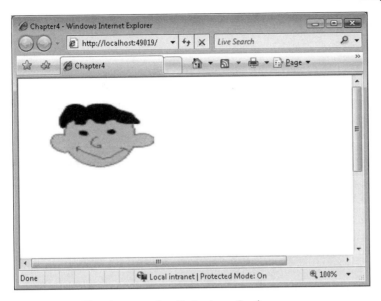

FIGURE 4-13 Filling the rectangle with the *ImageBrush*.

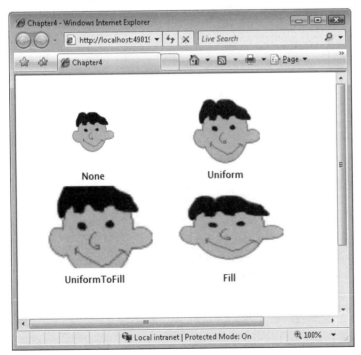

FIGURE 4-14 Using the different *Stretch* property modes in *ImageBrush*.

Aligning the Image

The alignment of the image along the x- and y-axes can be set with the *AlignmentX* and *AlignmentY* properties. You can align the image to the left, right, or center on the x-axis and to the top, center, or bottom on the y-axis. Note that if you are stretching the image to fill the surface, then setting the alignment will have no effect—it will only work when *Stretch* is set to *None*. Following is an example of aligning the image to the right and bottom:

```
<Rectangle Stroke="Black" Width="200" Height="128" x:Name="r1">
   <Rectangle.Fill>
      <ImageBrush ImageSource="smily.jpg" Stretch="None"
                  AlignmentX="Right" AlignmentY="Bottom" />
   </Rectangle.Fill>
</Rectangle>
```

You can see how it will appear in Figure 4-15.

FIGURE 4-15 Using image alignment.

VideoBrush

The *VideoBrush* allows you to fill an area with video. I'll discuss this brush in more detail in Chapter 11, "Media, Ink, and Deep Zoom," where I also describe the *MediaElement* control more completely.

XAML Visual Properties

Beyond brushes and *Canvas* settings, there are a number of other properties provided by XAML to help you to control the appearance of your object. These allow you to set an object's dimensions, opacity, cursor behavior, and stroke.

Using XAML Dimension and Position Properties

XAML dimensions are set using the *Height* and *Width* properties, each of which takes a *double* value. To create a rectangle that is 100 pixels wide and 200 pixels high, for example, you would define your XAML as follows:

```
<Rectangle Fill="Black" Width="100" Height="200" />
```

In addition, keep in mind that the *Top* and *Left* properties attached to the parent canvas are used to specify the relative position of the object.

Consider the following XAML:

```
<Canvas>
  <Canvas Canvas.Top="40" Canvas.Left="40">
    <Rectangle Canvas.Top="40" Fill="Black" Width="100" Height="200" />
  </Canvas>
</Canvas>
```

Assume the outmost *Canvas* is the root canvas for the page. The *Rectangle* will be drawn 80 pixels down from the top of the page as a result. Its parent canvas is 40 pixels down, and the *Rectangle* is 40 pixels down from its parent, for a total of 80 pixels.

Using Opacity

There are two ways that you can set the opacity of an object. The first is to use the alpha channel in the brush that is used to fill the object. The following XAML will create a black rectangle on top of an image:

```
<Image Source="smily.jpg" />
<Rectangle Fill="#FF000000" Width="100" Height="200" />
```

The *Fill* is set to black (because the red, green, and blue channels are all set to zero), and the alpha is set to opaque (filled with #FF). You can make the rectangle semitransparent by changing the alpha channel value:

```
<Image Source="smily.jpg" />
<Rectangle Fill="#77000000" Width="100" Height="200" />
```

You'll see that the rectangle now appears grey, and the image is visible underneath it.

The second method is to use the *Opacity* property, which takes a value from 0 (totally transparent) through 1 (totally opaque). This property is used in conjunction with the alpha channel in the brush. If you use the brush color #77000000 to fill the shape, for example, and then set *Opacity* to 1, the rectangle will still be somewhat opaque. If you set it to 0, the rectangle will be totally transparent.

Using the *Opacity* property is useful when it comes to animating the *opacity* of an object. It makes it easy to fade an object in or out using a *DoubleAnimation*. You can learn more about animation in Chapter 5, "XAML Transformation and Animation."

Cursor Behavior

Most XAML elements allow you to use the *Cursor* property to specify how the mouse will appear when it hovers over an item. This property is set to a value from the *MouseCursor* enumeration:

- **Arrow**   Displays the typical default arrow cursor
- **Default**   No cursor preference; use the parent's cursor if it is specified
- **Hand**   Displays a pointing hand cursor, usually used for a link
- **IBeam**   Specifies an I-beam cursor; typically used for text selection
- **None**   No cursor
- **Wait**   Specifies an icon that indicates a busy wait state

Controlling *Stroke*

The *Stroke* property is used to determine how a shape's outline is painted on the screen. This is different from how it is *filled* with a brush. In a rectangle, for example, the stroke determines how the outline of the rectangle is drawn.

The *Stroke* is set by using a brush. Following is an example of XAML that renders a rectangle using a simple stroke to specify a black outline:

```
<Rectangle Stroke="Black" Canvas.Left="40" Canvas.Top="40" Width="100" Height="200">
```

The *Stroke* property is in fact using a *Black SolidColorBrush* in this case. It is syntactically equivalent to the following XAML:

```
<Rectangle Canvas.Left="40" Canvas.Top="40" Width="100" Height="200">
   <Rectangle.Stroke>
      <SolidColorBrush Color="Black" />
   </Rectangle.Stroke>
</Rectangle>
```

Using this syntax (defining the brush as an attached *Stroke* property), it is possible to specify different types of brushes to draw the shape's stroke. Following is an example of using a *LinearGradientBrush* to paint the rectangle's stroke:

```
<Rectangle StrokeThickness="10" Canvas.Left="40"
          Canvas.Top="40" Width="100" Height="200">
  <Rectangle.Stroke>
    <LinearGradientBrush >
      <GradientStop Color="#FF000000" Offset="0"/>
      <GradientStop Color="#FFFFFFFF" Offset="0.5"/>
      <GradientStop Color="#FF000000" Offset="1"/>
    </LinearGradientBrush>
  </Rectangle.Stroke>
</Rectangle>
```

You can see how this appears on the screen in Figure 4-16.

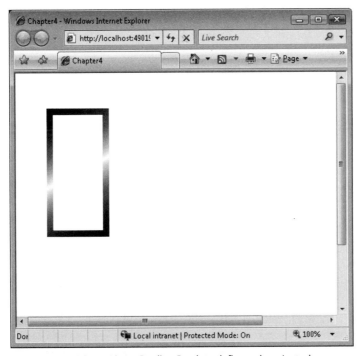

FIGURE 4-16 Using a *LinearGradientBrush* to define a shape's stroke.

Setting Stroke Width

You may have noticed in this example that the thickness of the stroke was set to 10. This was done to better demonstrate the gradient, which doesn't show up well using the default stroke thickness value of 1.

The stroke width is set using the *StrokeThickness* property. This specifies the stroke width in pixels:

```
<Rectangle StrokeThickness="10" Stroke="Black" Canvas.Left="40" Canvas.Top="40" Width="100"
Height="200" />
```

Setting Stroke Dash

The *StrokeDashArray* property is used to set the stroke dash pattern. This is combined with the *StrokeDashCap* and *StrokeDashOffset* properties to allow stroke dash fine-tuning.

To set the stroke of the rectangle to be dashed with a repeating pattern of dashes, you define an array of *double* values that represents the length of the dashes as well as the space between them. To define a dash pattern using a dash 4 units long, followed by a space 1 unit long, followed by a dash 2 units long, followed by a space 1 unit long before repeating, you would set the *StrokeDashArray* property to (4,1,2,1). Here's an example:

```
<Rectangle StrokeThickness="10" Stroke="Black" Canvas.Left="40" Canvas.Top="40" Width="100"
Height="200" StrokeDashArray="4,1,2,1"/>
```

Figure 4-17 shows how this is drawn on the screen.

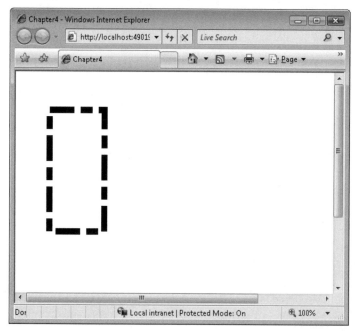

FIGURE 4-17 Setting the dash pattern for the stroke using *StrokeDashArray*.

You can see that these dashes are rectangular in shape, with squared dash edges. You can change this using the *StrokeDashCap* property. This property is set to a value from the *PenlineCap* enumeration. It can contain the following values:

- **Flat**   This is the default value, and it specifies that the cap doesn't extend beyond the end of the line—it is the same as not having a cap.

- **Round**   This specifies a semicircle with the same diameter as the line thickness.

- *Square* This specifies a square end cap.

- *Triangle* This specifies an isosceles triangle end cap, with the base length equal to the thickness of the stroke.

Following is an example of using the *StrokeDashCap* to set a rounded dash cap:

```
<Rectangle StrokeThickness="10" Stroke="Black" Canvas.Left="40" Canvas.Top="40" Width="100"
Height="200" StrokeDashArray="4,1,2,1" StrokeDashCap="Round"/>
```

Figure 4-18 shows how this will appear on the screen.

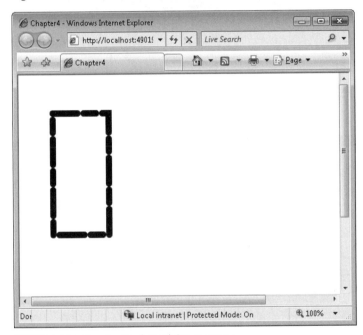

FIGURE 4-18 Using the *StrokeDashCap* property.

Controlling Line Joins

If you look at the previous examples, you will notice that the dash lines intersect at the corners and are drawn squared off. This is considered a line join, and the *StrokeLineJoin* property allows you to control how the pen behaves at this line join. This property is set to the *PenLineJoin* enumeration, which can contain one of three values:

- *Bevel* Shave off the edges of the join

- *Miter* Keep the sharp edges

- *Round* Round the edges of the join

This XAML creates a rectangle with the line join type set to *Bevel*:

```
<Rectangle StrokeThickness="10" Stroke="Black" Canvas.Left="40" Canvas.Top="40" Width="100"
Height="200" StrokeLineJoin="Bevel" />
```

You can see how this is drawn in Figure 4-19.

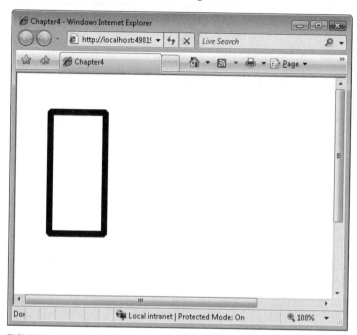

FIGURE 4-19 Using the *StrokeLineJoin* to specify a beveled corner.

Shapes in XAML

XAML supports a number of basic shapes that can be used to create more complex objects. These shapes are:

- **Ellipse**   Draws an ellipse—a circle is an ellipse with equal radius distances for *X* and *Y*

- **Rectangle**   Draws a rectangle—a square is a rectangle with equal distances for *X* and *Y*

- **Line**   Draws a line

- **Path**   Draws a series of connected lines and curves according to a path language

- **Polygon**   Draws a closed shape made up of a connected series of lines

- **Polyline**   Draws a series of connected straight lines

We'll look at how to create each of these shapes in the following subsections.

Using the *Ellipse* Object

The *Ellipse* shape is used to draw an ellipse or circle. You control the *Ellipse* by setting its height property to the desired vertical diameter (i.e., twice the desired vertical radius) and its width property to the desired horizontal diameter. If these values are equal in value, the XAML will render a circle. The *Ellipse* outline is drawn using a *Stroke*, and the *Ellipse* is filled using a *Brush*.

Using the *Rectangle* Object

The *Rectangle* shape is used to draw a rectangle or square. You control the size of the shape using the *Width* and *Height* properties. If these properties are equal, you end up with a square. Like the *Ellipse*, the outline of the *Rectangle* is drawn using a *Stroke*, and it is filled using a *Brush*.

You can round the corners of a *Rectangle* shape using the *RadiusX* and *RadiusY* properties. You set these to a *double* specifying the radius of the desired circle. They default to 0.0, indicating no rounding. As the *RadiusX* and *RadiusY* are set independently, you can obtain elliptical rounding effects by using different values.

Following is an example of a rectangle with rounded corners. *RadiusY* is set to 40, and *RadiusX* is set to 20, indicating that the corners will be smoother vertically than they are horizontally:

```
<Rectangle Fill="Black" Canvas.Left="40" Canvas.Top="40"
        Width="100" Height="200" RadiusX="20" RadiusY="40" />
```

You can see the results of these settings in action in Figure 4-20.

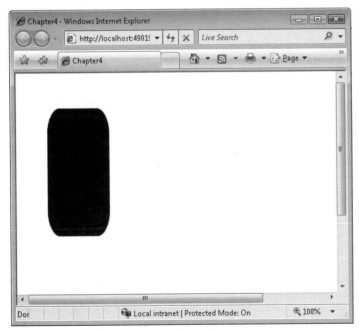

FIGURE 4-20 Rounding the corners of a rectangle.

Using the *Line* Object

You can draw a simple line in XAML using the *Line* object. This allows you to specify its (X1,Y1) and (X2,Y2) coordinates with the line to be drawn between them. These coordinates are relative to the upper-left position of the line, specified using *Canvas.Top* and *Canvas.Left* in the usual manner. Note that you need to specify the line stroke using at least a stroke color before the stroke will be drawn.

Consider the following XAML:

```
<Line X1="40" Y1="40" X2="100" Y2="100" Stroke="Black" />
```

This will draw a line from (40,40) to (100,100). However, if you add *Canvas.Top* and/or *Canvas.Left*, then the line will be drawn relative to that. So, the following XAML will draw the line from (40,140) to (100,200), assuming there is no positioning on the parent canvas. If there is, Silverlight will draw the line relative to the parent positioning.

```
<Line Canvas.Top="100" X1="40" Y1="40" X2="100" Y2="100" Stroke="Black" />
```

Using Paths and Geometries

The *Path* object draws a connected series of lines and curves. These lines and curves can be defined using a geometry type. We'll look at the various geometry types here.

The *EllipseGeometry* defines the path as a simple ellipse. Here's an example:

```
<Path Stroke="Black">
  <Path.Data>
    <EllipseGeometry RadiusX="100" RadiusY="100" />
  </Path.Data>
</Path>
```

The *EllipseGeometry* uses *RadiusX* and *RadiusY* to specify the dimensions of the ellipse that makes up the geometry. It also allows you to define the center point of the ellipse using the *Center* attribute. Following is an example:

```
<Path Stroke="Black">
  <Path.Data>
    <EllipseGeometry RadiusX="100" RadiusY="100" Center="50,50" />
  </Path.Data>
</Path>
```

The *LineGeometry* defines the path as a single line, starting at the *StartPoint* and ending at the *EndPoint*. These are set simply using string x- and y-coordinates, so the upper-left corner is specified as (0,0). Here's an example of a *LineGeometry*:

```
<Path Stroke="Black">
  <Path.Data>
    <LineGeometry StartPoint="10,10" EndPoint="100,100" />
```

```
    </Path.Data>
</Path>
```

The *RectangleGeometry* defines the path as a single rectangle, using the *Rect* property to define the dimensions of the rectangle. This is a string of four values, corresponding to the top, left, height, and width of the rectangle. So, to draw a rectangle that is 100 by 200 pixels with its upper-left corner at (0,0), you would use the following *Path*:

```
<Path Stroke="Black">
  <Path.Data>
    <RectangleGeometry Rect="0,0,100,200" />
  </Path.Data>
</Path>
```

The *PathGeometry* is used to put together a complex path of different segments, including arcs, Bezier curves, lines, poly-Bezier curves, polyquadratic Bezier curves, and quadratic Bezier curves. Segments can be collected into a *PathFigure*, and one or more *PathFigure* objects make up a *PathGeometry*. The *PathGeometry* also sets the starting point of the path. If you have multiple segments, the starting point for each segment will be the last point of the previous segment.

The *ArcSegment* Object

The *ArcSegment* object draws a simple elliptical arc between two points. You have a number of different properties to set to define the arc:

- **Point** Sets the starting point for the arc

- **Size** Sets the x and y radius of the arc

- **RotationAngle** Sets the rotation angle—that is, how far the angle is rotated around the x-axis

- **IsLargeArc** Sets the "largeness" of the arc, where an arc over 180 degrees is considered large

- **SweepDirection** Sets the drawing direction of the arc (*Clockwise* or *CounterClockwise*)

Here's an example of a *Path* with a single arc segment, with these properties demonstrated:

```
<Path Stroke="Black">
  <Path.Data>
    <PathGeometry>
      <PathFigure>
        <ArcSegment Point="100,100" Size="200,200"
          RotationAngle="10" IsLargeArc="False"
          SweepDirection="ClockWise" />
      </PathFigure>
    </PathGeometry>
  </Path.Data>
</Path>
```

The *LineSegment* Object

You can add a line to a *PathSegment* using the *LineSegment* object. This simply draws a line from the current or starting point to the point defined using its *Point* property. So, to draw a line from (100,100) to (200,200) and then another back to (200,0), you create a *PathFigure* containing multiple line segments like this:

```
<Path Stroke="Black">
   <Path.Data>
      <PathGeometry>
         <PathFigure StartPoint="100,100">
            <LineSegment Point="200,200" />
            <LineSegment Point="200,0" />
         </PathFigure>
      </PathGeometry>
   </Path.Data>
</Path>
```

The *PolyLineSegment* Object

As its name suggests, the *PolyLineSegment* allows a number of lines to be drawn simply by providing the points. The first line is drawn from the start point to the first defined point, the second line from this point to the second defined point, and so forth.

Following is the XAML that demonstrates a *PolyLineSegment*:

```
<Path Stroke="Black">
   <Path.Data>
      <PathGeometry>
            <PathFigure StartPoint="100,100">
               <PolyLineSegment
                 Points="50,50,150,150,250,250,
                         100,200,200,100,300,300" />
            </PathFigure>
      </PathGeometry>
   </Path.Data>
</Path>
```

The *BezierSegment* Object

This object allows you to define a Bezier curve, which is a curve between two points defined by one or two control points. The *BezierSegment* object takes three points as parameters, called *Point1*, *Point2*, and *Point3*. Depending on how many you use, you get different behavior. So, for example, if you set *Point1* and *Point2*, the curve will be rendered from the start point to *Point2*, using *Point1* as the control point. If you set *Point1*, *Point2*, and *Point3*, the curve will be rendered from the start point to *Point3*, using *Point1* and *Point2* as control points.

Following is an example of a *PathFigure* containing a *BezierSegment*:

```
<Path Stroke="Black">
   <Path.Data>
      <PathGeometry>
         <PathFigure StartPoint="100,100">
            <BezierSegment Point1="140,120" Point2="100,140" />
         </PathFigure>
      </PathGeometry>
   </Path.Data>
</Path>
```

The *PolyBezierSegment* Object

This object allows you to set a group of points that Silverlight will interpret into a set of control points for a group of Bezier curves. Consider the following XAML:

```
<Path Stroke="Black">
  <Path.Data>
     <PathGeometry>
        <PathFigure StartPoint="100,100">
           <PolyBezierSegment>
             <PolyBezierSegment.Points>
                <Point X="50" Y="50" />
                <Point X="150" Y="150" />
                <Point X="250" Y="250" />
                <Point X="100" Y="200" />
                <Point X="200" Y="100" />
                <Point X="300" Y="300" />
             </PolyBezierSegment.Points>
           </PolyBezierSegment>
        </PathFigure>
     </PathGeometry>
  </Path.Data>
</Path>
```

Alternatively, you can define the set of points using a points collection stored as comma-separated values in a string:

```
<Path Stroke="Black">
   <Path.Data>
      <PathGeometry>
         <PathFigure StartPoint="100,100">
            <PolyBezierSegment  Points="50,50,150,150,250,250,
                                  100,200,200,100,300,300" />
         </PathFigure>
      </PathGeometry>
   </Path.Data>
</Path>
```

The result of this XAML is shown in Figure 4-21. To interpret this, the starting point is defined as being at position (100,100), which is the upper-left side of the overall curve. The first Bezier then goes to the end point (250,250), using (50,50) and (150,150) as control points. As these control points effectively cancel each other out (they are equidistant from the line from [100,100] to [250,250]), the first Bezier ends up being a straight line ending at (250,250). The second Bezier then starts at this point (250,250) and is drawn to the last point at (300,300), through control points at (100,200) and (200,100), which gives it the distinctive "loop back and then forward" look.

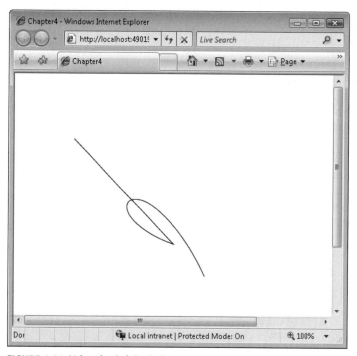

FIGURE 4-21 Using the *PolyBezierSegment*.

The *QuadraticBezierSegment* Object

A quadratic Bezier is a simple Bezier curve that is drawn as a regular quadratic curve using a single control point. It takes two point objects. If you only use one, it becomes the end point of the curve with no control point and is effectively a straight line from the start point to the point you defined. If you use two points, then the second point is the end point of the curve, and the first is the quadratic control point. Here's an example:

```
<Path Stroke="Black">
   <Path.Data>
      <PathGeometry>
         <PathFigure StartPoint="100,100">
            <QuadraticBezierSegment Point1="200,0" Point2="300,100"  />
         </PathFigure>
      </PathGeometry>
   </Path.Data>
</Path>
```

The curve rendered by this XAML can be seen in Figure 4-22.

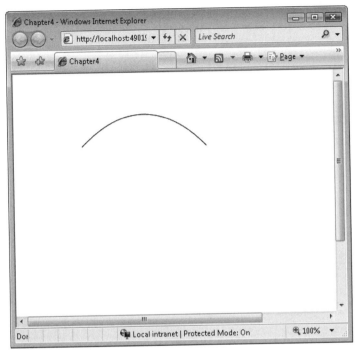

FIGURE 4-22 Simple quadratic Bezier curve.

The *PolyQuadraticBezierSegment* Object

As its name suggests, this is a collection of connected quadratic Bezier curves defined and parsed from a list of control points in a similar manner to that described for the *PolyBezierSegment* object earlier in this chapter. Following is an example of a *PolyQuadraticBezierSegment* in action:

```
<Path Stroke="Black">
   <Path.Data>
      <PathGeometry>
         <PathFigure StartPoint="100,100">
            <PolyQuadraticBezierSegment Points="50,50,150,150,250,250,
                                                100,200,200,100,300,300" />
         </PathFigure>
      </PathGeometry>
   </Path.Data>
</Path>
```

The result of this XAML is shown in Figure 4-23.

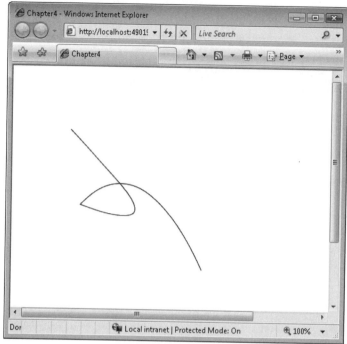

FIGURE 4-23 *PolyQuadraticBezier* object in action.

This code draws a number of quadratic Bezier curves. The first is from the starting point, (100,100), to (150,150), with a control point at (50,50), which yields a straight line ending at (150,150). The second is then a curve starting at (150,150) and ending at (100,200), with a control point at (250,250). This is shown as the curve sweeping toward the left. The third curve then starts at (100,200) and ends at (300,300), through a control point at (200,100), and this is rendered as the long smooth curve going from left to right in Figure 4-23.

Compound Path Segments

Each of these segment types can be compounded within a *PathFigure* segment within a collection. Additionally, *PathFigure* segments can be collected within a *PathGeometry* to create a complex set of segments.

Following is an example in which the *PathGeometry* contains two *PathFigure* objects. The first object has a *LineSegment*, a *PolyQuadraticBezierSegment*, and another *LineSegment*. The second object has a single *LineSegment*.

```
<Path Stroke="Black">
  <Path.Data>
    <PathGeometry>
      <PathFigure StartPoint="100,100">
        <LineSegment Point="200,200" />
        <PolyQuadraticBezierSegment Points="50,50,150,150,250,250,
                                            100,200,200,100,300,300" />
        <LineSegment Point="0,0" />
      </PathFigure>
      <PathFigure>
        <LineSegment Point="10,400" />
      </PathFigure>
    </PathGeometry>
  </Path.Data>
</Path>
```

Using the *GeometryGroup* Object

In the previous sections, you saw the various geometries that are available, from simple ones such as the *EllipseGeometry*, *LineGeometry*, and *RectangleGeometry*, to complex ones made up of many *PathSegments* within a *PathGeometry*. You can combine these together using a *GeometryGroup* object.

You simply define the geometries that you want as a collection within this object. Following is an example of a *GeometryGroup* containing an *EllipseGeometry*, a *RectangleGeometry*, and then the same complex *PathGeometry* that you used in the previous section:

```
<Path Stroke="Black">
  <Path.Data>
    <GeometryGroup>
      <EllipseGeometry RadiusX="100" RadiusY="100" Center="50,50" />
      <RectangleGeometry Rect="200,200,100,100" />
      <PathGeometry>
        <PathFigure StartPoint="100,100">
          <LineSegment Point="200,200" />
          <PolyQuadraticBezierSegment Points="50,50,150,150,250,250,
                                              100,200,200,100,300,300" />
          <LineSegment Point="0,0" />
        </PathFigure>
        <PathFigure>
          <LineSegment Point="10,400" />
        </PathFigure>
      </PathGeometry>
    </GeometryGroup>
  </Path.Data>
</Path>
```

Figure 4-24 shows how this will appear.

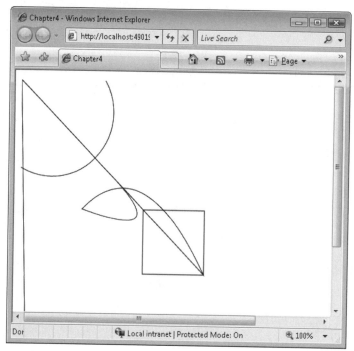

FIGURE 4-24 Using the *GeometryGroup* object to group many geometries together.

The *Path* Language

The *Path* object has a *Data* property that can use the *Path* language to define a complex path. This language uses the syntax of a command letter followed by a space, followed by a comma-separated list of numbers, followed by a space before the next command letter. Following is an example:

```
<Path Stroke="Black" Data="M 100,100 L 200,200" />
```

- In this instance, the path is drawn using the *M* command, for *Move*, to move to (100,100) and the *L* command, for *Line*, to draw a line between there and (200,200).These commands can either be uppercase (for example, *M*), which determines absolute coordinates, or lowercase (for example, *m*), which determines relative coordinates. The *M* command places the drawing pen at the specified point without drawing a line between the current point and the defined point; that is, it moves the starting point. It will draw the line from (100,100) to (200,200), assuming there is no positioning on the parent canvas. If there is, Silverlight will draw the line relative to the parent positioning.

- The *L* (for Line) command draws a line from the current point to the specified point.

- The *H* command takes a single number as a parameter and draws a horizontal line between the current point and the specified value on the x-axis.

- The *V* command takes a single number as a parameter and draws a vertical line between the current point and the specified value on the y-axis.

- The *C* command takes three points as parameters. It draws a cubic Bezier curve between the current point and the third of these points, using the first two points as control points.

- The *Q* command takes two points as parameters and draws a quadratic Bezier curve between the current point and the second one, using the first as a control point.

- The *S* command takes two points as parameters and draws a smooth cubic Bezier curve between the current point and the second of these. It uses two control points—the current point itself and the first of the two parameters—to generate a smoother curve.

- The *T* command works in the same way as the *S* command, except that it draws a smooth quadratic Bezier curve.

- The *A* command takes five parameters—for size, rotation angle, *isLargeArc*, *sweepDirection*, and end point. It uses these parameters to draw an elliptical arc.

- The *Z* command ends the current path and closes it to form a closed shape by drawing a line between the current point and the starting point of the path.

Clipping and Geometries in XAML

XAML elements may be clipped according to a rule defined by a geometry type. As we saw in the previous section, these types can be simple (*EllipseGeometry*, *LineGeometry*, or *RectangleGeometry*), complex (using a geometry defined by *PathGeometry*), or a group of any of these contained within a *GeometryCollection*.

To define how an object is clipped, you simply set its attached *Clip* property to a geometry type. The following example is an image being clipped by an *EllipseGeometry*:

```
<Image Source="smily.jpg" Width="300" Height="300">
<Image.Clip>
   <EllipseGeometry Center="150,150" RadiusX="100" RadiusY="100" />
</Image.Clip>

</Image>
```

You can see how this looks in Figure 4-25.

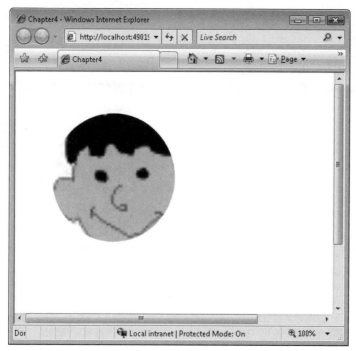

FIGURE 4-25 Clipping an image with a geometry.

XAML Controls in Silverlight

There are a number of XAML controls available to Silverlight developers. These include the following:

- *Canvas*

- *Image*

- *Glyphs*

- *TextBlock*

- *MediaElement*

What we have seen so far in this chapter—properties such as clipping, brushes, layout, and more—apply to all of these elements. We will discuss the first four in the following subsections; the *MediaElement* control is covered in detail in Chapter 11.

The *Canvas* Element

This element defines an area of the page in which you can place child elements. It can be used to group elements visually, with their layout and positioning relative to the canvas. In addition, the *Canvas* object can be used solely as a container for other objects, allowing them to be treated as a single object with respect to placement and events handling.

Here's an example of collecting rectangles into groups using *Canvas* elements:

```
<Canvas Width="144" Height="128" Canvas.Left="24" Canvas.Top="8">
    <Rectangle Fill="#FF000000" Stroke="#FF000000"
                    Width="144" Height="64" Canvas.Top="24"/>
    <Rectangle Fill="#FF000000" Stroke="#FF000000"
                    Width="56" Height="128" Canvas.Left="40"/>
</Canvas>
<Canvas Width="152" Height="144" Canvas.Left="24" Canvas.Top="184">
    <Rectangle Fill="#FFFF0000" Stroke="#FF000000"
                    Width="152" Height="72" Canvas.Top="32"/>
    <Rectangle Fill="#FFFF0000" Stroke="#FF000000"
                    Width="64" Height="144" Canvas.Left="48"/>
</Canvas>
```

The *Image* Element

The *Image* element is used to define a graphic. This is set to the Universal Resource Indicator (URI) of a valid image, such as a bitmap, .jpg or .png image.

Following is an example in which the layout of the image is set using *Height*, *Width*, *Canvas.Left*, and *Canvas.Top* properties and the *Source* points to "smily.jpg":

```
<Image Width="184" Height="128" Canvas.Left="56" Canvas.Top="32" Source="smily.jpg"/>
```

The *Glyphs* Element

The *Glyphs* element is used to render fixed text according to a defined font. It can also be used to render characters that have no fixed keystroke associated with them, such as many graphics characters in fonts including Wingdings or Unicode text.

One thing to be careful about when using *Glyphs* is that, for the glyph to work, the font will be downloaded to the target machine. As a result, you should ensure that you have distribution rights to the font that you are using.

To use the *Glyphs* element, you specify the font using the *FontUri* property. You then specify the characters to render using the *Indices* or *UnicodeString* properties. When using *Indices*, you specify characters based on their offset within the font definition using a semicolon-separated list.

In addition, you have to specify the font size using the *FontRenderingEmSize* property. Optionally, you can set the *StyleSimulations* property to emulate font styles. You can set this property to *BoldSimulation*, *ItalicSimulation*, or *BoldItalicSimulation*, as well as to the default setting, *None*.

Here's an example that uses a *Glyphs* element. It uses the Webdings font to draw some characters using their offset.

Note In order to run this application, you will need to have the webdings.ttf font file on your server in the same directory as the Silverlight application. If you don't have this font available, simply replace it with another font that you do have available that can render the desired characters. It is important to remember that if you use this technique in a production environment, you must have permission to distribute the fonts that you are using.

```
<Glyphs Canvas.Top="0" FontUri="webdings.ttf" Indices="133;134;135"
        Fill="Black" FontRenderingEmSize="48"/>
```

You can see how this will be rendered by Silverlight in Figure 4-26.

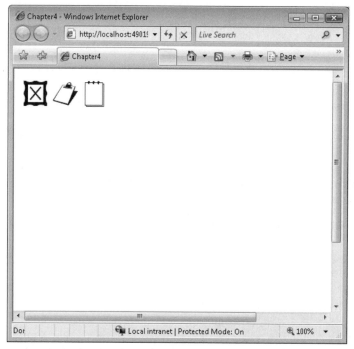

FIGURE 4-26 Using the *Glyphs* object.

The *TextBlock* Element

This is a lightweight object that displays single or multiline text with multiple formatting options. It differs significantly from the *Glyphs* element in that it does not require you to specify the font. Thus, regardless of the operating system or browser that you are using, the text will be rendered in the same way.

You specify the font family that you want the text to be rendered in using the *FontFamily* property. Silverlight supports nine basic fonts:

- Arial

- Arial Black

- Comic Sans MS

- Courier New

- Georgia

- Lucida Grande/Lucida Sans Unicode

- Times New Roman

- Trebuchet MS

- Verdana

These fonts are considered "Web-safe," meaning that if you use them, your results will be consistent regardless of the browser or operating system being used to display the text. If you use fonts that are not in this set, the browser will check to see if those fonts are on the system, and if they are, it will use them. If they are not, a set of font replacement rules will pick the best match from the system fonts.

The *FontSize* property is used to specify the size in pixels that you want the text to be rendered. The *FontStyle* property is used to determine the style that is rendered. This can be *Normal* or *Italic*.

The *FontWeight* property is used to determine the weight of the font when rendering. There are a number of possible values for this: *Thin, ExtraLight, Light, Normal, Medium, SemiBold, Bold, ExtraBold, Black*, or *ExtraBlack*.

The *TextDecorations* property is used to determine whether the text in the *TextBlock* is rendered with an underline or not. It can be set to *Underline* or *None*.

The *TextWrapping* property is used to determine whether or not the *TextBlock* wraps the text. It can be set to *NoWrap*, so the text is on a single line and is clipped to the width of the *TextBlock*, or to *Wrap* so the text flows onto a new line when it reaches the end of the available horizontal width. Text wrapping can affect the dimensions of the text box by changing the width through clipping the text and the height by adding extra lines. As a result, the default *Width* and *Height* properties may return an inaccurate value. So, the *TextBlock* exposes *ActualWidth* and *ActualHeight* properties, which return the correct value.

Runs and Line Breaks

The *Run* element is used to change formatting or styling of text within a *TextBlock*. If you want a block of text to set with three different styles or fonts, you'd define the first style on the text block and set its text property to the desired text. You'd then add a run with the second style and text, and then add another run with the third style and its text. Here's an example:

```
<TextBlock FontFamily="Arial" Width="400"
        Text="ArialText">
<Run Foreground="Blue" FontFamily="Comic Sans MS"
    FontSize="24">Large Comic Sans</Run>
<Run Foreground="Teal" FontFamily="Verdana"
    FontSize="12" FontStyle="Italic">Italic Verdana</Run>
</TextBlock>
```

The text "ArialTextLarge Comic SansItalic Verdana" is then loaded into the *TextBlock*, but as "Large Comic Sans" is in a *Run* defined with one font and style and "Italic Verdana" is defined in a different one, the rendered output will show the text as a single line with changing formats. You can see the results in Figure 4-27.

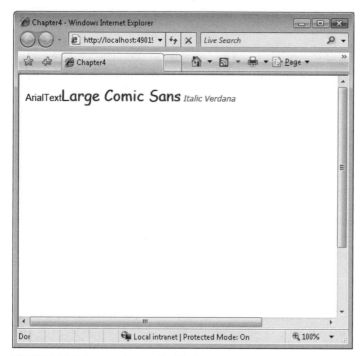

FIGURE 4-27 Using runs in your *TextBlock*.

You can create breaks in the text in your *TextBlock* using the *LineBreak* element. This is simply inserted between runs to create a break. Following is the previous example updated to use a line break:

```
<TextBlock FontFamily="Arial" Width="400"
        Text="ArialText">
<Run Foreground="Blue" FontFamily="Comic Sans MS"
    FontSize="24">Large Comic Sans</Run>
  <LineBreak />
<Run Foreground="Teal" FontFamily="Verdana"
    FontSize="12" FontStyle="Italic">Italic Verdana</Run>
</TextBlock>
```

Figure 4-28 shows how this is rendered. You can see that the break appears between the words "Sans" and "Italic."

FIGURE 4-28 Using *LineBreak* in the *TextBlock*.

Summary

In this chapter, you learned about many of the details involved in setting up visual elements using XAML. You were introduced to layout, positioning, filling, strokes, opacity, paths, geometries, and clipping, which give you control over what you see in your user interface. In addition, you took a look at the generic controls that provide containment of controls and elements as well as text rendering.

In the next chapter, you'll examine how XAML is used to bring life to the user interface by adding transformations and animation!

Chapter 5
XAML Transformation and Animation

In Chapter 4, "XAML Basics," you learned how you can use XAML to render graphics on the screen, whether they are vector graphics, raster graphics (using the *Image* object), or video graphics. In this chapter, we will examine how to enhance these graphics using different types of transformations (to change how the object appears) and animations (to change attributes of the object over time). In addition, we'll introduce key frames and explain how they can be used to fine-tune animation behavior, and then we'll take a quick look at Expression Blend again to see how it can be used to design animations visually.

Transformations

In graphics, a transform defines how to map points from one coordinate space to another. This is typically described using a *transformation matrix*, a special mathematical construct that allows for simple mathematical conversion from one system to another. Silverlight XAML abstracts this, and we will not go into detail about the mathematics in this book. Silverlight XAML supports four set transformations for rotation, scaling, skewing, and translation (movement), as well as a special transformation type that allows you to implement your own matrix, which is used to combine transformations.

Transformations are applied using transform properties. There are several different types of transform properties, which are applied to different object types.

Thus, when using a *Brush* type, you define your transformation using either the *Brush.Transform* property when you want to affect the brush's content—if you want to rotate an image before using it in an *ImageBrush*, for example—or you might use the *Brush.RelativeTransform* property, which allows you to transform a brush using relative values—something you might do if you are painting different areas of different sizes using the same brush, for example.

When using a *Geometry* type, you apply a simple transform using the *Geometry.Transform* property. This type does not support relative transforms.

Finally, when using a user interface (UI) element, you specify the transformation to use with the *RenderTransform* property. If you are transforming an ellipse, for example, you'll use the *Ellipse.RenderTransform* to define the desired transform.

In the following section, we'll take a look at the different transformation types to see how these properties are used within their specific object types.

Rotating with the *RotateTransform* Property

RotateTransform allows you to rotate an element by a specified angle around a specified center point. You set the angle of rotation using the *Angle* property to set the number of degrees that you want to rotate the item. Consider the horizontal vector pointing to the right to be 0 degrees, and rotation takes place *clockwise*, so the vertical vector pointing down is the result of a 90-degree rotation.

You set the center of transformation using the *CenterX* and *CenterY* properties to specify the coordinates of the pivot. These default to 0.0, which makes the default rotation pivot the upper-left corner of the container.

Consider this example XAML, in which a *TextBlock* is rotated using a *RenderTransform* that contains a *RotateTransform* specifying a 45-degree rotation:

```
<TextBlock Width="320" Height="40"
           Text="This is the text to rotate" TextWrapping="Wrap">
    <TextBlock.RenderTransform>
        <RotateTransform Angle="45" />
    </TextBlock.RenderTransform>
</TextBlock>
```

You can see how this appears in Figure 5-1.

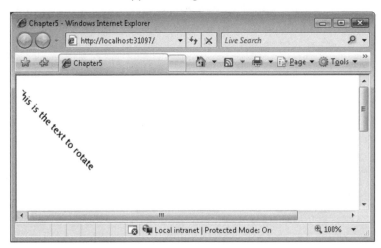

FIGURE 5-1 Using the *RotateTransform* property.

As you can see, this text is being rotated around a center point at (0,0) at the upper-left corner of the screen.

This XAML shows how to use *CenterX* and *CenterY* to rotate around a different point. In this case, the rotation is done around the (100,200) point:

```
<TextBlock Width="320" Height="40"
           Text="This is the text to rotate" TextWrapping="Wrap" >
    <TextBlock.RenderTransform>
        <RotateTransform Angle="45" CenterX="100" CenterY="200" />
    </TextBlock.RenderTransform>
</TextBlock>
```

The results of this transformation are shown in Figure 5-2.

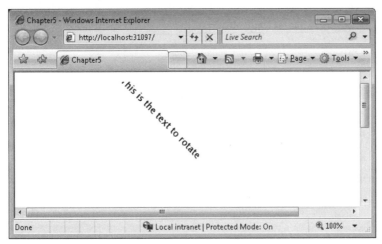

FIGURE 5-2 Rotating around a different center point.

Scaling with the *ScaleTransform* Property

The *ScaleTransform* property is used to change the size of an object based on the horizontal axis, the vertical axis, or both axes.

When scaling an object, you need to specify at least one of the axes around which you want to scale and by how much you want to scale against that axis. You use the *ScaleX* property to scale the object on the horizontal axis, the x-axis, and the *ScaleY* to scale it on the vertical axis, the y-axis. These are set to a *double* value, which represents the value by which you multiply the object's current size on the specified axis. Therefore, values greater than 1 will stretch the object by that multiple. For example, using a *ScaleX* value of 2 will double the size of the object horizontally. Values less than 1, but greater than 0, will shrink the object. Using a setting of 0.5, for instance, will reduce the size of the object by half along the specific dimension.

So, for example, consider this XAML that creates a red rectangle 96 pixels wide by 88 pixels high:

```
<Rectangle Fill="#FFFF0404" Stroke="#FF000000" Width="96" Height="88"
Canvas.Left="112" Canvas.Top="72" />
```

Figure 5-3 shows what this looks like when it is rendered in Silverlight.

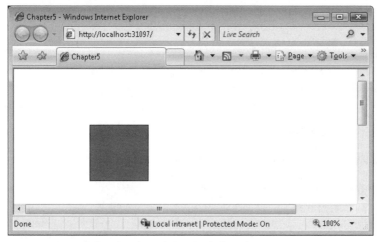

FIGURE 5-3 Rendering the rectangle in Silverlight.

To apply a *ScaleTransform* to this object, you use a *RenderTransform* and specify the transform to be a *ScaleTransform*. Here's the XAML:

```
<Rectangle Fill="#FFFF0404" Stroke="#FF000000"
        Width="96" Height="88" Canvas.Left="112" Canvas.Top="72">
  <Rectangle.RenderTransform>
    <ScaleTransform ScaleX="2" />
  </Rectangle.RenderTransform>
</Rectangle>
```

Figure 5-4 shows how this is rendered by Silverlight.

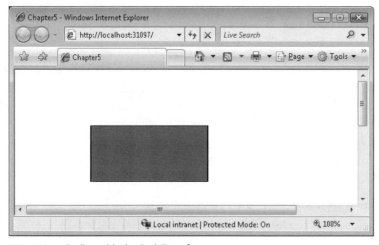

FIGURE 5-4 Scaling with the *ScaleTransform*.

You will notice that the rectangle increased in size horizontally to the right using this *ScaleTransform* because the center of scaling was not specified. You can specify it with the

CenterX property for horizontal scaling or the *CenterY* property for vertical scaling. These specify the coordinate of the center of scaling. This coordinate is relative to the upper-left corner of the rectangle. The coordinate default is 0, meaning that scaling will take place to the right on the horizontal axis and downward on the vertical axis.

If you set the *CenterX* property to a positive value (for example, 50), the scaling will be around the X point, 50 pixels to the right of the leftmost side of the rectangle. This will make it look like the rectangle has moved a number of pixels to the left of the one where the *CenterX* hasn't been changed (the number depends on the size of the scaling factor). This is because the stretching is centered on that point, pushing the left side of the rectangle to the left as well as pushing the right side to the right. You'll get similar effects by setting the *ScaleY* and *CenterY* values in the same way. Following is an example:

```
<Rectangle Fill="#FFFF0404" Stroke="#FF000000"
    Width="96" Height="88" Canvas.Left="80" Canvas.Top="80">
  <Rectangle.RenderTransform>
    <ScaleTransform ScaleX="2" CenterX="50"/>
  </Rectangle.RenderTransform>
</Rectangle>
```

You can see how this affects the rectangle in Figure 5-5.

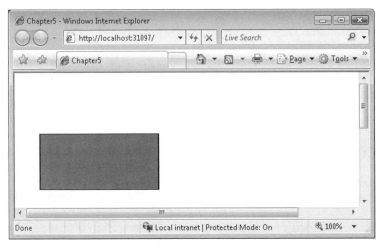

FIGURE 5-5 Scaling around a center point.

Moving an Object with the *TranslateTransform* Property

A *translation* is a transform that moves an object in a 2D plane from one position to another. It is defined by setting up vectors that define the object's motion along its x- and y-axes. These are set using the *X* and *Y* properties on the transform. To move an item two units horizontally (meaning it will move to the right), you set the *X* property to 2. To move it to the left, use a negative value, such as –2. Similarly, to move an object vertically, you would use the *Y* property, and positive values will cause the object to move down the screen, whereas negative values will move it up the screen.

Here's an example of a translate transform that moves the position of the red rectangle that we've been looking at by specifying *X* and *Y* values that move it up and to the left. These values effectively make up a *vector* that determines the transform.

```
<Rectangle Fill="#FFFF0404" Stroke="#FF000000"
          Width="96" Height="88" Canvas.Left="80" Canvas.Top="80">
  <Rectangle.RenderTransform>
    <TranslateTransform X="-50" Y="-50"/>
  </Rectangle.RenderTransform>
</Rectangle>
```

See the results of this transform in Figure 5-6. The rectangle has moved upward and to the left relative to its specified position compared with the position of the rectangle in Figure 5-3.

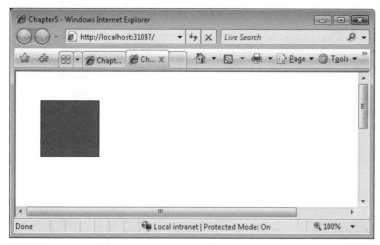

FIGURE 5-6 Using the *TranslateTransform* property.

Skewing an Object with the *SkewTransform* Property

Skewing an object involves changing it in a progressive, uniform manner along an axis. This has the effect of turning a square or rectangle into a parallelogram. This visual effect is very useful in creating the illusion of depth on a 2D surface.

You can apply a skew at a certain angle on either the x- or y-axis and around a center point. These can, of course, be combined so that you can skew on both axes at the same time.

Following is the XAML that skews our rectangle on the x-axis by 45 degrees:

```
<Rectangle Fill="#FFFF0404" Stroke="#FF000000"
          Width="96" Height="88" Canvas.Left="80" Canvas.Top="80">
  <Rectangle.RenderTransform>
```

```
        <SkewTransform AngleX="45"/>
    </Rectangle.RenderTransform>
</Rectangle>
```

You can see the result of this in Figure 5-7.

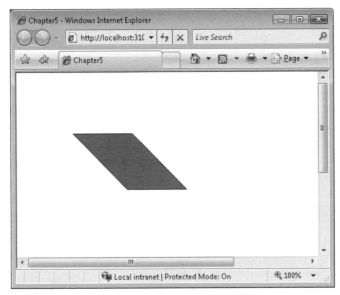

FIGURE 5-7 Skewing the rectangle using *SkewTransform*.

Simulating 3D Perspective with *SkewTransform*

Skewing is useful for simulating 3D effects in graphics. Following is an example of some XAML that uses three rectangles, two skewed on the x-axis and one on the y-axis, that create an illusion of a 3D perspective:

```
<Rectangle Fill="#FFFF0404" Stroke="#FF000000"
           Width="88" Height="88" Canvas.Left="80" Canvas.Top="80">
   <Rectangle.RenderTransform>
      <SkewTransform AngleX="45"/>
   </Rectangle.RenderTransform>
</Rectangle>
<Rectangle Fill="#FFFF0404" Stroke="#FF000000"
           Width="88" Height="88" Canvas.Left="80" Canvas.Top="168">
   <Rectangle.RenderTransform>
      <SkewTransform AngleX="45"/>
   </Rectangle.RenderTransform>
</Rectangle>
<Rectangle Fill="#FFFF0404" Stroke="#FF000000"
           Width="88" Height="88" Canvas.Left="80" Canvas.Top="80">
   <Rectangle.RenderTransform>
      <SkewTransform AngleY="45"/>
   </Rectangle.RenderTransform>
</Rectangle>
```

You can see the results of this in Figure 5-8.

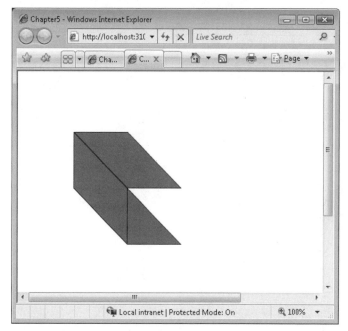

FIGURE 5-8 Simulating perspective with *SkewTransform*.

Defining Your Own Transforms with *MatrixTransform*

All transformations, at their heart, are performed by multiplying the coordinate space of the object by a transformation matrix. Each of the transforms that you've seen so far in this chapter is a well-known and well-defined transform.

Matrix mathematics and how transforms are implemented are beyond the scope of this book, but for the sake of syntactic completeness, we will look at how you can define them in Silverlight XAML.

Note that the matrix used in the *MatrixTransform* is an *affine* matrix, which means that the bottom row of the matrix is always set to (0 0 1), and as such you set only the first two columns. These are set using the transform's *Matrix* property, which takes a string containing the first two rows of values separated by spaces. Following is an example:

```
<Rectangle Fill="#FFFF0404" Stroke="#FF000000"
        Width="96" Height="88" Canvas.Left="80" Canvas.Top="80">
  <Rectangle.RenderTransform>
    <MatrixTransform Matrix="1 0 1 2 0 1" />
  </Rectangle.RenderTransform>
</Rectangle>
```

Figure 5-9 shows the impact of the transform using this matrix, which renders a combined stretched and skewed rectangle.

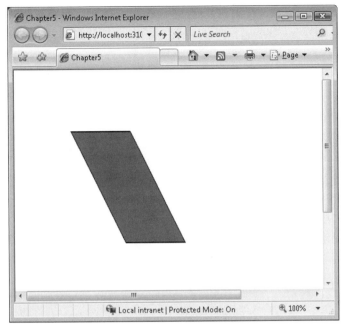

FIGURE 5-9 Using the *MatrixTransform*.

Combining Transformations

As you saw in the previous example, you can create a complex transformation by using a transformation affine matrix and specifying that using the *MatrixTransform* type. However, if you aren't an expert in matrix mathematics, another technique for using transforms is to combine them by means of the *TransformGroup* element. This simply allows you to specify multiple transforms, and the combined effect of each will be applied to the object. Here's an example:

```
<Rectangle Fill="#FFFF0404" Stroke="#FF000000"
      Width="96" Height="88" Canvas.Left="80" Canvas.Top="80">
  <Rectangle.RenderTransform>
    <TransformGroup>
      <ScaleTransform ScaleX="1.2" ScaleY="1.2" />
      <SkewTransform AngleX="30" />
      <RotateTransform Angle="45" />
    </TransformGroup>
  </Rectangle.RenderTransform>
</Rectangle>
```

This example combines a *ScaleTransform* that increases the size of the shape on both axes by 20 percent, with a 30-degree skew on the x-axis and a rotation of 45 degrees. You can see the results of this transformation in Figure 5-10.

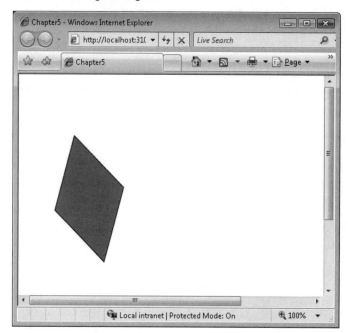

FIGURE 5-10 Combining transforms with a *TransformGroup*.

Animation

The word *animation* literally means "imparting life onto something." So, with animation you can bring your creations to life by changing the attributes of your objects, such as their color, size, opacity, and other properties, over time or in response to user actions.

In XAML, you animate an item by changing one or more of its properties over time. This time is defined using a timeline. For example, to move an item across the screen in 5 seconds, you'd specify a 5-second timeline that animates the *Canvas.Left* property from 0 to the width of the screen. In the next sections, we'll discuss each type of animation available, as well as the difference in animating these properties using key frames.

Before you look into the different animation types, you should know that there is a framework around animations that involves *Triggers*, *EventTriggers*, and *Storyboards*. First, let's take a look at these concepts, and then we'll examine the different animation types in more detail.

Using Triggers and Event Triggers

Animations in Silverlight take place in response to an event, which is defined using a trigger. At present, there is only one trigger type supported in Silverlight XAML, the *EventTrigger*. Each UI property has a *Triggers* collection that is used to define one or more triggers (i.e., one or more *EventTriggers*).

So, the first step in adding an animation to an element is to define its triggers collection; then you'll need to add at least one event trigger to the collection you've created. For example, if you are animating a rectangle, the first step—specifying the triggers collection—will look like this:

```
<Rectangle x:Name="rect" Fill="Red" Canvas.Top="100"
          Canvas.Left="100" Width="100" Height="100">
   <Rectangle.Triggers>
   </Rectangle.Triggers>
</Rectangle>
```

Next, you will need to define an *EventTrigger* to add to this collection. On this *EventTrigger*, you will use the *RoutedEvent* property to specify the event to run the animation in response to. Chapter 6, "The Silverlight Browser Control," has details on each event supported by each object in XAML, but note that *RoutedEvent* only supports the *Loaded* event.

To implement an animation that will begin when the rectangle is loaded, you would specify the *EventTrigger* as follows:

```
<EventTrigger RoutedEvent="Rectangle.Loaded">
</EventTrigger>
```

The XAML snippet to run this animation looks like this:

```
<Rectangle x:Name="rect" Fill="Red" Canvas.Top="100"
          Canvas.Left="100" Width="100" Height="100">
   <Rectangle.Triggers>
     <EventTrigger RoutedEvent="Rectangle.Loaded">
     </EventTrigger>
   </Rectangle.Triggers>
</Rectangle>
```

The next step is to define the animation that you want to use. Animations are contained within *storyboards*, which are covered in the next section.

Using *BeginStoryboard* and *Storyboard*

BeginStoryboard is a trigger action that contains a *Storyboard* object. *Storyboard* objects contain the animation definitions. When you define an animation, you simply embed these objects within the *EventTrigger* definition. Here's how this would be accomplished using the rectangle example that we've been working with so far:

```
<Rectangle x:Name="rect" Fill="Red" Canvas.Top="100"
          Canvas.Left="100" Width="100" Height="100">
   <Rectangle.Triggers>
     <EventTrigger RoutedEvent="Rectangle.Loaded">
        <BeginStoryboard>
           <Storyboard>
           </Storyboard>
        </BeginStoryboard>
     </EventTrigger>
```

```
    </Rectangle.Triggers>
</Rectangle>
```

Defining the Animation Parameters

Now that the framework for the animation is set up, you can specify the animation that you want to perform. At its most basic level, animation defines the changing of a property over time. You can animate three different property types:

- Double types are animated using the *DoubleAnimation* or *DoubleAnimationUsingKey-Frames*. This method is used to animate properties that contain a *double* value—for example, dimensions such as *Canvas.Left* or visual attributes such as *Opacity*.

- Point types are animated using a *PointAnimiation* or *PointAnimationUsingKeyFrames* type. This method is used to animate properties that contain a *point* value, such as line segments or curves that are defined using points.

- Color types are animated using a *ColorAnimation* or *ColorAnimationUsingKeyFrames* type. This method is used to animate properties that contain a *color* value—the background or stroke of an element, for instance.

Each of these property types is animated from a value specified in the *From* attribute (or its current value if this is not set) either to a value specified in the *To* attribute or by a value specified in the *By* attribute.

Targeting the Animation

To define which object you want to apply the animation to, you use the *Storyboard.TargetName* property on these animation types, and you need to pass it the name of the object in question, which is set on the object using the *x:Name* property. Additionally, you specify the property that will be animated using the *Storyboard.TargetProperty*. Note that if you are specifying a complex or attached property (such as *Canvas.Left*), you place it in parentheses. So, for example, to specify a *Double* animation to target the *Canvas.Left* of a rectangle named *rect*, the resulting XAML will look like this:

```
<DoubleAnimation Storyboard.TargetName="rect"
Storyboard.TargetProperty="(Canvas.Left)" />
```

Setting the Duration

To define how long it will take to transition the properties in question from one value to another, you use the *Duration* property. It is defined in the HH:MM:SS format, wherein a 5-second time duration for the animation is specified as 00:00:05, abbreviated to 0:0:5. Following is an example:

```
<DoubleAnimation Storyboard.TargetName="rect"
Storyboard.TargetProperty="(Canvas.Left)" Duration="0:0:5" />
```

Setting the Begin Time

If you do not want the animation to begin right away, you can insert a delay using the *BeginTime* property. It uses the same syntax as *Duration*.

```
<DoubleAnimation Storyboard.TargetName="rect"
Storyboard.TargetProperty="(Canvas.Left)" BeginTime="0:0:5" />
```

Using the *SpeedRatio* Property

You can also tweak the animation behavior by multiplying the duration by a speed ratio. This is achieved using the *SpeedRatio* property. For example, in the previous case, the duration was set to 5 seconds. You can change the speed ratio to make the animation last 10 seconds by setting *SpeedRatio* to 2, or, alternatively, you can speed the animation up to 1 second by setting *SpeedRatio* to 0.2.

```
<DoubleAnimation Storyboard.TargetName="rect"
Storyboard.TargetProperty="(Canvas.Left)" SpeedRatio="2" Duration="0:0:5" />
```

Using the *AutoReverse* Property

Silverlight animation provides the facility to reverse the changes made as part of the animation. For example, if you are moving a *double* value from 0 to 500 over a specific time frame, an *AutoReverse* will cause the animation to move from 500 back to 0.

Note that if the animation is set to run for 5 seconds as previously stated, and the *AutoReverse* is set to *true*, then the complete animation will take 10 seconds. Following is an example of XAML containing the *AutoReverse* property:

```
<DoubleAnimation Storyboard.TargetName="rect"
    Storyboard.TargetProperty="(Canvas.Left)" AutoReverse="True"
    Duration="0:0:5" />
```

Setting the *RepeatBehavior* Property

When the animation has finished running, you can apply a number of options to control how you want it to behave. You specify these using the *RepeatBehavior* property. This property can take three different types of values:

- A time defined in seconds. The timeline will wait for this period and then start the animation again.

- Constant repetition by setting *Forever* as the repeat behavior.

- A discrete number of repetitions by specifying a number followed by *x*. For example, if you want the animation to run three times, you specify the value *3x*.

Following is the complete XAML for our animated rectangle to move it from 100 to 500 and back to 100 on the x-axis and then repeat that behavior three times:

```
<Rectangle x:Name="rect" Fill="Red"
    Canvas.Top="100" Canvas.Left="100" Width="100" Height="100">
  <Rectangle.Triggers>
    <EventTrigger RoutedEvent="Rectangle.Loaded">
      <BeginStoryboard>
        <Storyboard>
          <DoubleAnimation RepeatBehavior="3x"
                           Storyboard.TargetName="rect"
                           Storyboard.TargetProperty="(Canvas.Left)"
                           To="500" Duration="0:0:5"
                           AutoReverse="True" />
        </Storyboard>
      </BeginStoryboard>
    </EventTrigger>
  </Rectangle.Triggers>
</Rectangle>
```

Let's look at each of these animation types in a little more detail. First, we'll examine the attributes needed to animate each of the various types, and then we'll address where the associated key frame type of animation fits into the picture.

Animating a Value with *DoubleAnimation*

The *DoubleAnimation* object allows you to specify how a *double* value will change over a specified timeline. The animation is calculated as a linear interpolation between the property values over time.

When animating a *double*, you specify the value at the start of the animation using the *From* value and then change it to either the *To* value, which is an absolute destination, or the *By* value, which is a relative destination.

For example, if you are moving the *Canvas.Left* property of an item from 100 (near the left of the screen) to 500, you can set *From* to 100 and *To* to 500 or *By* to 400. Note that if you set both, the *To* property takes precedence and the *By* property is ignored. Also, if the rectangle is already located at the desired *From* position, you do not need to specify the *From* property.

The previous XAML example displayed this behavior. The rectangle is located with a *Canvas.Left* value of 100, and the *DoubleAnimation* specifies the *To* value as 500. Hence, the animation will move the value from 100 to 500, which will cause the rectangle to move across the screen to the right.

Animating a Color with *ColorAnimation*

ColorAnimation operates in a manner that is very similar to *DoubleAnimation*. You use it to specify how the *color* value of an element will change over time. The animation is then calculated as a linear interpolation between the *color* values over the specified time.

When animating a color, you specify the value at the start of the animation using the *From* property. If you do not specify this, then the current color is used. You specify the desired end color using the *To* attribute. You can also specify a *By* attribute, which will provide the end color that is the result of adding the values of the *From* color (or the starting color) to the *By* color.

When you animate a color-based property, you do not animate the contents of the property directly because the content of the property is usually a brush and not a color. So, if you want to animate the fill color of a rectangle, for example, you don't use the rectangle's *Fill* property as your target. Instead, you specify that you intend to animate the *Color* property of the *SolidBrush* that is used to perform the fill.

Following is an example of how to animate the color of a rectangle, changing it from black to white over a time duration of 5 seconds using a color animation:

```
<Rectangle x:Name="rect" Canvas.Top="100" Canvas.Left="100"
           Width="100" Height="100" Fill="Black">
   <Rectangle.Triggers>
      <EventTrigger RoutedEvent="Rectangle.Loaded">
         <BeginStoryboard>
            <Storyboard>
               <ColorAnimation Storyboard.TargetName="rect"
                               Storyboard.TargetProperty=
                                 "(Shape.Fill).(SolidColorBrush.Color)"
                               To="#00000000" Duration="0:0:5" />
            </Storyboard>
         </BeginStoryboard>
      </EventTrigger>
   </Rectangle.Triggers>
</Rectangle>
```

As you can see, this XAML snippet specifies the *Color* property of the *SolidColorBrush* that is filling the shape as its target property. This is the typical XAML syntax used in addressing complex properties like this.

Animating a Point with *PointAnimation*

To change a value that is defined as a point over time, you use the *PointAnimation* type. The animation is then calculated as a linear interpolation between the values over the specified time.

In a manner similar to the *Color* and *Double* animations, you specify the start value using *From* and the destination either as a relative direction (using *By*) or an absolute point (using *To*). Following is an example of how you could animate the end point of a Bezier curve:

```
<Path Stroke="Black" >
   <Path.Data>
      <PathGeometry>
         <PathFigure StartPoint="100,100">
```

```
                  <QuadraticBezierSegment x:Name="seg"
                              Point1="200,0" Point2="300,100"  />
              </PathFigure>
          </PathGeometry>
      </Path.Data>
      <Path.Triggers>
          <EventTrigger RoutedEvent="Path.Loaded">
              <BeginStoryboard>
                  <Storyboard>
                      <PointAnimation Storyboard.TargetName="seg"
                                  Storyboard.TargetProperty="Point2"
                                  From="300,100" To="300,600" Duration="0:0:5" />
                  </Storyboard>
              </BeginStoryboard>
          </EventTrigger>
      </Path.Triggers>
  </Path>
```

In this case, the Bezier curve is defined with a start point at (100,100), an end point at (300,100), and a control point at (200,0). An animation is set up to trigger after the path loads, and it animates the end point of the curve (*Point2*) from (300,100) to (300,600) over a time duration of 5 seconds.

Using Key Frames

The three animation types that you've just learned about, *ColorAnimation*, *DoubleAnimation*, and *PointAnimation*, all work by changing a defined property over time using linear interpolation. For example, if you are moving a *double* value from 100 to 500 over 5 seconds, it will increment by 80 each second.

Each of these can have this transition defined through a set of milestones called *key frames*. To change the linear behavior of the animation from the starting property to the ending property, you insert one or more key frames. Then you define the style of animation that you want between the various points.

Key frames are defined using *key times*. These are times that are specified relative to the start time of the animation, and they specify the end time of the key frame. So, imagine you need a 9-second animation with three evenly spaced key frames. Using key frames, you can specify the first key frame to end at 0:0:3, the second to end at 0:0:6, and the third to end at 0:0:9. You do not specify the *length* of the key time—instead, you specify the end time for each key frame.

As another example, consider a *Double* animation that you want to span half the range of 100 to 500. The animation should move very quickly in the first half and very slowly in the second half, requiring a 6-second total transition. Since 350 is the midpoint between 100 and 500, you would define a key frame to begin at point 350. You'd tell it to go for 1 second between the start point and the midpoint, using a key time of 0:0:1, and then set a time duration of 5 seconds between the midpoint and the end point by using a second key time of 0:0:6. Now the item will zip across the screen to the midpoint and then will crawl the rest of the way.

In the previous example, both animated segments will be linearly interpolated. To provide extra flexibility, two other types of key frames are provided: a discrete key frame that instantly "jumps" the value between the two values, and a spline key frame that moves the value between the first and end points using a quadratic curve to define the interpolation. (In the following sections, you'll look at how to define an animation using key frames for the *Double* type. The same principles apply for *Point* and *Color* animation types.)

To specify key frames, you use the *UsingKeyFrames* postfix on your animation. That is, to define *Double* animations and use key frames, you'll use *DoubleAnimationUsingKeyFrames* on which you specify your target and property (in the same way you use *DoubleAnimation*). *DoubleAnimationUsingKeyFrames* contains the key frame definitions. (And as I mentioned, the same applies to *PointAnimationUsingKeyFrames* or *ColorAnimationUsingKeyFrames*.)

Using Linear Key Frames

The default method for animation between two property values is linear interpolation in which the amount is divided evenly over time. You can also define linear steps between frames using the *LinearKeyFrame* type in which linear interpolation is still used, but it is used between key frames so you can have an acceleration/deceleration effect.

Consider the following animation. Here, a *DoubleAnimationUsingKeyFrames* is used, and it defines two key frames. One defines a linear interpolation between 0 and 300 for *Canvas.Left* changes over 1 second, and the next defines a linear interpolation between 300 and 600 for *Canvas.Left* changes over 8 seconds. This has the effect of making the rectangle move quickly to the halfway point and then slowly the rest of the way across. Similar principles apply for the *LinearPointKeyFrame* and *LinearColorKeyFrame*.

```
<Rectangle Fill="#FFFF0000" Stroke="#FF000000"
        Width="40" Height="40" Canvas.Top="40" x:Name="rect">
  <Rectangle.Triggers>
    <EventTrigger RoutedEvent="Rectangle.Loaded">
      <BeginStoryboard>
        <Storyboard>
          <DoubleAnimationUsingKeyFrames
              Storyboard.TargetName="rect"
              Storyboard.TargetProperty="(Canvas.Left)" >
            <LinearDoubleKeyFrame KeyTime="0:0:1" Value="300" />
            <LinearDoubleKeyFrame KeyTime="0:0:9" Value="600" />
          </DoubleAnimationUsingKeyFrames>
        </Storyboard>
      </BeginStoryboard>
    </EventTrigger>
  </Rectangle.Triggers>
</Rectangle>
```

Using Discrete Key Frames

If you want to change the property from one value to another and *not* use linear interpolation, you can use a discrete key frame. This causes the object to "jump" to the value at the specified key frame time. Following is the same example as the previous one except that it uses a discrete key frame. At 1 second into the animation, the rectangle will jump halfway across the screen. Then at 9 seconds into the animation, it will jump to the right of the screen.

```
<Rectangle Fill="#FFFF0000" Stroke="#FF000000"
    Width="40" Height="40" Canvas.Top="40" x:Name="rect">
  <Rectangle.Triggers>
    <EventTrigger RoutedEvent="Rectangle.Loaded">
      <BeginStoryboard>
        <Storyboard>
          <DoubleAnimationUsingKeyFrames
              Storyboard.TargetName="rect"
              Storyboard.TargetProperty="(Canvas.Left)" >
            <DiscreteDoubleKeyFrame KeyTime="0:0:1" Value="300" />
            <DiscreteDoubleKeyFrame KeyTime="0:0:9" Value="600" />
          </DoubleAnimationUsingKeyFrames>
        </Storyboard>
      </BeginStoryboard>
    </EventTrigger>
  </Rectangle.Triggers>
</Rectangle>
```

Similar principles apply for the *DiscretePointKeyFrame* and *DiscreteColorKeyFrame*.

Using Spline Key Frames

To change the property from one value to another using a curved value that provides for acceleration and deceleration, you use a spline key frame. To do this, first you define a quadratic Bezier curve, and then the speed of the property as it moves from one value to another is determined by a parallel projection of that curve.

If this is hard to visualize, consider the following scenario: The sun is right overhead, and you hit a baseball into the outfield. You look at the shadow of the ball. As it is climbing into the air, the movement of the shadow appears to accelerate. As it reaches its apex, you'll see the shadow decelerate. As the ball falls, you'll see the speed of the shadow accelerate again until it is caught or hits the ground.

Imagine your animation in this case is the ball's shadow, and the spline is the curve of the baseball. You define the trajectory of the baseball, a spline, using a *KeySpline*. The *KeySpline* defines control points for a quadratic Bezier curve. It is normalized so that the first point of the curve is at 0 and the second is at 1. For a parabolic arc, which is the trajectory the baseball would follow, the *KeySpline* will contain two comma-separated normalized values.

To define a curve like the flight of a baseball, you can specify the spline using a *KeySpline*, such as 0.3,0 0.6,1. This defines the first point of the curve at (0.3,0) and the second at (0.6,1). This will have the effect of making the animation accelerate quickly until approximately one-third of the movement of the baseball is complete, then it will move at a uniform speed until approximately two-thirds of the ball's trajectory is reached, and then it will decelerate for the rest of the flight of the animated baseball as the animation simulates the ball's fall to earth.

Following is an example of using a *KeySpline* to define the spline for this simulation using *DoubleAnimationUsingKeyFrames*:

```
<Ellipse Fill="#FF444444" Stroke="#FF444444"
      Width="40" Height="40" Canvas.Top="40" x:Name="ball">
   <Ellipse.Triggers>
      <EventTrigger RoutedEvent="Ellipse.Loaded">
         <BeginStoryboard>
            <Storyboard>
               <DoubleAnimationUsingKeyFrames
                     Storyboard.TargetName="ball"
                     Storyboard.TargetProperty="(Canvas.Left)" >
                  <SplineDoubleKeyFrame KeyTime="0:0:5"
                        KeySpline="0.3,0 0.6,1" Value="600" />
               </DoubleAnimationUsingKeyFrames>
            </Storyboard>
         </BeginStoryboard>
      </EventTrigger>
   </Ellipse.Triggers>
</Ellipse>
```

This example animates the ellipse so that it moves across the screen in a manner similar to the shadow of a baseball, as if you were above the baseball looking down toward the ground as the ball flies through the air.

Animation and Expression Blend

Animation can be defined graphically in Expression Blend. This generates the XAML for you to perform the animation, providing the different types of animation for you automatically.

When using Blend, select Animation Workspace from the Window menu. This will give you the tools to graphically design timelines, and when you edit the properties that you want changed using the visual editor, then the XAML code for the animation will be generated. You can see this in Figure 5-11.

At the bottom of the screen, you can see the Objects And Timeline view. This allows you to add a timeline and then visually add key frames. To add a new timeline, click the + button in the Objects And Timeline view. See Figure 5-12.

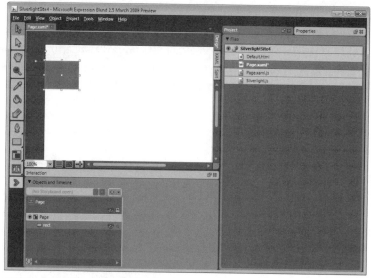

FIGURE 5-11 Expression Blend in Animation Workspace mode.

FIGURE 5-12 Adding a new timeline.

When you click the + button, you'll see a dialog box that asks you for the name of the story-board to create. You can see the Create Storyboard dialog box illustrated in Figure 5-13. In this case, I've changed the default name from Storyboard1 to Timeline1 and cleared the Create As Resource check box.

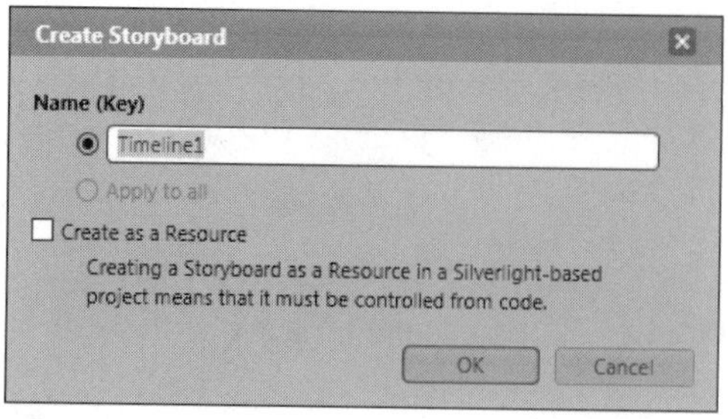

Create Storyboard

Name (Key)

⦿ Timeline1

○ Apply to all

☐ Create as a Resource

Creating a Storyboard as a Resource in a Silverlight-based project means that it must be controlled from code.

OK   Cancel

FIGURE 5-13 Creating the storyboard.

When using Blend, you can create an animation at the *Canvas* level or as a *Resource*. In the case of the former, animations then run in response to triggers on the canvas. Following is an example of the XAML created by Blend from the Create Storyboard dialog box, where the user specified that they did not want to create the animation as a *Resource*:

```
<Canvas.Triggers>
    <EventTrigger RoutedEvent="Canvas.Loaded">
        <BeginStoryboard>
            <Storyboard x:Name="Timeline1"/>
        </BeginStoryboard>
    </EventTrigger>
</Canvas.Triggers>
```

Note that if the user checked the Create As Resource check box (see Figure 5-13), then the *Storyboard* would be created within *<Canvas.Resources>*, and you would have to run it from JavaScript. You'll see more on this in Chapter 6.

The Objects And Timeline view will change to show the timeline that you've just created. You can see this in Figure 5-14.

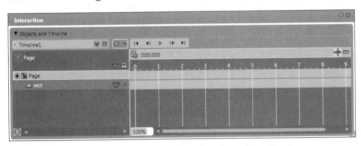

FIGURE 5-14 Objects And Timeline view showing a new timeline.

The vertical line at time zero that you see in Figure 5-14 denotes the current time. (In Blend, this line will be yellow.) To add a key frame, you simply drag this line to the time where you want a key frame, and click the Record Keyframe button. This button is located just above the timeline to the left of 0:00:000 in Figure 5-14.

Drag the line to the 4-second mark, and add a key frame. You'll see the key frame added as a small oval on the timeline, as shown in Figure 5-15.

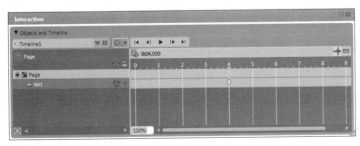

FIGURE 5-15 Adding a key frame.

Now that the timeline is on the 4-second frame and you have added a key frame, you can edit the rectangle's color, location, opacity, or shape, and Blend will calculate the correct transformations necessary to facilitate the animation. As an example, Figure 5-16 shows the same rectangle in Figure 5-11, but now it has been moved, filled with a different color, and resized.

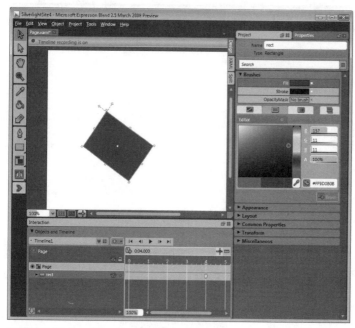

FIGURE 5-16 Specifying the key frame changes.

Finally, you may notice that if you drag the timeline indicator around, you can preview the animation and see how it appears at any particular time. Figure 5-17 shows how our rectangle appears at the 2-second key time, achieved by dragging the yellow vertical line to the 2-second point.

Following is the complete XAML that was generated by Blend when designing this animation:

```
<Canvas
  xmlns="http://schemas.microsoft.com/client/2007"
  xmlns:x="http://schemas.microsoft.com/winfx/2006/xaml"
  Width="640" Height="480"
  Background="White"
  x:Name="Page">
  <Canvas.Triggers>
    <EventTrigger RoutedEvent="Canvas.Loaded">
      <BeginStoryboard>
        <Storyboard x:Name="Timeline1">
          <DoubleAnimationUsingKeyFrames BeginTime="00:00:00"
            Storyboard.TargetName="rect"
            Storyboard.TargetProperty="(UIElement.RenderTransform).
                (TransformGroup.Children)[3].(TranslateTransform.X)">
```

```
            <SplineDoubleKeyFrame KeyTime="00:00:04" Value="141"/>

        </DoubleAnimationUsingKeyFrames>

        <DoubleAnimationUsingKeyFrames BeginTime="00:00:00"
          Storyboard.TargetName="rect"
          Storyboard.TargetProperty="(UIElement.RenderTransform).
              (TransformGroup.Children)[3].(TranslateTransform.Y)">
          <SplineDoubleKeyFrame KeyTime="00:00:04" Value="163"/>
        </DoubleAnimationUsingKeyFrames>

        <DoubleAnimationUsingKeyFrames BeginTime="00:00:00"
          Storyboard.TargetName="rect"
          Storyboard.TargetProperty="(UIElement.RenderTransform).
              (TransformGroup.Children)[2].(RotateTransform.Angle)">
          <SplineDoubleKeyFrame KeyTime="00:00:04" Value="35.107"/>
        </DoubleAnimationUsingKeyFrames>

        <ColorAnimationUsingKeyFrames BeginTime="00:00:00"
            Storyboard.TargetName="rect"
            Storyboard.TargetProperty="(Shape.Fill).(SolidColorBrush.Color)">
          <SplineColorKeyFrame KeyTime="00:00:04" Value="#FF9D0B0B"/>
        </ColorAnimationUsingKeyFrames>

        <DoubleAnimationUsingKeyFrames BeginTime="00:00:00" Storyboard.TargetName="rect"
          Storyboard.TargetProperty="(UIElement.RenderTransform).
              (TransformGroup.Children)[0].(ScaleTransform.ScaleX)">
          <SplineDoubleKeyFrame KeyTime="00:00:04" Value="1.7"/>
        </DoubleAnimationUsingKeyFrames>

        <DoubleAnimationUsingKeyFrames BeginTime="00:00:00"
          Storyboard.TargetName="rect"
          Storyboard.TargetProperty="(UIElement.RenderTransform).
              (TransformGroup.Children)[0].(ScaleTransform.ScaleY)">
          <SplineDoubleKeyFrame KeyTime="00:00:04" Value="1.549"/>
        </DoubleAnimationUsingKeyFrames>
      </Storyboard>
    </BeginStoryboard>
  </EventTrigger>
</Canvas.Triggers>
<Rectangle Width="87" Height="69" Fill="Red" Stroke="#FF000000"
          Canvas.Top="41" RenderTransformOrigin="0.5,0.5" x:Name="rect">
  <Rectangle.RenderTransform>
    <TransformGroup>
      <ScaleTransform ScaleX="1" ScaleY="1"/>
      <SkewTransform AngleX="0" AngleY="0"/>
      <RotateTransform Angle="0"/>
      <TranslateTransform X="0" Y="0"/>
    </TransformGroup>
  </Rectangle.RenderTransform>
</Rectangle>
</Canvas>
```

FIGURE 5-17 Previewing the animation.

Summary

In this chapter, you learned how transformations and animations are defined in Silverlight XAML. You were introduced to different types of transformation used to rotate, scale, or skew an object, as well as to free-form transformations using an affine matrix as applied to a shape. You then learned about animations and saw how to define an animation to run based on an XAML trigger. You saw how animations change property values over time, and you looked at the XAML types that support animating *double*, *point*, and *color* values. You also learned how to use key frames for finer control over your animations. Finally, you took a look at the Expression Blend animation designer to see how easily animations can be generated visually using Blend.

In Chapter 6, you'll look at the Silverlight control itself and learn more about its full set of properties, methods, and events that you can use.

Chapter 6
The Silverlight Browser Control

In this chapter, we'll take an in-depth look at programming the Silverlight plug-in object and the XAML it contains using JavaScript within the browser. We'll investigate how to host the Silverlight plug-in object in the browser, as well as the full property, method, and event model that the control supports. We'll also look at how to support loading and error events on the control and how to handle parameterization and context for the control. You'll see how Silverlight provides a default error handler and how you can override this with your own error handlers. We'll delve into the *Downloader* object that is exposed by Silverlight and find out how this can be used to dynamically add content to an application. Finally, we'll explore the programming model for the user interface (UI) elements that make up the XAML control model, and you will learn how you can use the methods and events that they expose from within the JavaScript programming model.

Hosting Silverlight in the Browser

You don't need any special software to be able to use and build Silverlight applications other than the Silverlight plug-in itself and the Silverlight.js file that manages downloading and in-stalling the plug-in for clients that don't have it. You can use any software for building Web sites to build Silverlight sites, from Notepad to Eclipse to Expression Web or Expression Blend—it's really up to you.

This section presents a basic primer that will show you what you need to do to begin to use Silverlight. So far in this book, you've been using an Expression Blend or Microsoft Visual Studio template to do the hard work for you, but now let's take a look at what it takes to get a simple Silverlight site up and running without any tools other than Windows Explorer and Notepad.

The first and most important file that you will need is the standard Silverlight.js file. This is available in the Silverlight Software Development Kit (SDK), which you can download from the Web site *http://www.microsoft.com/silverlight*.

Next, you'll need to create an HTML file that will reference this JavaScript file. You'll host the Silverlight control in this page. Here's an example:

```
<HTML>
   <HEAD>
      <script type="text/javascript" src="Silverlight.js" />
   </HEAD>
   <BODY>
   </BODY>
</HTML>
```

The Silverlight.js file contains methods called *createObject* and *createObjectEx* that you can use to instantiate Silverlight. The difference between these is that *createObjectEx* can use the JavaScript Object Notation (JSON) to serialize the parameters.

These functions take a set of parameters that are used to instantiate the control. The parameters are described in Table 6-1.

TABLE 6-1 **Parameters for *createObject* and *createObjectEx***

Parameter Name	Description
source	This sets the source for the XAML code or XAP application that the control renders. It can be a file reference (i.e., "source.xap"), a URI (i.e., *http://server/generatexaml.aspx*), or a reference to inline XAML contained within a DIV (i.e., *#xamlcontent* for a DIV named *xamlcontent*).
parentElement	This is the name of the DIV that contains the Silverlight control on your HTML page.
ID	This is the unique ID that you assign to an instance of the Silverlight control.
width	This sets the width of the control in pixels or by percentage.
height	This sets the height of the control in pixels or by percentage.
background	This determines the background color of the control. See the section titled *"SolidColorBrush"* in Chapter 4, "XAML Basics," for more details on how to set colors. You can use an *ARGB* value, such as #FFAA7700, or a named color, such as *Black*.
framerate	This sets the maximum frame rate to allow for animation. It defaults to 24.
isWindowless	This is set to *true* or *false* and defaults to *false*. When it is set to *true*, the Silverlight content is rendered behind the HTML content so that HTML content can be written on top of it.
enableHtmlAccess	This determines if the content that is hosted in the Silverlight control is accessible from the browser DOM. It defaults to *true*.
inplaceInstallPrompt	Silverlight has two modes of installation. An *inplace* install involves accepting the software license and downloading the control directly without leaving the site hosting it. An *indirect* install involves having the user transfer to the Microsoft download site for Silverlight. From there, they accept the license and download the control. You control which method will be presented to the user with this property. Setting the property to *true* allows the user direct *inplace* installation; a *false* setting leads to the *indirect* installation.

version	This determines the minimum version of Silverlight to support.
onLoad	This specifies the function to run when the control is loaded.
onError	This specifies the function to run when the control hits an error.
onFullScreenChange	This event is fired when the *FullScreen* property of the Silverlight control changes.
onResize	This event is fired when the *ActualWidth* or *ActualHeight* property of the Silverlight control changes.
initParams	This specifies a user-definable set of parameters to load into the control. For more details on this, see the section titled "Handling Parameters" later in this chapter.
userContext	This specifies a unique identifier that can be passed as a parameter to the *onLoad* event handler function. You'll see more of this in the "Responding to Page Load Events" section later in this chapter.

Please note that the *width*, *height*, *background*, *framerate*, *isWindowless*, *enableHtmlAccess*, *version*, and *inplaceInstallPrompt* properties are handled within a properties array when creating an instance of the control, and the *onLoad* and *onError* are handled within the events array.

Following is an example:

```
Silverlight.createObject(
    "Scene.xaml",
    document.getElementById("SilverlightControlHost"),
    "mySilverlightControl",
    {
        width:'300',
        height:'300',
        inplaceInstallPrompt:false,
        background:'#D6D6D6',
        isWindowless:'false',
        framerate:'24',
        version:'2.0'
    },
    {
        onError:null,
        onLoad:null
    },
    null);
```

Now let's return to our HTML page and set it up so that it can handle this Silverlight control. You see that when the Silverlight component was named, it was expecting a parent DIV called *SilverlightControlHost* to host it. This is achieved using the *ID* property of the DIV. Here's the full HTML code:

```html
<html>
<head>
    <script type="text/javascript" src="Silverlight.js"></script>
    <script type="text/javascript">
    function createSilverlight()
    {
    Silverlight.createObject(
      "Page.xaml",
      document.getElementById("SilverlightControlHost"),
      "mySilverlightControl",
      {
        width:'300',
        height:'300',
        inplaceInstallPrompt:false,
        background:'#D6D6D6',
        isWindowless:'false',
        framerate:'24',
        version:'2.0'
      },
      {
        onError:null,
        onLoad:null
      },
      null);
    }
    </script>
</head>

<body>
    <div id="SilverlightControlHost">
        <script type="text/javascript">
            createSilverlight();
        </script>
    </div>
</body>
</html>
```

Finally, you'll need the XAML source for your Silverlight control. This sample calls for an XAML file called Scene.xaml.

Following is a simple XAML file that contains a "Hello, World!" *TextBlock*:

```xml
<Canvas
        xmlns="http://schemas.microsoft.com/client/2007"
        xmlns:x="http://schemas.microsoft.com/winfx/2006/xaml"
        Width="640" Height="480"
        Background="White"
        x:Name="Page">
  <TextBlock Text="Hello, World!"></TextBlock>
</Canvas>
```

And that's everything that you need to get a Silverlight application set up and ready to go. As you add more functionality to your application, your code will become more complex, but these three files—the HTML host, the XAML file, and Silverlight.js—are generally common to every project.

Using the Object Tag Directly

The previous example created an instance of the Silverlight control by using the *Silverlight.createObject* function that resides in Silverlight.js. If you want to avoid using this function and want to instantiate the Silverlight plug-in directly instead, you can do so. This is done using the standard *<object>* tag, which uses *<param>* children to set the parameters. Here's an example of how this works:

```
<object data="data:application/x-silverlight,"
  type="application/x-silverlight-2-b1"
  width="100%" height="100%">
  <param name="source" value="Page.xaml"/>
  <param name="onerror" value="onSilverlightError" />
  <param name="background" value="white" />
</object>
```

> **Note** The data attribute in this example is set to "data:application/x-silverlight," which is the *MIME* type for Silverlight 1.0. The expected final *MIME* type for Silverlight 2 when it is released is "application/x-silverlight2". Please note that the betas will have a different *MIME* type, with Beta 2 having the *MIME* type "application/x-silverlight-2-b2". If you are having trouble getting the browser to recognize your Silverlight object, make sure that this is set correctly based on the version that you are using.

One nice feature of the *<object>* tag is that it is stackable in the sense that, if the initial *<object>* instantiation fails, the browser will render the next piece of HTML in its place, provided that the HTML is located before the closing *</object>* tag. This makes it easy to make a simple banner to put on the screen if Silverlight is not installed.

Here's an example:

```
<object data="data:application/x-silverlight,"
  type="application/x-silverlight-2-b1"
  width="100%" height="100%">
  <param name="source" value="Page.xaml"/>
  <param name="onerror" value="onSilverlightError" />
  <param name="background" value="white" />

  <a href="…" style="text-decoration: none;">
    <img src="…" alt="Get Microsoft Silverlight"
        style="border-style: none"/>
  </a>
</object>
```

In this situation, a hyperlink (<*a*> tag) is embedded within the object, so if Silverlight is not present in the system, this tag would provide a clickable installation for it.

This approach is extremely useful if you want to embed Silverlight into a Web site, such as a blogging engine, for example, where JavaScript is not available because it isn't necessary for the application when it is coded this way.

Responding to Page Load Events

You specify a JavaScript event handler to manage page load events using the *onLoad* parameter introduced in Table 6-1. This fires after the XAML content within the Silverlight control has completely loaded. Note that if you have defined a loaded event on any XAML UI element, those events will fire before the Silverlight control's *onLoad* event does. In addition to this, the control has a read-only *IsLoaded* property that is set immediately before the *onLoad* event fires.

When using an *onLoad* event handler, your JavaScript function should take three parameters: The first is a reference to the control, the second is the user context, and the third is a reference to the root element of the XAML. Following is an example:

```
function handleLoad(control, userContext, rootElement)
{
    ...
}
```

Handling Parameters

When you call the *createObject* function to instantiate Silverlight, you can pass parameters to it using the *initParams* property. This property is a string value, so if you have multiple values, you can encode them into a comma-separated string that can be easily sliced back up in JavaScript. Following is an example of setting up the Silverlight control that has three parameters:

```
function createSilverlight()
{
    Silverlight.createObject(
        "Scene.xaml",
        document.getElementById("SilverlightControlHost"),
        "mySilverlightControl",
        {
            width:'300',
            height:'300',
            inplaceInstallPrompt:false,
            background:'#D6D6D6',
            isWindowless:'false',
            framerate:'24',
            version:'2.0'
```

```
    },
    {
        onError:null,
        onLoad:handleLoad
    },
    "p1, p2, p3", // Parameter List
    null);
}
```

Here the parameters *p1, p2,* and *p3* are encoded into a comma-separated string. JavaScript has a string *split* method that allows you to split a comma-separated string into an array of values.

Following is an example of an *onLoad* event handler that uses this method to split the parameter list into an array of strings and to display each one in an alert box:

```
function handleLoad(control, userContext, rootElement)
{
    var params = control.initParams.split(",");
    for (var i = 0; i< params.length; i++)
    {
        alert(params[i]);
    }
}
```

User Context

An additional parameter that can be passed to the Silverlight control is the context parameter. This will be included directly in the *onLoad* event as the second parameter, typically named *userContext*. It behaves exactly the same as the previous parameters you've seen in that it is a property value that can be queried after the control has rendered. Typically, user context is not used for control parameters, however. It is instead used as a reference variable to distinguish different controls, although there is nothing to prevent you from using it to parameterize your control.

Following is an example of a page that hosts three Silverlight controls. Note that the name and context variables are set in this host page and then passed as parameters to the JavaScript that creates the Silverlight control:

```
<html>
<head>
    <script type="text/javascript" src="Silverlight.js"></script>
    <script type="text/javascript">
    function handleLoad(control, userContext, rootElement)
    {
        alert(userContext);
    }

    function createSilverlight(parentElement, cid, context)
    {
```

```
            Silverlight.createObject(
             "Page.xaml",
             document.getElementById(parentElement),
             cid,
             {
                 width:'300',
                 height:'300',
                 inplaceInstallPrompt:false,
                 background:'#D6D6D6',
                 isWindowless:'false',
                 framerate:'24',
                 version:'2.0'
             },
             {
                 onError:null,
                 onLoad:handleLoad
             },
             "p1,p2,p3",
             context,
             null);
    }
    </script>
</head>

<body>
    <div id="SilverlightControlHost1">
        <script type="text/javascript">
            createSilverlight("SilverlightControlHost1",
                "ctrl1","the first control");
        </script>
    </div>
    <div id="SilverlightControlHost2">
        <script type="text/javascript">
            createSilverlight("SilverlightControlHost2",
                "ctrl2","the second control");
        </script>
    </div>
    <div id="SilverlightControlHost3">
        <script type="text/javascript">
            createSilverlight("SilverlightControlHost3",
                "ctrl3","the third control");
        </script>
    </div>

</body>
</html>
```

The HTML page contains the *onLoad* event handler, which you can see here:

```
<script type="text/javascript">
    function handleLoad(control, userContext, rootElement)
    {
        alert(userContext);
    }
</script>
```

This takes the *userContext* parameter and displays the context value in an alert box. You can see how this appears on screen in Figure 6-1, where the HTML page is displaying the context for the first control.

FIGURE 6-1 Displaying user context.

Responding to Page Error Events

Silverlight provides several methods for error handling, depending on the type of error. Errors are raised when the XAML parser hits a problem, loading isn't completed properly, run-time errors are encountered, and when event handlers defined in the XAML document do not have a JavaScript function associated with them.

When initializing a control using the *onError* event handler, you specify a JavaScript function that will be called when an error occurs. However, if you do not specify one (or if you specify it as *null*), the default JavaScript event handler will fire.

The Default Event Handler

The JavaScript default event handler will display an error message alert box that contains basic details about the Silverlight error, including the error code and type as well as a message defining the specific problem and the method name that was called.

Following is an example of a badly formed XAML document, in which the closing tag of the *TextBlock* element is misnamed *</TextBlok>*:

```
<Canvas xmlns="http://schemas.microsoft.com/client/2007"
        xmlns:x="http://schemas.microsoft.com/winfx/2006/xaml">
  <TextBlock>Hello, World!</TextBlok>
</Canvas>
```

If the error handler is set to *null*, then the default error handler will fire and display the default Silverlight error message, as shown in Figure 6-2.

FIGURE 6-2 Default error message.

Using Your Own Error Handler

You can use your own error handler by setting the *onError* property of the Silverlight control to a custom event handler function. Your error handler function will need to take two parameters: the sender object and the event arguments that define the specifics of the error that occurred.

There are three types of event argument that you can receive. The first is the basic *ErrorEventArgs* object that contains the error message type and code. The *errorType* property defines the type of error as a string containing *RuntimeError* or *ParserError*. Based on this information, you can use one of the two associated derived error types.

When processing a parsing error in XAML, the *ParserErrorEventArgs* is available. This contains a number of properties:

- The *charposition* property contains the character position where the error occurred.
- The *linenumber* property contains the line where the error occurred.
- The *xamlFile* identifies the file in which the error occurred.
- The *xmlAttribute* identifies the xml attribute in which the error occurred.
- The *xmlElement* defines the element in which the error occurred.

Run-time errors are defined in the *RuntimeErrorEventArgs* object. This object also contains a number of properties:

- The *charPosition* property identifies the character position where the error occurred.
- The *lineNumber* property identifies the line in which the error occurred.
- The *methodName* identifies the method associated with the error.

In the previous section, you saw a parsing error as trapped by the default error handler. Here's how you could capture the same error with your own error handler. First, you create the *createSilverlight()* method that sets up the error handler:

```
function createSilverlight()
{
    Silverlight.createObject(
        "Scene.xaml",
        document.getElementById("firstControl"),
        "agc1",
        {
            width:'300',
            height:'300',
            inplaceInstallPrompt:false,
            background:'#D6D6D6',
            isWindowless:'false',
            framerate:'24',
            version:'2.0'
        },
        {
            onError:handleError,
            onLoad:null
        },
        null);
}
```

Following is the HTML file that calls this revised Silverlight creation method and contains the *handleError* function that was defined as the error handler using the *onError* attribute:

```html
<html>
<head>
    <script type="text/javascript" src="Silverlight.js"></script>
    <script type="text/javascript" src="createSilverlight.js"></script>
    <script type="text/javascript">
        function handleError(sender, errorArguments)
        {
            var strError = "Error Details: \n";
            strError+= "Type: " + errorArguments.errorType + "\n";
            strError+= "Message: " + errorArguments.errorMessage + "\n";
            strError+= "Code: " + errorArguments.errorCode + "\n";
            // We know (in this case) that its a parser error.
            // For a more generic error handler
            // you should trap on error type before calling
            // properties on a specific argument type.
            strError+= "Xaml File: " + errorArguments.xamlFile + "\n";
            strError+= "Xaml Element: " + errorArguments.xmlElement + "\n";
            strError+= "Xaml Attribute: " + errorArguments.xmlAttribute + "\n";
            strError+= "Line: " + errorArguments.lineNumber + "\n";
            strError+= "Position: " + errorArguments.charPosition + "\n";
            alert(strError);
        }
    </script>
</head>

<body>
    <div id="firstControl">
        <script type="text/javascript">
            createSilverlight();
        </script>
    </div>
</body>
</html>
```

When this is executed and the error is tripped, the alert box will display the contents of the error. Figure 6-3 shows an example of a customized alert box.

FIGURE 6-3 Using your own event handler.

Silverlight Control Properties

The Silverlight control has a number of properties, some of which were discussed in the section titled "Hosting Silverlight in the Browser." In addition to being able to set them when you initialize the control, you can also set the control's properties using script. The control splits properties into three types: direct, content, and settings properties. *Direct* properties are properties of the control itself that are accessible using the *control.propertyname* syntax. *Content* properties and *settings* properties are accessed using the *control.content.propertyname* and *control.settings.propertyname* syntax respectively.

Direct Properties

Following are the direct properties that are supported:

- **initParams**   The initialization parameters that are passed to the control are stored in this property. It can only be set as part of the control initialization.

- **isLoaded**   This property is *true* after the control is loaded; otherwise, it is *false*. It is read-only.

- **source**   This is the XAML content that you want to render. It can be a reference to a file, a URI to a service that generates XAML, or, when prefixed with a # character, a DIV containing XAML code in a script block.

Content Properties

When accessing content properties, you use the *control.content.propertyname* syntax. For example, if you want to access the *actualHeight* property, you use the *control.content.actualHeight* syntax. The following content properties are available:

- **actualHeight**   This returns the height of the rendering area of the Silverlight control in pixels. The value returned depends on a number of different criteria. First, it depends on how the height of the control was initially set. Recall that it can be a percentage or an absolute pixel value. In the case of the former, the *actualHeight* property is the current height of the control, but if the user changes the browser dimensions, this will change. If the height was set using an absolute pixel value, this will be returned. When the control is used in full screen mode, this will return the current vertical resolution of the display.

- **actualWidth**   This returns the width of the display. The value returned depends on a number of criteria and is similar to the *actualHeight* parameter.

- **fullScreen**   This switches the Silverlight control display between embedded and full screen mode. It defaults to *false*, which is the embedded mode. When set to *true*, Silverlight will render to the full screen.

Settings Properties

The control also contains a number of properties that are defined as settings properties, where they are accessed using the *control.settings.propertyname* syntax:

- **background** This sets the background color of the Silverlight control. It can take several different formats, including a named color (such as *Black*), 8Bit *Red/Green/Blue* (*RGB*) values with or without alpha, and 16Bit *RGB* values with or without alpha.

- **enableFrameRateCounter** When set to *true*, Silverlight will render the current frame rate (in frames per second) in the browser's status bar. It defaults to *false*.

- **enableHtmlAccess** When set to *true*, this will allow the XAML content to be accessible from the browser DOM. The default value is *true*.

- **enableRedrawRegions** When set to *true*, this shows the areas of the plug-in that are being redrawn upon each frame. It's a useful tool to help you optimize your application. The default value is *false*.

- **maxFrameRate** This specifies the maximum frame rate to render it. It defaults to 24 and has an absolute maximum of 64.

- **version** This reports the version of the Silverlight control that is presently being used. It is a string containing up to four integers, separated by dots, that contains the major, minor, build, and revision number, although only the first two values (major and minor version number) are required.

- **windowless** This determines whether the property is displayed as a windowless or windowed control. When set to *true*, it is windowless, meaning the Silverlight content is effectively rendered "behind" the HTML content on the page.

Silverlight Control Methods

The Silverlight control has a number of methods that you can use to control its behavior and function. Similar to Silverlight property groups, the Silverlight methods are grouped into "families" of methods. At present, one direct and three content methods are supported. You'll see which is which in the following sections, including samples showing their syntax and how to access them.

The *createFromXaml* Method

The *createFromXaml* method is a Silverlight content method that allows you to define XAML content to dynamically add to your Silverlight control. It takes two parameters. The first is a string containing the XAML that you want to use, and the other is the *namescope* parameter that, when *true* (it defaults to *false*), will create unique *x:Name* references within the provided XAML that will not conflict with any existing XAML element names.

There is a constraint around the XAML that you can add using *createFromXaml*. The XAML you add has to have a single root node. So, if you have a number of elements to add, make sure that they are all contained within a single node containing the *Canvas* element.

Additionally, *createFromXaml* does not add the XAML to the Silverlight control until it has been added to the children of one of the *Canvas* elements within the control. So, when you call *createFromXaml*, you get a reference to the node returned, and this reference is then used to add the node into the render tree. Following is an example:

```
function handleLoad(control, userContext, sender)
{
    var xamlFragment = '<TextBlock Canvas.Top="60" Text="A new TextBlock" />';
    textBlock = control.content.createFromXaml(xamlFragment);
    sender.children.add(textBlock);
}
```

Here the XAML code for a *TextBlock* control is created, containing the text "A new TextBlock". This is then used to create an XAML node within the control content; after it is complete, Silverlight will return a reference to the *TextBlock*. This reference is then added to the Silverlight control's render tree and is used to render the context of the *TextBlock*.

The *createFromXamlDownloader* Method

The *createFromXamlDownloader* method is a content method used in conjunction with a *Downloader* object, which you will learn about later in this chapter. It takes two parameters. The first parameter is a reference to the *Downloader* object that downloads the XAML code or a package containing the XAML code. The second parameter is the name of the specific part of the download content package to use. If this is a .zip file, then you specify the name of the file within the .zip file that contains the XAML code you want to use. When the downloaded content is not in a .zip package, then this parameter should be set to an empty string.

The *createObject* Method

The *createObject* method is a direct method designed to allow you to create a disposable object for a specific function. In Silverlight, the only object that is supported is the *Downloader* object. We'll cover this in greater detail later in this chapter.

The *findName* Method

This content method allows you to search for a node within your XAML code based on its *x:Name* attribute. If *findName* finds a node with the provided name, it returns a reference to it; otherwise, it returns *null*.

The *Downloader* Object

The Silverlight control provides an object that lets you download additional elements using asynchronous downloading functionality. This allows you to download individual assets or assets that are packaged in a .zip file.

Downloader Object Properties

The *Downloader* object supports the following properties:

- **downloadProgress**   This property provides a normalized value (between 0 and 1) representing the percentage progress of the content downloaded, where 1 is equal to 100 percent complete.

- **status**   This property gets the HTTP status code for the current status of the downloading process. It returns a standard HTTP status code, such as "404" for "Not Found" or "200" for "OK".

- **statusText**   This property gets the HTTP status text for the current status of the downloading process. This corresponds to the status code for the *status* property. For a successful request, the *status* will be "200," and the *statusText* will be "OK." For more information about HTTP status codes, check out the standard HTTP codes provided by W3C (*http://www.w3.org/Protocols/rfc2616/rfc2616-sec10.html*).

- **uri**   This property contains the URI of the object that the downloader is presently accessing.

Downloader Object Methods

The *Downloader* object supports the following methods:

- **abort**   This cancels the current download and resets all properties to their default state.

- **getResponseText**   This returns a string representation of the downloaded data. It takes an optional parameter that is used to name the contents of the filename within a downloaded package.

- **open**   This initializes the download session. It takes three parameters. The first is the verb for the action. The set of HTTP verbs is documented by the W3C; however, only the *GET* verb is supported in Silverlight. The second parameter is the URI for the resource that is to be downloaded.

- **send**   This executes the download request that was initialized with the *Open* command.

Downloader Object Events

The *Downloader* object supports the following events:

- **completed**   This event will fire when the download is complete. It takes two parameters. The first is the object that raised the event (in this case, the downloader control itself), and the second is a set of event arguments (*eventArgs*).

- **downloadProgressChanged**   This event will fire while content is being downloaded. It fires every time the progress (which is a value between 0 and 1) changes by 0.05 (5 percent) or more, as well as when it reaches 1.0 (100 percent). When it reaches 1.0, the *completed* event will also fire.

Using the *Downloader* Object

The *Downloader* object allows you to access network resources from JavaScript. Please note that this object will only work if you are running your Silverlight application from a Web server, and it will throw an error if you are simply loading the page from the file system.

You create a *Downloader* object using the *createObject* method provided by the Silverlight control. Here's an example:

```
<script type="text/javascript">
    function handleLoad(control, userContext, sender)
    {
        var downloader = control.createObject("downloader");
    }
</script>
```

The next step is to initialize the download session by using the *Downloader* object's *open* method to declare the URI of the file and then to call the *send* method to kick off the download. Following is an example that will download a movie file called *movie.wmv*:

```
function handleLoad(control, userContext, sender)
{
    var downloader = control.createObject("downloader");
    downloader.open("GET","movie.wmv";
    downloader.send();
}
```

In order to trap the download progress and completion, you'll need to wire the appropriate event handlers. Following is the same function, updated accordingly:

```
function handleLoad(control, userContext, sender)
{
    var downloader = control.createObject("downloader");
    downloader.addEventListener("downloadProgressChanged","handleDLProgress");
    downloader.addEventListener("completed","handleDLComplete");
    downloader.open("GET","movie.wmv";
    downloader.send();
}
```

Now you can implement these event handlers. In this example, the *DownloadProgressChanged* event is wired to a JavaScript function called *handleDLProgress,* and the *Completed* event is wired to the *handleDLComplete* JavaScript function. You can see these functions here:

```
function handleDLProgress(sender, args)
{
    var ctrl = sender.getHost();
```

```
        var t1 = ctrl.content.findName("txt1");
        var v = sender.downloadProgress * 100;
        t1.Text = v + "%";
    }

    function handleDLComplete(sender, args)
    {
        alert("Download complete");
    }
```

> **Note** You can only use the *Downloader* object on applications that are hosted on a Web Server. If you try to use it from a page that is loaded from the file system, you'll get an error.

Programming UI Elements

XAML provides a number of visual elements for creating your UIs. These are listed in detail in Chapter 4 and in Chapter 5, "XAML Transformation and Animation," where their properties are discussed. The set of UI elements includes *Canvas, Ellipse, Glyphs, Image, Line, MediaElement, Path, Polygon, Polyline, Rectangle, Run, Shape,* and *TextBlock.*

Each of these elements supports a rich set of methods and events, and these will be listed and discussed in the next several sections.

In addition, Silverlight 2 has a rich control set. These controls are used from .NET code to produce a rich UI, and they are discussed in detail in Chapter 7, "Silverlight Controls: Presentation and Layout."

UI Element Methods

UI elements provide functions that can be called from JavaScript to allow you to manipulate them to create rich application interaction. These methods are common to all of the UI elements.

The *AddEventListener* and *RemoveEventListener* Methods

The *AddEventListener* method is used to add an event listener at run time to the UI element. This is useful for separating design and development—the developer doesn't add anything directly to the XAML that the designer produces. Instead, the developer adds event handling code to a JavaScript file (or block). UI element events you might handle are discussed later in this chapter.

Following is an example that shows you how to add an event listener at run time. This example adds an event handler that traps the mouse click and specifies that the event should be handled by a JavaScript function called *handleMouse.* This function, like most event handlers, takes two parameters: a sender and event arguments. Because it is a mouse event, it takes an instance of *MouseEventArgs,* which allows us to get the x- and y-coordinates of the mouse at the time of the event:

```
<script type="text/javascript">
    function handleLoad(control, userContext, sender)
    {
        sender.addEventListener("mouseLeftButtonDown",handleMouse);
    }
    function handleMouse(sender, mouseEventArgs)
    {
        alert(mouseEventArgs.getPosition(null).x + ":"
            + mouseEventArgs.getPosition(null).y);
    }
</script>
```

You can destroy the connection at run time using the *RemoveEventListener* method. You can either pass it the integer token that was returned by *addEventListener*, or you can pass it the event name.

The *findName* Method

This method is used to search through the XAML tree to find a named object. It will return a reference to the specified object if it exists; otherwise, it will return *null*. For example, take a look at this XAML code:

```
<Canvas xmlns="http://schemas.microsoft.com/client/2007"
        xmlns:x="http://schemas.microsoft.com/winfx/2006/xaml"
        Height="400" Width="400">
  <TextBlock Canvas.Top="0" x:Name="txt1" Text="TextBlock1" />
  <TextBlock Canvas.Top="20" x:Name="txt2" Text="TextBlock2" />
  <TextBlock Canvas.Top="40" x:Name="txt3" Text="TextBlock3" />
</Canvas>
```

This code defines three T*extBlocks* called *txt1*, *txt2*, and *txt3* using the *x:Name* property. You can now use the *findName* method to find a named node, obtain a reference to it, and then edit it using that reference. In this case, it is done within the *handleLoad* event handler.

```
<script type="text/javascript">
    function handleLoad(control, userContext, sender)
    {
        var t1 = sender.findName("txt1");
        t1.Text = "TextBlock1 has changed";
    }
</script>
```

Accessing the Control with the *GetHost* Method

UI elements provide a *GetHost* method that can be used to access the containing Silverlight control. This can be particularly useful if you want to query the object for information, such as its version number.

Accessing a Parent Element with the *getParent* Method

You may have cases in which you want to access a UI element's parent. It is inefficient to get a reference to the Silverlight control and then to use *findName* to get the parent, so the *get-Parent* method is available. It will return a reference to the parent upon success; otherwise, it will return *null*.

Using the *GetValue* and *SetValue* Methods

You can always access properties with the traditional dot syntax, *object.propertyname*, but an alternative methodology, using the *GetValue* method, exists to support attached properties. So, for example, if you want to access the *Canvas.Top* property, you cannot do it with *object.Canvas.Top*. You must use the *object.GetValue("Canvas.Top")* syntax. *GetValue* can also be used to access nonattached properties, even though in that case the dot notation is equivalent.

In a similar way, you can use the *SetValue* method to set a property value for either a simple or attached property. This method takes two parameters. The first is the name of the property, and the second is the value to assign. Following is an example:

```
var t1 = ctrl.content.findName("txt1");
t1.setValue("Canvas.Top",20);
```

> **Note**   You can also use a square bracket syntax to access and set attached properties. Here's an example: t1["Canvas.Top"] = 20.

Using *SetFontSource*

The *TextBlock* element supports an additional method, *SetFontSource*, that allows you to use a downloaded font for the *TextBlock*. So, if you want to use a new font to render the text—for example, if you need to support a foreign character set (such as a font used for East Asian languages), then you can download the font with a *Downloader* object and use the *SetFont-Source* method, passing it the *Downloader* object, and then the *TextBlock* will use that font. To use this method, you must have the rights to distribute the font (or a subset thereof).

Following is an example using the *SetFontSource* method. In this case, I have an XAML document that was defined using Expression Blend and that uses some Chinese text:

```
<Canvas
  xmlns="http://schemas.microsoft.com/client/2007"
  xmlns:x="http://schemas.microsoft.com/winfx/2006/xaml"
  Width="640" Height="480" Background="White">
  <TextBlock x:Name="myTextBlock" Width="152" Height="64"
    Canvas.Left="184" Canvas.Top="56" Text="你好吗? "
    TextWrapping="Wrap" MouseLeftButtonDown="handleIt" />
</Canvas>
```

In Silverlight 2, the default font for these characters is used. If you want to render them in a *specific* font that may not be available on every user's computer, then you can use a *Downloader* object to download this font. The previous XAML code defines a *MouseLeftButtonDown* event handler function called *handleIt*. You can see that function here:

```
// Event handler for initializing and executing a font file download request.
function handleIt(sender, eventArgs)
{
   // Retrieve a reference to the control.
   var control = sender.getHost();
   // Create a Downloader object.
   var downloader = control.createObject("downloader");
   // Add Completed event.
   downloader.addEventListener("Completed", "onCompleted");
   // Initialize the Downloader request.
   downloader.open("GET", "MyFontName.TTF");
   // Execute the Downloader request.
   downloader.send();
}
```

This creates a download object that downloads the font and defines an event handler *onCompleted* that will handle the *Completed* event that fires when the download is complete. This event will then set the font source for the *TextBlock* to the supporting font, and then Silverlight will render the Chinese characters using the new font source.

```
// Event handler for the Completed event.
function onCompleted(sender, eventArgs)
{
   // Retrieve the TextBlock object.
   var myTextBlock = sender.findName("myTextBlock");

   // Add the font files in the downloaded object
   // to the TextBlock's type face collection.
   myTextBlock.setFontSource(sender);

   // Set the FontFamily property to the friendly name of the font.
   myTextBlock.fontFamily = "Simhei";
}
```

UI Element Events

UI elements support a number of events that may be wired to JavaScript functions either by using the *AddEventListener* methodology to add them at run time or by using the appropriate XAML attribute to add them at design time. For example, if you want to wire a control's *MouseLeftButtonDown* event using JavaScript, you do it with the *AddEventListener* method:

```
t1.addEventListener("MouseLeftButtonDown", handleMouseDown);
```

To wire the event in XAML, you can use the attribute that has the same name as the desired event (such as "MouseLeftButtonDown"). Following is an example:

```
<TextBlock Canvas.Top="0" x:Name="txt1" Text="Status"
MouseLeftButtonDown="handleMouseDown"/>
```

The events that are supported on the UI element are as follows:

- **GotFocus**   This is fired when the element receives mouse focus.

- **KeyDown**   This occurs on an element when it has focus and a key is pressed. The event handler takes two attributes. The first of these is the *sender*, representing a reference to the object that raised the event. The second is a *KeyEventArgs* object. This has a number of properties of its own. The first is *key*, which is an integer value that represents the key that was pressed. It is not operating system specific, and specific details about how this maps to actual keys can be found in the Silverlight SDK. Another property is the *platformKeyCode*, which *is* operating system specific. In addition to the actual key, the Boolean properties *shift* and *ctrl* are exposed. These indicate whether or not the Shift and Ctrl keys are pressed. (Note that this event does not fire when Silverlight is in full screen mode.)

- **KeyUp**   This occurs on an element when it has focus and the key is released. It provides for the same two attributes as the *KeyDown* event. (Note that this event does not fire when Silverlight is in full screen mode.)

- **Loaded**   This fires when the Silverlight content is loaded into the host Silverlight control and parsed, but before it is rendered.

- **LostFocus**   This is the opposite of the *GotFocus* event; it fires when the object loses focus.

- **MouseEnter**   This fires when the mouse enters the bounding area of the object.

- **MouseLeave**   This is the opposite of *MouseEnter* event; it fires when the mouse leaves the area of the bounding object.

- **MouseLeftButtonDown**   This occurs when the user presses the left mouse button over the UI element.

- **MouseLeftButtonUp**   This occurs when the left mouse button is released.

- **MouseMove**   This occurs when the cursor moves over the UI element.

Implementing Drag and Drop

You can use the mouse event handlers and Silverlight's *CaptureMouse* and *ReleaseMouseCapture* methods to implement drag and drop in Silverlight.

First of all, let's take a look at an XAML document containing several shapes that may be dragged and dropped around the canvas. These shapes wire their mouse event handlers (*MouseLeftButtonDown, MouseLeftButtonUp,* and *MouseMove*) to the *onMouseDown, onMouseUp,* and *onMouseMove* functions respectively.

```
<Canvas xmlns="http://schemas.microsoft.com/client/2007"
        xmlns:x="http://schemas.microsoft.com/winfx/2006/xaml"
        Height="400" Width="400">
```

```
<Ellipse Canvas.Top="0" Height="10" Width="10" Fill="Black"
         MouseLeftButtonDown="onMouseDown"
         MouseLeftButtonUp="onMouseUp"
         MouseMove="onMouseMove" />
<Ellipse Canvas.Top="20" Height="10" Width="10" Fill="Black"
         MouseLeftButtonDown="onMouseDown"
         MouseLeftButtonUp="onMouseUp"
         MouseMove="onMouseMove"/>
<Ellipse Canvas.Top="40" Height="10" Width="10" Fill="Black"
         MouseLeftButtonDown="onMouseDown"
         MouseLeftButtonUp="onMouseUp"
         MouseMove="onMouseMove"/>
<Ellipse Canvas.Top="60" Height="10" Width="10" Fill="Black"
         MouseLeftButtonDown="onMouseDown"
         MouseLeftButtonUp="onMouseUp"
         MouseMove="onMouseMove"/>
</Canvas>
```

Now, let's take a look at each of the event handler functions. First, let's examine the *Mouse-Down* event handler. When dragging, you want that control to "own" the mouse events, so you use the *captureMouse* method. You'll also want to remember the starting points for the dragging, so these will be recorded by the event handler. Finally, you'll flag that the mouse is down using a Boolean variable *isMouseDown*.

```
var beginX;
var beginY;
var isMouseDown = false;
function onMouseDown(sender, mouseEventArgs)
{
    beginX = mouseEventArgs.getPosition(null).x;
    beginY = mouseEventArgs.getPosition(null).y;
    isMouseDown = true;
    sender.captureMouse();
}
```

Now, in a drag-and-drop operation, you want to move the item with the mouse. So, when the *MouseMove* event fires, you will record the current mouse coordinates and use them to figure out where the item should be moved as well.

The *mouseEventArgs* allow us to retrieve the current x- and y-coordinates of the mouse. Because the *Ellipse* object that is being dragged in the example is the *sender*, you can set its left and top properties by adding the delta on the x- and y-coordinates to their respective initial values.

Also note that *onMouseMove* will fire whether you are dragging or not, so we use the *isMouseDown* to check if we are currently dragging. (Remember, it was set in the previous *MouseDown* event handler.)

```
function onMouseMove(sender, mouseEventArgs)
{
  if (isMouseDown == true)
```

```
    {
        var currX = mouseEventArgs.getPosition(null).x;
        var currY = mouseEventArgs.getPosition(null).y;
        sender["Canvas.Left"] += currX - beginX;
        sender["Canvas.Top"] += currY - beginY;
        beginX = currX;
        beginY = currY;
    }
}
```

Finally, when the mouse button is released, you will release the mouse capture and reset *isMouseDown*. The ellipses will stay in their new positions.

```
function onMouseUp(sender, mouseEventArgs)
{
    isMouseDown = false;
    sender.releaseMouseCapture();
}
```

Figure 6-4 shows the four ellipses with drag and drop enabled, and Figure 6-5 shows the position of the ellipses after the drag-and-drop operation has been completed.

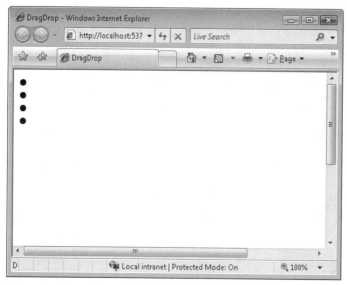

FIGURE 6-4 Four ellipses with drag and drop enabled.

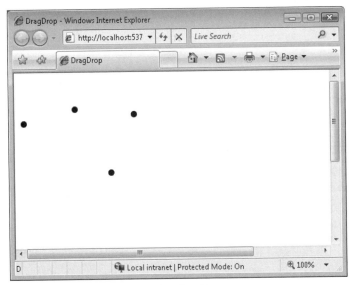

FIGURE 6-5 Dragging and dropping the ellipses.

Summary

In this chapter, you looked at the Silverlight object model and how it can be programmed using JavaScript. You learned how the Silverlight control is hosted within the browser, including how to initialize it and how to set up its initial state using its property model. You saw how it can be customized with context and custom parameters, as well as the full property, method, and event model that it supports. In addition, you learned how to implement a custom error handler on the control, as well as how to use the basic default error handler.

You discovered how you can add external content to your control using the *Downloader* object and how to trap the events that it exposes to provide feedback as to download progress. You were introduced to the UI elements that XAML offers and learned about the methods, events, and properties that they expose and how you can program them.

Now that you have been introduced to Silverlight and its features, it's time to take your skills to the next level, where you will learn about the rich and powerful control set and programming model offered by Silverlight 2. We'll start in the next chapter with a look at the base control set for Silverlight.

Part II
Programming Silverlight 2

Chapter 7
Silverlight Controls: Presentation and Layout

Silverlight 2 comes with two main assemblies containing controls for use in your applications: the *core controls* and the *extended controls*. These are in addition to the *System.Windows.Forms* namespace that contains basic controls.

In this chapter, we will introduce the following core controls, and you will learn how you can use them in Silverlight:

- *Button*
- *CheckBox*
- *HyperlinkButton*
- *Image*
- *ListBox*
- *RadioButton*
- *TextBlock*
- *TextBox*

You'll look at the specific properties, methods, and events that each of these controls expose, as well as the general ones that are shared across all controls. The information in this chapter is not intended to be an exclusive reference for everything associated with each control, but there should be more than enough basics to get you started, making it easier for you to experiment with these controls on your own.

The *Button* Control

In Silverlight, you implement a push button using the *Button* control. A button reacts to user input from input devices such as the mouse, keyboard, or stylus, raising a *Click* event when it does so. There are several configurable ways in which a button raises the *Click* event. These are set using the *ClickMode* property, which can contain the values of *Hover, Press*, and *Release*. These values determine when the *Click* event is raised. In the first case, *Hover*, it is raised when the mouse enters the button. In the second, *Press,* it is raised when the mouse button is held down over the button. In the third, *Release*, the event is raised when the user has pressed *and* released the mouse button over the button.

```
<Canvas x:Name="LayoutRoot" Background="White">
  <Button x:Name="b1" ClickMode="Hover"
      Content="Button1" Click="Button_Click"></Button>
  <Button x:Name="b2" Canvas.Top="40" ClickMode="Press"
      Content="Button2" Click="Button_Click"></Button>
  <Button x:Name="b3" Canvas.Top="80" ClickMode="Release"
      Content="Button3" Click="Button_Click"></Button>
</Canvas>
```

You can see that the *Click* event handler has been defined on these buttons and that the same function, *Button_Click*, is defined for each.

Here is the code that handles the event:

```
private void Button_Click(object sender, RoutedEventArgs e)
{
  Button b = (Button)sender;
  string strTest = b.Name;
}
```

This code follows a typical event handler pattern. It receives an object sender that contains a reference to the control on which the event was raised, in this case one of the buttons, and a set of arguments associated with the event (*RoutedEventArgs*) that contains metadata about the event.

You'll notice that only one event handler is declared in this instance. This is particularly useful in keeping your code tidy. You will, of course, want to figure out which item raised the event, and that's where the sender comes in.

The sender is of type *Object*, so in order to figure out some of the button-specific properties, you'll simply cast it to a *Button*. So, in this case, you can see that it is cast to a *Button*, and from there the name can be derived. If you run the application now, you'll see three buttons, and you'll see how the *ClickMode* property associated with each of the buttons causes each of them to behave differently!

An additional, useful property is *IsEnabled*. When this is set to *false*, the button will still be rendered, but it will appear shaded on the screen and will not raise any events.

The label on your button is set using the *Content* property. This can be set to some simple text to create a caption for the button. However, *Button* is also a container control, so you can customize the content of your button with XAML.

Here's an example of a (very ugly) button that contains XAML as its content:

```
<Button x:Name="b1" Click="Button_Click" Width="100" Height="100">
  <Canvas>
    <Ellipse Fill="Green" Width="50" Height="50"></Ellipse>
    <TextBlock Text="Hello"></TextBlock>
  </Canvas>
</Button>
```

As you can see, this gives you great flexibility in how your button is presented, so you can easily put together rich buttons—similar to those on the Microsoft Office 2007 toolbar—within your Web applications.

The *CheckBox* Control

The *CheckBox* control is a control that gives the user a selectable option that typically takes the form of a box that the user can check or uncheck. It is used when a set of options is presented to the user and more than one option is allowed.

A *CheckBox* raises the *Checked* event when it has been selected, the *Unchecked* event when it has been cleared, or the *Click* event whenever it is clicked. Similar to the *Button* control, *CheckBox* has a *ClickMode* property that can be set to *Hover, Press,* or *Release,* which configures it to raise the event in different circumstances.

The *CheckBox* can also be a three-state check box with an indeterminate state between checked and unchecked. You turn this on or off using the *IsThreeState* property. When you are in this mode, if the user puts the check box into the indeterminate state, the *IsChecked* property will be *null*.

You can get the value of the *CheckBox* using the *IsChecked* property. Be careful when using this if you are using the *CheckBox* in the three-state mode because the *IsChecked* property value will be *null* when the *CheckBox* is in the indeterminable state.

Similar to the *Button* control, the *CheckBox* is a *Content* container, so you can use the *Content* property to hold a simple text string as the caption for a check box in your application, or you can use XAML within the *<Content>* child tag to get something richer.

Following is an example that shows each type:

```
<StackPanel>
  <CheckBox Checked="CheckBox_Checked"
      Unchecked="CheckBox_Unchecked"
      IsThreeState="True" Content="Test1">
  </CheckBox>
  <CheckBox Checked="CheckBox_Checked"
      Unchecked="CheckBox_Unchecked"
      IsThreeState="True">
    <CheckBox.Content>
      <StackPanel Orientation="Horizontal"></StackPanel>
        <TextBlock Text="The Caption"></TextBlock>
        <Image Source="..."/>
    </CheckBox.Content>
  </CheckBox>
</StackPanel>
```

When handling the *Clicked, Checked,* and *Unchecked* events, the *sender* will be an object that you should cast to the *CheckBox* type in order to get access to the properties.

Here's an example:

```
private void CheckBox_Checked(object sender, RoutedEventArgs e)
{
  CheckBox c = (CheckBox)sender;
  bool b = (bool)c.IsChecked;
}

private void CheckBox_Unchecked(object sender, RoutedEventArgs e)
{
  CheckBox c = (CheckBox)sender;
  bool b = (bool)c.IsChecked;
}
```

The *HyperlinkButton* Control

The *HyperlinkButton* provides a clickable element on the page that navigates to a URI specified in the *NavigateUri* property.

Here's an example:

```
<HyperlinkButton Content="Microsoft"
    NavigateUri="http://www.microsoft.com" />
```

The *HyperlinkButton* is a content control, meaning that it can have a simple *Content* property containing text to render for the hyperlink, or it can contain much richer—and more exciting—content.

For example, if you want a hyperlink button that appears as an image, it's very easy to do using the *<Hyperlink.Content>* child, which can contain an image. Here's an example:

```
<HyperlinkButton NavigateUri="http://www.silverlight.net" >
  <HyperlinkButton.Content>
    <Image Source="sl.jpg"/>
  </HyperlinkButton.Content>
</HyperlinkButton>
```

Now when you run the application, you'll get a clickable image that navigates to the specified URL.

The *TargetName* property is used to specify where the content at the URL will be rendered. The options that you can use to display the URL content include the following:

- **_blank** Opens a new browser window with no name.

- **_self** Replaces the current HTML page with the new content. If it is within a frame, it will only replace that frame.

- **_top**   Replaces the current HTML page with the new content. If it is within a frame, the entire browser will still have the new content.

- **_parent**   Replaces the entire HTML page.

If you are in a frameset, you can also specify the name of the frame to use.

Here's an example in which we specify that a new browser should open when the user selects the control:

```
<Grid x:Name="LayoutRoot" Background="White">
  <HyperlinkButton NavigateUri="http://www.silverlight.net"
       TargetName="_blank" >
    <HyperlinkButton.Content>
      <Image Source="sl.jpg"/>
    </HyperlinkButton.Content>
  </HyperlinkButton>
</Grid>
```

Note that the *Click* event for the *HyperlinkButton* will fire before the navigation takes place. This can be very useful so that any preprocessing is completed prior to the new content loading.

Here's an example with the *Click* event configured. Notice that the *NavigateUri* is set to *http://www.microsoft.com*, but the page actually navigates to *http://www.silverlight.net* because the *Click* runs before the navigation and then changes the *NavigateUri*.

First, here is the XAML:

```
<HyperlinkButton NavigateUri="http://www.microsoft.com"
    TargetName="_blank" Click="HyperlinkButton_Click"  >
  <HyperlinkButton.Content>
    <Image Source="sl.jpg"/>
  </HyperlinkButton.Content>
</HyperlinkButton>
```

And now here is the C# code-behind that handles the *HyperlinkButton_Click* event:

```
private void HyperlinkButton_Click(object sender, RoutedEventArgs e)
{
  HyperlinkButton h = (HyperlinkButton)sender;
  string strTest = h.NavigateUri.AbsoluteUri;
  if (strTest == "http://www.microsoft.com/")
  {
    h.NavigateUri = new Uri("http://www.silverlight.net");
  }
}
```

When you run this code, you'll now see that despite the fact that the *HyperlinkButton* is configured for one URL, this will be changed as part of the *Click* event handler to another URL, and the new URL will be opened instead.

The *Image* Control

The *Image* control is used to render an image. It can handle .bmp, .jpg, and .png file formats. You specify the path to the image using the *Source* property. Here's an example:

```
<Image Source="sl.jpg"//>
```

> **Note** If the code references an invalid format or if the *Source* is improperly set, then an *ImageFailed* event will be raised.

When the actual image has different dimensions from those that you specify for an *Image* control (i.e., if you have a 100 × 100 *Image* element that loads a 2000 × 2000 pixel .jpg), you can control the rendering behavior using the *Stretch* property. This can take the following values:

- **Fill** Scales the image to fit the output dimensions using independent scaling on the x- and y-axes.

- **Uniform** Scales the underlying image to fit the dimensions of the *Image* control, but leaves the aspect ratio untouched.

- **UniformToFill** Scales the image to completely fill the output area, clipping it where necessary.

- **None** Renders the image completely untouched, causing clipping if the underlying image is larger than the *Image* element.

You will often have cases in which you don't want to set the image at design time, hardcoding a URI into the XAML, but will want to set it at run time, perhaps as the result of a database call or something similar. In these instances, you will use the *BitmapImage* class (from the *System.Windows.Media.Imaging* namespace) as the source for the *Image* control. Following is an example of how this would work.

First the XAML:

```
<Image x:Name="theImage"/>
```

And here is the code that will load the image from a URL when the page loads:

```
public Page(){
  InitializeComponent();
  this.Loaded += new RoutedEventHandler(Page_Loaded);
}

void Page_Loaded(object sender, RoutedEventArgs e)
{
  Uri uri = new Uri("sl.jpg",UriKind.Relative);
  theImage.Source = new BitmapImage(uri);
}
```

In this case, a new *Uri* object is constructed using the path of the image. The second parameter in the constructor is the option for how the path to the Uri should be calculated. The URI referenced here can be relative (in which case the specified resource will be sought in the same directory as the one in which the component resides), absolute (in which case the specified resource will be sought directly, so you should specify the location using syntax such as *http://server/resource*), or a combination of the two.

After the Uri is constructed, it can be used to construct a new *BitmapImage*, which is set to the source of the *Image* control.

The *ListBox* Control

The *ListBox* control is used to present content as an ordered list. The *ListBox* is flexible enough so that list items can be created from any type of content, but the typical list is made up of *ListBoxItem* elements as in the following example:

```
<ListBox x:Name="theList" SelectionChanged="ListBox_SelectionChanged">
  <ListBoxItem Content="1"/>
  <ListBoxItem Content="2"/>
  <ListBoxItem Content="3"/>
  <ListBoxItem Content="4"/>
  <ListBoxItem Content="5"/>
</ListBox>
```

You can manage the user's selection of the items that make up the *ListBox* using the *Selection-Changed* event and the *SelectedItem* property. In the previous XAML, you can see that the *SelectionChanged* event will be handled by a method handler called *ListBox_SelectionChanged*. Here's the code:

```
private void ListBox_SelectionChanged(
    object sender, SelectionChangedEventArgs e)
{
  ListBoxItem x = theList.SelectedItem as ListBoxItem;
  string strTest = x.Content.ToString();
}
```

Note that the *SelectedItem* from the *ListBox* returns an *object* and not a *ListBoxItem* because (as mentioned earlier) the *ListBox* can host many different types of content, so in this case we cast the *SelectedItem* to a *ListBoxItem* in order to use it.

Remember that a *ListBox* can contain different types of items. Following is an example in which the *ListBox* contains compound items made up of *StackPanel* components containing a *Rectangle*, an *Image*, and a *TextBlock* each.

```
<ListBox x:Name="theList" SelectionChanged="ListBox_SelectionChanged">
  <StackPanel Orientation="Horizontal">
    <Rectangle Fill="Black" Height="100" Width="100"></Rectangle>
    <Image Height="100" Width="100" Source="s1.jpg"/>
```

```
            <TextBlock Text="Item 1"></TextBlock>
        </StackPanel>
        <StackPanel Orientation="Horizontal">
            <Rectangle Fill="Black" Height="100" Width="100"></Rectangle>
            <Image Height="100" Width="100" Source="sl.jpg"/>
            <TextBlock Text="Item 2"></TextBlock>
        </StackPanel>
    </ListBox>
```

You can see how this *ListBox* will be rendered in Figure 7-1.

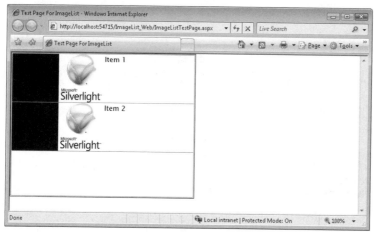

FIGURE 7-1 *ListBox* with complex items.

When you have a complex item like this, you can easily pull the content out by using the *SelectedItem* to get the container (in this case a *StackPanel*) and then deriving the content that you want from it. Here's an example:

```
StackPanel s = theList.SelectedItem as StackPanel;
TextBlock t = s.Children[2] as TextBlock;
string strTest = t.Text;
```

The *RadioButton* Control

The *RadioButton* control is similar to the *CheckBox* in that it is used for catching user selections. However, it is different from the *CheckBox* in that it is typically used for situations in which the user makes a *single* selection from a range of options.

One way you can control the range of options that allow a single selection is by setting up the *RadioButton* controls for the options as siblings within a container. Consider this example:

```
<StackPanel Orientation="Vertical" Background="Yellow">
  <RadioButton Content="Option 1" IsChecked="true" ></RadioButton>
  <RadioButton Content="Option 2"></RadioButton>
  <RadioButton Content="Option 3"></RadioButton>
```

```
    <RadioButton Content="Option 4"></RadioButton>
    <StackPanel Orientation="Vertical" Background="White">
      <RadioButton Content="Option 5" IsChecked="true"></RadioButton>
      <RadioButton Content="Option 6"></RadioButton>
      <RadioButton Content="Option 7"></RadioButton>
      <RadioButton Content="Option 8"></RadioButton>
    </StackPanel>
</StackPanel>
```

This XAML contains two *StackPanel* containers, one within the other. The first contains options 1, 2, 3, and 4, and the second contains options 5, 6, 7, and 8. As a result, the user can select only one from options 1 through 4 and only one from options 5 through 8. You can see how this works in Figure 7-2.

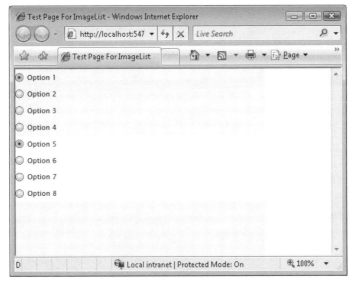

FIGURE 7-2 Using the *RadioButton* control.

Additionally, you can assign a *GroupName* to each *RadioButton* to subdivide the options into logical groups. In the previous example, you had options 1 through 4 in a *StackPanel*, and Silverlight allowed the user of the application to select only one of those four options.

If you wanted to subdivide this set of options into two groups so that the user could select one from options 1 and 2 and one from options 3 and 4, then instead of using a container, you can use *RadioButton* groups.

```
<StackPanel Orientation="Vertical" Background="Yellow">
  <RadioButton Content="Option 1" IsChecked="true"
      GroupName="G1" ></RadioButton>
  <RadioButton Content="Option 2" GroupName="G1" />
  <RadioButton Content="Option 3" GroupName="G2" />
  <RadioButton Content="Option 4" GroupName="G2" />
  <RadioButton Content="Option 5" GroupName="G3"
```

```
        IsChecked="true" />
  <RadioButton Content="Option 6" GroupName="G3" />
  <RadioButton Content="Option 7" GroupName="G3" />
  <RadioButton Content="Option 8" GroupName="G3" />
</StackPanel>
```

You can see this in action in Figure 7-3.

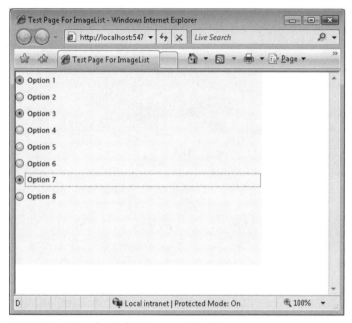

FIGURE 7-3 Using the *RadioButton* control with groups.

Similar to the *Button* and *CheckBox* controls, a *RadioButton* has a *ClickMode* property that determines what type of user interaction causes the *Click* event to be raised. This can be *Hover*, so that just moving the mouse over it will generate the event; *Press*, which raises the event when the mouse button is pressed down; and *Release*, in which the mouse button must be pressed and then released over the option button. Also similar to the *CheckBox* control, the *IsChecked* property can be evaluated for a particular *RadioButton* option to see if it is set.

The *TextBlock* Control

The *TextBlock* control is used to render text in Silverlight applications.

In its simplest case, the *TextBlock* is used along with its *Text* property to render the text. Here's an example:

```
<TextBlock Text="1234"></TextBlock>
```

You change the size of the rendered text using the *FontSize* property in pixels. You change the font that you are going to use with the *FontFamily* property; for example, if you want to use the Arial Black font at size 20, the XAML would look like this:

```
<TextBlock Text="1234" FontFamily="Arial Black" FontSize="20" />
```

The *FontStyle* property is used to set the text to be either italicized or normal. To use italics, set the property to *Italic* like this:

```
<TextBlock Text="1234" FontFamily="Arial Black"
    FontSize="20" FontStyle="Italic"></TextBlock>
```

To use normal text, you can set it to *Normal* or just leave the *FontStyle* property unset.

You can control line breaking and mixed text using the *<LineBreak>* and *<Run>* subelements of the *TextBlock*. As its name suggests, the *<LineBreak>* will create a break in the text, with the text that follows it setting on a new line.

However, the *TextBlock* is not a content presenter control as are some of the controls you saw earlier in this chapter, so if you want to continue text beyond the bounds of the original contents of the *Text* property, you must use the *Run* control:

```
<TextBlock Width="400" Text="My first text">
  <LineBreak/>
  <Run>My Second Text</Run>
  <LineBreak/>
  <Run>My Third Text</Run>
  <LineBreak/>
  <Run>My Fourth Text</Run>
</TextBlock>
```

The nice thing about the *Run* control is that it supports the same properties as the *TextBlock* for font, size, color, and so forth, so you have the same level of control over its content as you have with the *TextBlock*, which means there is no disparity between the *TextBlock* text and the text that displays using the *Run* control.

One way that Silverlight 2 differs from Silverlight 1.0 when using the *TextBlock* control is that the *TextBlock* is no longer restricted to the nine fonts that are built into Silverlight. Instead, Silverlight 2 uses a set of system font fallback rules, so if the font exists on the system, the text will be rendered in that font; if the font is not available on the system, a fallback font, defined by the operating system, will be used to render the text.

So, take a look at this example of some XAML created to display a *TextBlock* containing Webdings as well as some Chinese and Hebrew text:

```
<StackPanel Orientation="Vertical" Background="Yellow">
    <TextBlock Width="400" Text="My first text">
      <LineBreak/>
      <Run FontFamily="Webdings">My Second Text</Run>
```

```
        <LineBreak/>
        <Run>微软助力基础教育</Run>
        <LineBreak/>
        <Run>מרכז זכיפה חותיב בישראהקלילות וקבוצות דייו</Run>
        </Run>
    </TextBlock>
</StackPanel>
```

You can see how this appears in Figure 7-4. This new feature will make the development of internationalized applications in Silverlight very straightforward.

FIGURE 7-4 Using characters from special fonts in Silverlight.

The *TextBox* Control

You provide an area for your users to enter text using the *TextBox* control. In its simplest form, the *Text Box* control provides an area that is capable of being filled by the user with a single line of text. Here's an example:

```
<StackPanel>

  <TextBox />
  <TextBox />

</StackPanel>
```

This is very simply a *StackPanel* that contains two *TextBox* controls. Figure 7-5 shows what these will display, and I have typed some values into them to show you how a user would fill in the *TextBox* in an application.

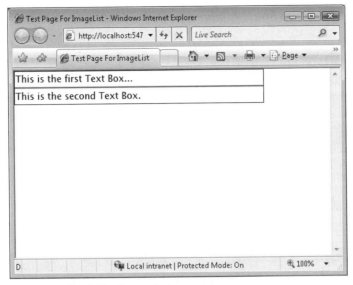

FIGURE 7-5 Simple *TextBox* controls.

To make these *TextBox* controls capable of accepting multiline input, you'll need to do two things. First, you'll have to specify a height or place them in a container that gives them the nondefault height. Then you'll have to use the *AcceptsReturn* property, set to *True*, to allow them to accept carriage return characters. You can see this in action in Figure 7-6.

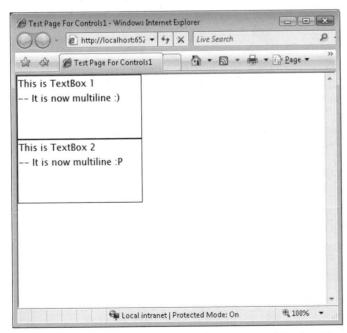

FIGURE 7-6 Amending the *TextBox* controls to accept multiline input from the user.

When you use the *TextBox* like this, the *Text* property will return a string with each line separated by a '\r'.

Whenever the text changes on the *TextBox*, the *TextChanged* event will fire. Note that this will happen after every keystroke, so if you want to capture all the changes, it might be better to capture the *LostFocus* event and manage the text from there.

Your *TextBox* controls automatically accept Input Method Editor (IME) input for foreign language support. If you have the system keyboards and language support already installed, then IME will work the same in Silverlight 2 as it does for any HTML control. You can see this in Figure 7-7, where IME languages are actually being mixed in the same *TextBox*—amazing!

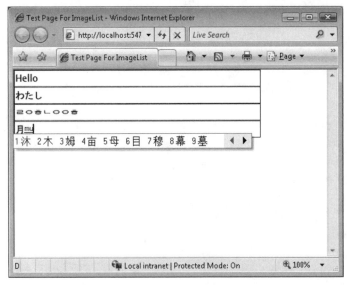

FIGURE 7-7 *TextBox* control with international text input.

In this case, the *Text* property will return a Unicode-encoded string that contains all the characters with '\r' denoting the line separators.

TextBox controls allow you to select ranges of *Text*, and they also allow you to configure how the selection appears. You use the *SelectedText* property to set or get the text in the current selection. The start of the current selection may be read with *SelectionStart* and the length with *SelectionEnd*. Whenever the selection changes, the *SelectionChanged* event will fire. Take a look at the following example.

First, here is the XAML:

```
<TextBox Height="100" AcceptsReturn="True"
  LostFocus="TextBox_LostFocus"
  Text="ABCDEFGHIJKLMNOPQRSTUVWXYZ"
```

```
    SelectionChanged="TextBox_SelectionChanged">
</TextBox>
```

This defines the *SelectionChanged* event, which is handled in code by the *Text-Box_SelectionChanged* event handler. You can see that here:

```
private void TextBox_SelectionChanged(object sender, RoutedEventArgs e)
{
  TextBox t = sender as TextBox;
  int st = t.SelectionStart;
  int ln = t.SelectionLength;
  string strT = t.SelectedText;
}
```

In this case, the *st* variable is an *int* containing the index of the starting character in the selection (which is zero based), *ln* is the length of the selection, and *strT* is a string containing the selection. So, for example, if you make a selection like the one shown in Figure 7-8, *st* will be 9, *ln* will be 8, and *strT* will be JKLMNOPQ.

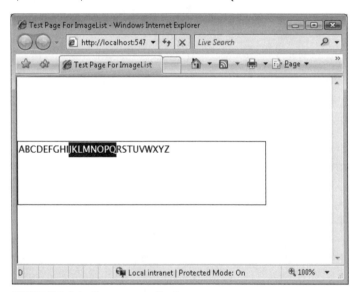

FIGURE 7-8 Selecting a range of text.

The *TextBox* also allows you to control the font that is used in the *TextBox*, using exactly the same method as the *TextBlock*. For details about how to do this, take a look at the section titled "The *TextBlock* Control" earlier in this chapter.

Common Properties, Events, and Methods

The previous sections detailed many of the basic controls that are available with Silverlight, highlighting their specific properties, methods, and events. However, there are a number of items of common functionality that all or most of these controls share, and you will need to know about them when you begin to develop your Silverlight applications.

Handling Focus

Controls that can receive input expose *GotFocus* and *LostFocus* events. They are an important addition in Silverlight 2—in Silverlight 1.0, only the overall control was able to accept these events.

The *GotFocus* and *LostFocus* events fire whenever the user enters or leaves a control, either by selecting it with the mouse or by moving to a control using the Tab key. Both of these events are *bubbling* events, meaning that if the control receives the event but doesn't handle it, the event is passed up to its parent, and it continues to be passed on until it is caught by an event handler.

Handling the Mouse

Silverlight controls expose several mouse events:

- **MouseEnter** This event will fire when the mouse enters the drawing area of a control.

- **MouseLeave** This event will fire when the mouse leaves the drawing area of a control.

- **MouseLeftButtonDown** This event will fire when the left button of the mouse is pressed down over the control.

- **MouseLeftButtonUp** This event will fire when the left button of the mouse is released over the control.

- **MouseMove** This event will fire when the mouse moves over the control.

In addition to these events, you may want to use the *captureMouse* and *releaseMouse* methods on a control for maximum control. The *captureMouse* method, when called on a control, will cause all mouse events to be directed to that control whether the mouse is in its bounds or not. The *releaseMouse* will, as its name suggest, set event capturing back to normal. These are very useful methods for implementing drag and drop. Let's take a look at an example that achieves this.

Using the Mouse Events for Drag and Drop

Following is a XAML document that gives us four ellipses on a page. Note that the ellipses all define the same event handlers for their mouse events:

```
<UserControl x:Class="MouseEvents.Page"
  xmlns="http://schemas.microsoft.com/winfx/2006/xaml/presentation"
  xmlns:x="http://schemas.microsoft.com/winfx/2006/xaml"
  FontFamily="Trebuchet MS" FontSize="11"
  Width="400" Height="300">
  <Grid x:Name="LayoutRoot" Background="White">
    <Canvas Width="400" Height="300" Background="Wheat">
```

```
    <Ellipse Canvas.Top="0" Fill="Black" Width="20" Height="20"
      MouseLeftButtonDown="Ellipse_MouseLeftButtonDown"
      MouseLeftButtonUp="Ellipse_MouseLeftButtonUp"
      MouseMove="Ellipse_MouseMove" />
    <Ellipse Canvas.Top="40" Fill="Black" Width="20" Height="20"
      MouseLeftButtonDown="Ellipse_MouseLeftButtonDown"
      MouseLeftButtonUp="Ellipse_MouseLeftButtonUp"
      MouseMove="Ellipse_MouseMove" />
    <Ellipse Canvas.Top="80" Fill="Black" Width="20" Height="20"
      MouseLeftButtonDown="Ellipse_MouseLeftButtonDown"
      MouseLeftButtonUp="Ellipse_MouseLeftButtonUp"
      MouseMove="Ellipse_MouseMove" />
    <Ellipse Canvas.Top="120" Fill="Black" Width="20" Height="20"
      MouseLeftButtonDown="Ellipse_MouseLeftButtonDown"
      MouseLeftButtonUp="Ellipse_MouseLeftButtonUp"
      MouseMove="Ellipse_MouseMove" />
  </Canvas>
 </Grid>

</UserControl>
```

Now let's look at the code-behind for this. First, we need some variables to hold the state of the x and y-coordinates of the mouse when we begin dragging, and another variable to indicate whether or not the mouse button is currently being held down.

```
double beginX = 0;
double beginY = 0;
bool isMouseDown = false;
```

When the mouse button is held down over any of the buttons, the *Ellipse_MouseLeftButtonDown* function will execute.

```
private void Ellipse_MouseLeftButtonDown(object sender,
        MouseButtonEventArgs e)
{
    Ellipse b = sender as Ellipse;
    beginX = e.GetPosition(this).X;
    beginY = e.GetPosition(this).Y;
    isMouseDown = true;
    b.CaptureMouse();
}
```

Because the sender is a generic object, the first thing we'll need to do is cast it as an ellipse. We then use the *MouseButtonEventArgs* argument to derive the current x and y-coordinates and set them to the beginning values. Then, as the mouse button is held down, we want to keep track of it, so the *isMouseDown* variable is set to *True*. Finally, we want to capture the mouse events for this ellipse (whichever one it is) so that, even if the user drags the mouse off this ellipse, it will continue to receive the events.

So, as the user drags the mouse, we want a *MouseMove* event to fire. This is handled by the *Ellipse_MouseMove* event handler function. Here it is:

```
private void Ellipse_MouseMove(object sender,
        MouseEventArgs e)
{
    if (isMouseDown)
    {
        Ellipse b = sender as Ellipse;
        double currX = e.GetPosition(this).X;
        double currY = e.GetPosition(this).Y;
        b.SetValue(Canvas.LeftProperty, currX);
        b.SetValue(Canvas.TopProperty, currY);
    }
}
```

Because this event will fire when the mouse moves over an ellipse, regardless of whether the user is dragging or not, we are only interested in doing something if the user is dragging, which, by definition, means that our *isMouseDown* variable is *True*. So in this case, we get the current coordinates of the mouse and use them to set the value of the *Top* and *Left* attached properties of the ellipse. The effect of this will be to move the ellipse to the location of the mouse coordinates, giving us a drag.

Finally, when we release the mouse button, we get *MouseLeftButtonUp* event firing, which is captured by the *Ellipse_MouseLeftButtonUp* function. Here it is:

```
private void Ellipse_MouseLeftButtonUp(object sender,
        MouseButtonEventArgs e)
{
    Ellipse b = sender as Ellipse;
    isMouseDown = false;
    b.ReleaseMouseCapture();
}
```

This will then reset our *isMouseDown* variable and release the mouse capture from the control that had captured it. The effect is that mouse behavior will have returned to normal, and the ellipse will have moved to the drop location. You can see this in action in Figures 7-9 and 7-10.

Figure 7-9 shows how the application looks in its default state. If the user moves the mouse over any of the ellipses in the application and then holds down the mouse button and moves the mouse, it will cause the ellipse in the application to move, and the user can use drag and drop to rearrange them on the screen. You can see this in Figure 7-10.

In addition to mouse events, there are keyboard events that can fire on many controls. You'll learn more about these in the next section.

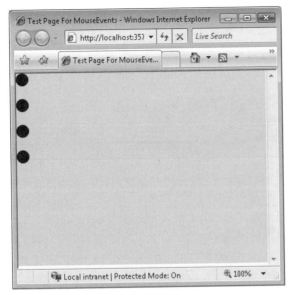

FIGURE 7-9 Drag-and-drop application.

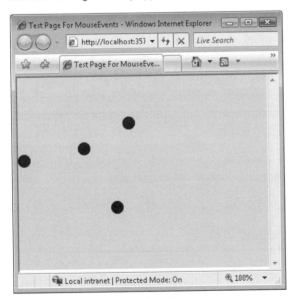

FIGURE 7-10 Dragging and dropping.

Using the Keyboard

In addition to the *TextBox* control that offers your user the ability to input text using the full keyboard, many controls expose the *KeyDown* and *KeyUp* properties that may be used to capture keyboard input. The *KeyDown* property fires whenever an element has focus and a key is pressed on it. Its *Event Handler* function takes a generic sender object and a *KeyEventArgs* object that can be used to extract information about the key that was pressed. This has a *key* property that returns a *Key* object that contains information about the key. This is a platform-independent property, so it is the best choice for you to use in your applications. Another property that the *KeyEventArgs* offers is the *platformKeyCode* property, which can be used with the *key* property to get operating system–specific keys.

Additionally, the *Keyboard.Modifers* event will return a *ModifierKeys* value that can be used to derive if any modifier key (Alt, Control, Shift, Windows, or Apple) is pressed. Simply assign the return to a *ModifierKeys* value, and check its return value for the string that corresponds to the desired modifier key (i.e., Shift).

Summary

In this chapter, we introduced some of the basic Silverlight controls, and you learned how you can use these core controls to build your Silverlight applications. You looked at the *Button, CheckBox, HyperlinkButton, Image, ListBox, RadioButton, TextBlock,* and *TextBox* controls. Additionally, we examined some of the common properties, methods, and events that are shared across all controls, giving you a good overview to get started using presentation and layout controls in Silverlight.

In the next chapter, you will find out about more advanced Silverlight controls and learn how you can use these extended controls to enhance your applications.

Chapter 8
Silverlight Controls: Advanced Controls

Chapter 7, "Silverlight Controls: Presentation and Layout," introduced you to the Silverlight control set and provided you with a tour through some of the basic controls, such as *TextBox* and *CheckBox*. However, modern rich interactive applications (RIAs) tend to require controls that are much more sophisticated, such as data-bound grids, calendars, and more. In this chapter, you'll learn about how to use these controls in your Silverlight applications. Some of these controls, such as the *DataGrid*, are worthy of a book of their own, so you won't get the full control API here, but you should gain enough knowledge about these advanced controls to understand what is going on when you use them. Then you can begin experimenting and learning more about how they work on your own.

The *DataGrid* Control

The *DataGrid* control is designed to assist you in displaying data in a row/column format, similar to a spreadsheet. It is a *Data* grid, as opposed to just a grid, because it is bindable to a data source. We'll be looking at how to display data in more detail in Chapter 10, "Building Connected Applications with Silverlight," but to understand the power of the *DataGrid*, we'll also be using some of those techniques here.

When you add a *DataGrid* control to your XAML surface, you'll end up with XAML like this:

```
<UserControl
  xmlns:my="clr-namespace:System.Windows.Controls;
        assembly=System.Windows.Controls.Data"
        x:Class="SilverlightApplication1.Page"
  xmlns="http://schemas.microsoft.com/client/2007"
  xmlns:x="http://schemas.microsoft.com/winfx/2006/xaml"
  Width="400" Height="300">
  <Grid x:Name="LayoutRoot" Background="White">
    <my:DataGrid></my:DataGrid>
  </Grid>
</UserControl>
```

This *DataGrid* isn't very functional at the moment, so let's add two properties to it—a name and *AutoGenerateColumns*, which, when the grid is bound to the *DataGrid*, will instruct the grid to automatically generate the required columns for the data. Here's how the *DataGrid* XAML should look after these additions:

```
<my:DataGrid x:Name="GrdHeadline" AutoGenerateColumns="True">
</my:DataGrid>
```

That's all it takes to get a *DataGrid* ready to use bound data. Before we continue to look at more of the properties, methods, and events associated with the control, let's do a simple data binding. We'll bind to an RSS feed at *http://feeds.reuters.com/reuters/oddlyEnoughNews?format=xml*.

So, first add a reference to System.Net at the top of your Page.xaml.cs code:

```
using System.Net;
```

Next, in the *Page* constructor, add the following code to set up a *WebClient* object to read from the URI and add an event handler to manage the completion of the download:

```
WebClient client = new WebClient();
Uri uri =
    new Uri("http://feeds.reuters.com/reuters/topNews?format=xml");
client.DownloadStringCompleted +=
    new DownloadStringCompletedEventHandler(
        client_DownloadStringCompleted);
client.DownloadStringAsync(uri);
```

Now, after the download of the data is complete, the event handler at *client_DownloadStringCompleted* will fire. In this function, we'll be using a custom class of type *NewsHeadline*. Here is the code for this class:

```
public class NewsHeadLine
{
  public string strHead { get; set; }
  public string strLine { get; set; }
}
```

Also, the client *_DownloadStringCompleted* uses the System.Xml.Linq libraries, so you'll need to add a reference to these by right-clicking References and selecting Add Reference. On the .NET Tab, you'll see System.Xml.Linq library, as shown in Figure 8-1. Select it and click OK.

You'll also need to instruct your code to use this in order to compile. To do this, you simply need to add this statement at the top of Page.xaml.cs:

```
using System.Xml.Linq;
```

Now, here is the code for the *client_DownloadStringCompleted* event handler:

```
void client_DownloadStringCompleted(
  object sender, DownloadStringCompletedEventArgs e)
{
  XDocument xmlHeadlines = XDocument.Parse(e.Result);
  var headlines = from story in xmlHeadlines.Descendants("item")
                  select new NewsHeadLine
                  {
                    strHead = (string)story.Element("title"),
                    strLine = (string)story.Element("link")
                  };
  GrdHeadline.ItemsSource = headlines;
}
```

This parses the return from the service call (stored in e.Result) into an *XDocument* object. It then uses Linq to select the data from the *XDocument*, creating a collection of headlines. This collection is then set to the *ItemsSource* property of the *DataGrid*. The results can be seen in Figure 8-2.

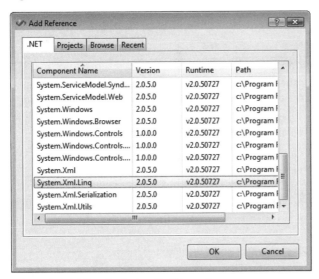

FIGURE 8-1 Adding the System.Xml.Linq reference.

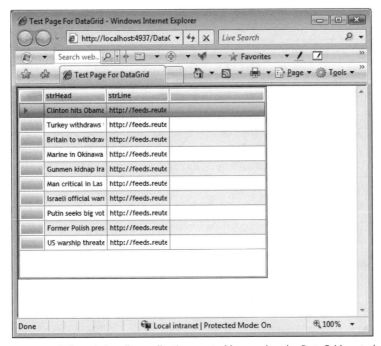

FIGURE 8-2 Sample headline collection created by running the *DataGrid* control.

The *DataGrid* has two selection modes: single, in which only one row at a time may be selected; and multiple, in which several rows may be selected by holding down the Ctrl and/or
Shift keys and clicking.

You set these modes using the *SelectionMode* property, which can be set to *DataGridSelec-
tionMode.Single* for single selection and *DataGridSelectionMode.Extended* for multiple selection.

When using single selection mode, the *SelectedItem* mode contains the selection. It is of type
object, so it needs to be cast to the correct type before it can be used. Previously, you saw that
we filled this grid with items of the *NewsHeadLine* class that we defined.

So, for a single selection, you can get the data from the selection like this:

```
NewsHeadLine theHeadline = GrdHeadline.SelectedItem as NewsHeadLine;
```

When the list is set to allow multiple items, you can use the *SelectedItems* property that returns a list collection. This is very straightforward to manage. Here's the code:

```
string strHead;
string strLink;
System.Collections.IList listOfItems = GrdHeadline.SelectedItems;
foreach(NewsHeadLine newsHead in listOfItems)
{
  strHead = newsHead.strHead;
  strLink = newsHead.strLine;
}
```

In this case, the *SelectedItems* method returns a *System.Collections.IList*. You can then iterate
through it, pulling out each *NewsHeadline* object and getting its data.

When using any kind of grid, and the *DataGrid* is no exception, it is always useful to make
your grid more readable with striping—that is, distinguishing alternate rows with different
colors or shading. In this case, you can use the *RowBackground* and *AlternatingRowBack-
ground* to set striping for your *DataGrid*. These are set to a brush color with the following
code:

```
GrdHeadline.RowBackground =
    new SolidColorBrush(Colors.LightGray);
GrdHeadline.AlternatingRowBackground =
new SolidColorBrush(Colors.Yellow);
```

You can see the effect of this formatting on the output shown in Figure 8-3.

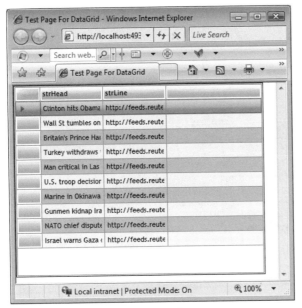

FIGURE 8-3 Using alternating row colors.

You may have noticed that the columns are added in the order that the data was defined in the *NewsHeadLine* class. You aren't limited to having the columns appear in this order, however, and you can override the default setting by using the *DisplayIndex* property. For example, our *DataGrid* has two columns, with the headlines listed in the first column and the links listed in the second. You could flip these around like this:

```
GrdHeadline.Columns[0].DisplayIndex = 1;
GrdHeadline.Columns[1].DisplayIndex = 0;
```

You can further manipulate how the grid renders your data by using a data template. This is XAML that defines how you want the data to be laid out, including binding to specific fields. For example, the previous output samples had each cell in the grid bound to a particular element within the RSS feed. If you prefer to have two fields from the RSS feed within the same cell, you would achieve this by using a data template. Consider the following XAML:

```
<UserControl
xmlns:my="clr-namespace:System.Windows.Controls;
  assembly=System.Windows.Controls.Data"
x:Class="DataGrid.Page"
  xmlns="http://schemas.microsoft.com/client/2007"
  xmlns:x="http://schemas.microsoft.com/winfx/2006/xaml"
  Width="400" Height="300">

  <Grid x:Name="LayoutRoot" Background="White">
    <my:DataGrid x:Name="GrdHeadline" AutoGenerateColumns="True">
      <my:DataGrid.Columns>
        <my:DataGridTemplateColumn>
```

```
        <my:DataGridTemplateColumn.CellTemplate>
          <DataTemplate>
            <StackPanel Orientation="Vertical">
            <TextBlock Text="123"></TextBlock>
            <TextBlock Text="{Binding strHead}"></TextBlock>
            <TextBlock Text="{Binding strPubDate}"></TextBlock>
            </StackPanel>
          </DataTemplate>
        </my:DataGridTemplateColumn.CellTemplate>
          </my:DataGridTemplateColumn>
            <my:DataGridTemplateColumn>
              <my:DataGridTemplateColumn.CellTemplate>
                <DataTemplate>
                    <TextBlock Text="{Binding strLine}"></TextBlock>
                </DataTemplate>
              </my:DataGridTemplateColumn.CellTemplate>
            </my:DataGridTemplateColumn>
        </my:DataGrid.Columns>
      </my:DataGrid>
  </Grid>
</UserControl>
```

In this XAML, the *DataGrid* has its columns predefined using *<my:DataGrid.Columns>*. Within this, we can override the default columns template of one field per cell by defining a new *<my:DataGridTemplateColumn.CellTemplate>* for each cell, which will contain the code to define how we want the cell to be rendered.

As you can see, we've defined only two cells, so this grid, regardless of the number of data fields, will have only two columns. The first column, defined by the first cell template, will be a *StackPanel* containing three text fields—a hard coded "123," the data-bound *strHead* property of our *NewsHeadline* class, and the data-bound *strPubDate* of our *NewsHeadline* class. The *StackPanel* stacks these fields vertically.

The second column, defined by the second cell template, is a simple *TextBlock* that binds to the *strLine* field. You may have noticed that we've added another field here, *strPubDate*, which wasn't in the initial class sample, so the class definition and binding code need to be updated. Here's the new class definition:

```
public class NewsHeadLine
    {
        public string strHead { get; set; }
        public string strLine { get; set; }
        public string strDescription { get; set; }
        public string strPubDate { get; set; }
    }
```

And following is the new data binding code that binds the additional fields:

```
void client_DownloadStringCompleted(object sender, DownloadStringCompletedEventArgs e)
{
  XDocument xmlHeadlines = XDocument.Parse(e.Result);
```

```
var headlines = from story in xmlHeadlines.Descendants("item")
            select new NewsHeadLine
            {
              strHead = (string)story.Element("title"),
              strLine = (string)story.Element("link"),
              strDescription = (string)story.Element("description"),
              strPubDate = (string)story.Element("pubDate")
            };
  GrdHeadline.ItemsSource = headlines;
}
```

One more quick change you'll need to make in order to see the new data is to change the default row height because it is currently capable of showing only one line, which would cause the vertical content in the first cell to be cropped. You'll also want to turn off the automatic column definition because you want to override how the *DataGrid* automatically binds the data. You do this with the following code (put it in the *Page* constructor):

```
GrdHeadline.AutoGenerateColumns = false;
GrdHeadline.RowHeight = 60;
```

Now when you execute this code, you'll see the *DataGrid* containing the defined column templates shown in Figure 8-4. It's not very pretty, but it does illustrate how you can control the appearance of your output from the *DataGrid* control.

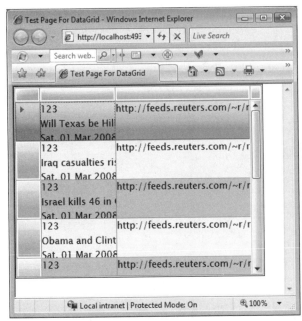

FIGURE 8-4 Using a data template to define how the data will be rendered.

The *DataGrid* control has a huge API that would deserve a book in its own right. However, what you've learned about it over the last few pages should give you an appreciation of the flexibility that it provides, and you will be able to use this basic information to take it to the next level as you build your Silverlight applications!

The *Calendar* and *DatePicker* Controls

When you need to select dates for use in your Silverlight applications, you can use the *Calendar* and *DatePicker* controls. The *Calendar* control displays the days in a given month or the months in a given year, and it provides arrow buttons that allow the user to control the current month or year by moving to the next or previous month. The *DatePicker* combines this display with a text box that allows you to enter the date according to a format or gives you access to a drop-down list that lets you select a specific date.

Let's take a look at the *Calendar* control first. It is simple to get started with this control:

```
<UserControl
xmlns:my="clr-namespace:System.Windows.Controls;assembly=System.Windows.Controls.Extended"
x:Class="cal.Page"
  xmlns="http://schemas.microsoft.com/client/2007"
  xmlns:x="http://schemas.microsoft.com/winfx/2006/xaml"
    Width="400" Height="300">
    <Grid x:Name="LayoutRoot" Background="White">
        <my:Calendar x:Name="cal"></my:Calendar>
    </Grid>
</UserControl>
```

This will render the *Calendar* in the default Month view, with today's date highlighted. See Figure 8-5 for an example—you can see I created this figure on a Sunday in March.

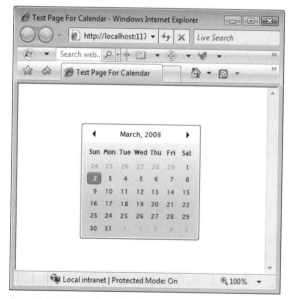

FIGURE 8-5 Using the *Calendar* control.

You use the *DisplayDate* property to set the *month* of the date to display. For example, the following code selects the date January 1, 2009:

```
DateTime d = new DateTime(2009, 1, 1);
cal.DisplayDate = d;
```

This displays the month of the date you selected, but it does not select the specific date. Look at the calendar displayed in Figure 8-6.

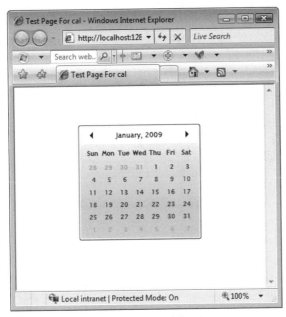

FIGURE 8-6 Changing the displayed date.

Compare Figure 8-6 and Figure 8-5, and you'll notice that there is no date selected on the calendar in Figure 8-6. By setting the display date, the selected date has been nullified, so the *SelectedDate* property is *null*. If you make a selection, this will be set for you (as a *DateTime* type), or you can set it in code by setting the *SelectedDate* property. Here's an example:

```
DateTime s = new DateTime(2009, 1, 31);
cal.SelectedDate = s;
```

You can see how this appears in Figure 8-7. Now there is a date—January 31—selected in the calendar that displays.

You can specify the range of unselectable dates with the *BlackoutDates* collection. This collection contains a *CalendarDateRangeCollection* type to which ranges of dates may be added. Any dates falling within these ranges will appear dimmed and thus are unselectable. The

SelectableDateStart and *SelectableDateEnd* properties can also give you the range of displayable dates. For example, if you want one range to be displayable and another range (usually a subset) to be selectable, you can use these properties to define the appearance of your calendar.

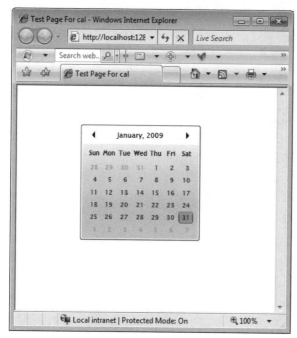

FIGURE 8-7 Using the *SelectedDate* property.

The *DatePicker* combines this functionality with a text field. The *Text* property of this field contains whatever the user enters as a date. If the data the user enters cannot be parsed, the *TextParseError* will be raised.

To the right of the text box, you'll see an icon that can be used to show a *Calendar* control for picking the date. When the user selects this icon, the *CalendarOpened* event will fire, and when they dismiss it, the *CalendarClosed* event will fire. The *Calendar* and *DatePicker* controls provide you with the basic tools you need to create applications that require input based on dates and that can also display calendar information.

The *RepeatButton* and *ToggleButton* Controls

The *RepeatButton* control provides a button that raises multiple click events when the user holds down the mouse button over it. The frequency of events being fired depends on the *Delay* property, which is specified in milliseconds. For example, consider the following XAML:

```
<RepeatButton x:Name="rpt" Delay="100"
  Content="0" Click="rpt_Click">
</RepeatButton>
```

This defines a Repeat button called *rpt* with a delay of 100 milliseconds, which defaults its content to 0. The code to handle the user clicking the button can be found in the *rpt_Click* event handler function. Following is the code for this event handler:

```
private void rpt_Click(object sender, RoutedEventArgs e)
{
  int n = Convert.ToInt16(rpt.Content);
  n++;
  rpt.Content = n.ToString();
}
```

As the user clicks the button, the current value of the *Content* property is retrieved, converted to an integer, incremented, and added back to the value. This causes the caption of the button to be incremented as the user holds down the mouse button over the *RepeatButton*. This can provide a useful type of control for handling multiple repeated actions, such as spinner-type controls, where a button containing an arrow is presented to the user, and as the user holds down the spinner, a value is incremented.

In all other regards, a *RepeatButton* is just a *Button* control, so you can find more details about how to use it in Chapter 7, where the generic *Button* control is introduced.

The *ToggleButton* is a button that, when clicked, remains depressed until you click it again, and then it is returned to its default state. It is effectively a combination of a radio control and a typical button. The properties associated with a *ToggleButton* control are very similar to those used with radio buttons and generic buttons in that it contains an *IsChecked* property that can be used to derive its current value and an *IsThreeState* property that allows a third state with the value *Null*, which is between the normal and depressed states.

Like the default *Button* control (see Chapter 7), these are *content* controls, so they can be used to render complex content to create image buttons, video buttons, or whatever you would like for your Silverlight applications.

The *ScrollViewer* Control

The *ScrollViewer* control is a container control for other information; it provides horizontal and/or vertical scroll bars so the viewer can move the display to see all the information when the dimensions of the content exceed that of the container. The visibility of the scroll bars are set by the *HorizontalScrollBarVisibility* and *VerticalScrollBarVisibility* properties. By default, the vertical scroll bar will display and the horizontal will not display, regardless of the content. Consider the following XAML example:

```
<UserControl x:Class="sviewer.Page"
    xmlns="http://schemas.microsoft.com/client/2007"
    xmlns:x="http://schemas.microsoft.com/winfx/2006/xaml"
    Width="400" Height="300">
    <Grid x:Name="LayoutRoot" Background="White">
        <ScrollViewer>
            <Image Source="mix08_1280.jpg" Stretch="None" />
        </ScrollViewer>
    </Grid>
</UserControl>
```

In this case, the *ScrollViewer* is the only child control on the 400 × 300 surface, so it will also be 400 × 300. It contains an image, which in this case is 1280 × 1024. You can see the result in Figure 8-8.

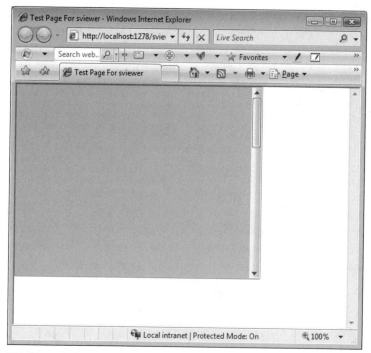

FIGURE 8-8 Using the *ScrollViewer* control.

As you can see, the image shown in Figure 8-8 is grey all along its left side, so all you can see is grey. You cannot scroll to the colorful part of the image that is on the right because there is no horizontal scroll bar.

But if you add *HorizontalScrollBarVisibility="True"* to the *ScrollViewer* definition in XAML, you'll be able to see the rest of the image. Here's the XAML:

```
<ScrollViewer HorizontalScrollBarVisibility="Visible">
    <Image Source="mix08_1280.jpg" Stretch="None" />
</ScrollViewer>
```

And you can see the results in Figure 8-9.

FIGURE 8-9 Using the *ScrollViewer* with horizontal scrollbar.

TIP You can override the visibility of the vertical scroll bar, too. By default, it is visible, but you can turn it off (so it does not display) by changing the *VerticalScrollBarVisibility* to *False*.

The *Slider* Control

A *Slider* control is used to allow the user to select a value from a fixed range by sliding a visual element (called a *thumb*) along a line from the low value in the range to the high value in the range. The value is accessible in the *Value* property, which returns a *Double*.

You can customize the *Slider* control in a number of ways. For example, the *Minimum* and *Maximum* properties are used to determine the minimum and maximum values in the range. If you want to have the user select a value in a range from 0 to 100, set the *Minimum* property to 0 and the *Maximum* property to 100.

Another property associated with the *Slider* control is the *Orientation* property, which is used to determine the direction the user will slide the thumb. It can be set to *Horizontal* or *Vertical*.

The low-high direction of movement of the *Slider* defaults to left-right when the *Orientation* property is set to *Horizontal* and bottom-top when it is set to *Vertical*. You can override these default settings with the *IsDirectionReversed* property, which, when set to *True*, will change the direction of movement for the *Slider*.

In addition to being able to drag the thumb, the user can also click on the sliding track in a typical *Slider* control to change the value by a fixed amount. This is determined by the *LargeChange* property, which, when set to a numeric value, will increase or decrease the value of the slider by that amount.

Following is an example of a *Slider* control in XAML:

```
<Slider x:Name="sldr" Maximum="100"
Orientation="Vertical"
IsDirectionReversed="True"
LargeChange="10">
</Slider>
```

The *Slider* created here will be vertical, with the low value at the top and the high value at the bottom. It will allow the user to select values from 0 through 100 by dragging the thumb, and the user can change the value in increments of 10 by clicking on the track.

The *WatermarkedTextBox* Control

A common piece of user interface enhancement involves creating a *watermark*, which is a subtle, shaded image or text in a text box that provides a hint to the user about the type of content that is expected. For example, if you want to let users know that they are expected to type a user name in one text box and a password in another text box, you can use the *Text-Block* and *WatermarkedTextBox* controls to create a user interface, such as the one shown in Figure 8-10.

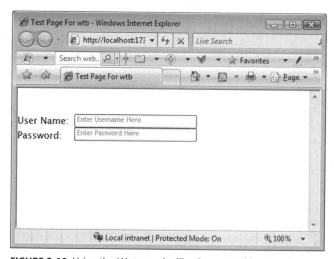

FIGURE 8-10 Using the *WatermarkedTextBox* control in a text box.

As you can see, the user is provided with hints in the form of text that appears dimmed and reads *Enter Username Here* and *Enter Password Here* within the appropriate text boxes. When the user begins to enter data in a text box, the watermark disappears.

You can create a simple watermark like this by using the *WatermarkedTextBox* property:

```
<Canvas>
  <StackPanel Orientation="Horizontal" Canvas.Top="40">
    <StackPanel>
      <TextBlock Text="User Name:   "></TextBlock>
      <TextBlock Text="Password:    "></TextBlock>
    </StackPanel>
    <StackPanel>
      <WatermarkedTextBox
        Watermark="Enter Username Here" Width="200">
      </WatermarkedTextBox>
      <WatermarkedTextBox
        Watermark="Enter Password Here" Width="200">
      </WatermarkedTextBox>
    </StackPanel>
  </StackPanel>
</Canvas>
```

The *Watermark* is a content property, so you aren't limited to using simple text as shown in the previous example. If you want to use content such as an XAML standard shape (an *Ellipse*, for example), an image, a video, or any other content as the watermark, you can do so easily.

Following is an example using a watermark as a content property. Note the syntax where you use *WatermarkedTextBox.Watermark* and then host content within it. In this case, the content consists of a horizontal *StackPanel* control with ellipses and a text block.

```
<Canvas>
  <StackPanel Orientation="Horizontal" Canvas.Top="40">
  <StackPanel>
   <TextBlock Text="User Name:   "></TextBlock>
   <TextBlock Text="Password:    "></TextBlock>
  </StackPanel>
  <StackPanel>
   <WatermarkedTextBox Width="240">
     <WatermarkedTextBox.Watermark>
       <StackPanel Orientation="Horizontal">
        <Ellipse Width="20" Fill="Green"></Ellipse>
        <TextBlock Text=" Enter Username Here "
           Foreground="LightGray"></TextBlock>
        <Ellipse Width="20" Fill="Green"></Ellipse>
       </StackPanel>
     </WatermarkedTextBox.Watermark>
   </WatermarkedTextBox>
   <WatermarkedTextBox Width="240">
     <WatermarkedTextBox.Watermark>
       <StackPanel Orientation="Horizontal">
        <Ellipse Width="20" Fill="Green"></Ellipse>
```

```
        <TextBlock Text=" Enter Password Here "
            Foreground="LightGray"></TextBlock>
        <Ellipse Width="20" Fill="Green"></Ellipse>
      </StackPanel>
     </WatermarkedTextBox.Watermark>
    </WatermarkedTextBox>
   </StackPanel>
   </StackPanel>
 </Canvas>
```

You can see the results in Figure 8-11.

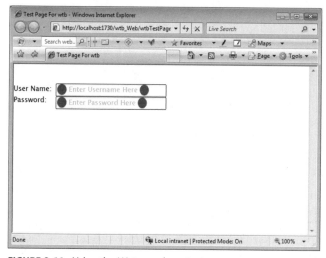

FIGURE 8-11 Using the *Watermark* content property.

Note that this does not automatically make the contents of the watermark appear dimmed in the way that the *WatermarkedTextBox* property did earlier, so the *TextBlock* controls have their *Foreground* property set to *LightGray* to simulate the effect.

Summary

In this chapter, we continued to explore the Silverlight control set. You spent a lot of time learning about the *DataGrid* and its associated properties, methods, and events because it is an important control that provides functionality similar to that of a spreadsheet for your applications. In our discussion of the *DataGrid* control, you were introduced to some of the code that Silverlight offers for easy data binding, as well as how to define data templates to use for your grid layouts. In addition, you looked through some of the other advanced tools available with Silverlight, including the *Calendar*, *DatePicker*, *ScrollViewer*, *Slider*, and *Watermarked-TextBox* controls.

Now, our summary of the base controls available in Silverlight is complete, and in the next chapter, we will take a look at what you need to know to build your own controls.

Chapter 9
Building Your Own Silverlight Control

In Chapter 7, "Silverlight Controls: Presentation and Layout," you got your first glimpse at using Microsoft Visual Studio to create Silverlight applications in C#. In Chapter 8, "Silverlight Controls: Advanced Controls," you looked at some of the controls available in Silverlight. At this point, you are probably interested in finding out about more controls than are available in the basic set, so you have two choices: you can either buy or build custom controls. You can buy controls from many vendors—check out *http://www.silverlight.net* for more details. Additionally, you can build your own controls for Silverlight using Silverlight. This chapter will take you through a hands-on approach to building such controls.

Creating the Project

Let's get started—the first step is to create a new Silverlight project in Visual Studio. You do this by selecting New Project on the File menu (see Figure 9-1).

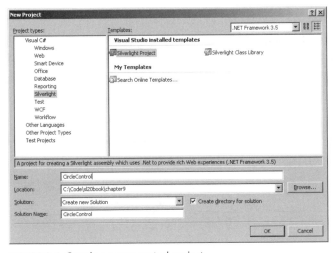

FIGURE 9-1 Creating a new control project.

As you can see in Figure 9-1, this project is going to be called CircleControl. If you refer back to Chapter 4, "XAML Basics," you'll see that XAML does not have a *Circle* shape available, but it does have an *Ellipse*, which takes width and height properties. You'll derive the shape you want from the *Ellipse*, but hide the width and height properties, instead exposing a *Radius* property that allows Silverlight to draw a circle.

Click OK, and the Silverlight Application Wizard will open (see Figure 9-2). Accept the defaults, and Visual Studio will create everything you need for a Silverlight application. For more details about Silverlight applications and information on what each file does, refer back to Chapter 3, "Using Visual Studio with Silverlight 2." You're now ready for the next step—adding the control itself.

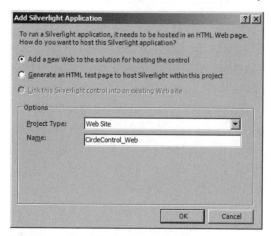

FIGURE 9-2 Silverlight Application Wizard.

Adding the Control Template

You build a Silverlight control in the same manner as anything else—using XAML and, if neces-sary, some code behind it. The template that you just used created a test project that contains App.xaml, for application-specific code, and Page.xaml, which provides your main UI. The con-trol that you build will be added to Page.xaml, and you'll see how to do that shortly.

First, let's create the control itself. Right-click the project (CircleControl in this case), select Add, and then select New Item. The Add New Item dialog box appears, as shown in Figure 9-3.

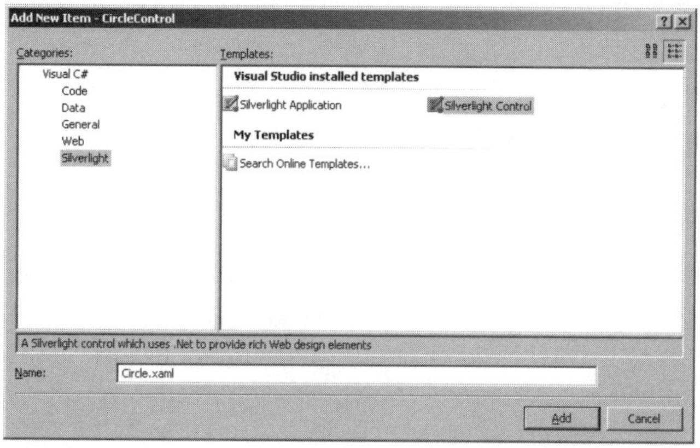

FIGURE 9-3 Adding a new Silverlight control.

In this dialog box, select Silverlight from the categories, select the Silverlight Control template, and then name it. Click Add when you're done.

A basic *UserControl* will be created for you. Here is,what the XAML looks like for the Circle control, placed within the CircleControl project:

```
<UserControl x:Class="CircleControl.Circle"
        xmlns="http://schemas.microsoft.com/client/2007"
        xmlns:x="http://schemas.microsoft.com/winfx/2006/xaml"
        Width="400" Height="300"
        >

    <Grid x:Name="LayoutRoot" Background="White">

    </Grid>
</UserControl>
```

Note that namespacing is used, so that the *x:Class*, which defines the object to Silverlight, is set to *CircleControl.Circle*. Because the circle will only have one visual element—and this inherits from the *Ellipse* base type—you should add that to the *LayoutRoot* Grid like this:

```
    <Grid x:Name="LayoutRoot">
        <Ellipse x:Name="BaseEllipse"></Ellipse>
    </Grid>
```

Writing the Control Code

The task of writing the control code is very straightforward. The *Circle* is a *UserControl* that renders the specified XAML that contains an *Ellipse*. On this we want to add a *Radius* property to specify the radius of the *Circle* and a *FillColor* property that will allow us to paint the circle. *UserControl* doesn't expose the *Fill* property, so you'll have to implement your own.

Here's the code—this should be in the .cs code-behind for your control, so if your control was called Circle.xaml, this will be Circle.xaml.cs:

```
using System;
using System.Collections.Generic;
using System.Linq;
using System.Windows;
using System.Windows.Controls;
using System.Windows.Documents;
using System.Windows.Input;
using System.Windows.Media;
using System.Windows.Media.Animation;
using System.Windows.Shapes;

namespace CircleControl
{
    public partial class Circle : UserControl
    {
        public Circle()
```

```
        {
            // Required to initialize variables
            InitializeComponent();


        }
        public double Radius
        {
            get
            {
                return BaseEllipse.Width / 2;
            }
            set
            {
                BaseEllipse.Width = value * 2;
                BaseEllipse.Height = value * 2;
            }

        }
        public SolidColorBrush Fill
        {
            get
            {
                return (SolidColorBrush)BaseEllipse.Fill;
            }
            set
            {
                BaseEllipse.Fill = (SolidColorBrush)value;
            }
        }
    }
}
```

As you can see, this is very straightforward stuff. The *Radius* property is a *double*, which for its *get* will return the width of the *BaseEllipse* divided by 2. When dealing with the *Ellipse* type, you always specify a width and height, and of course for a circle, the radius is half of the width or height of the shape.

Similarly, when you set the *Radius* value, you want to set the width and height of the underlying *Ellipse* so that each is double the value of the radius, which you can do in the property setter.

To set the *Fill*, you simply cast the inbound value to a *SolidColorBrush* and set the *Fill* of the underlying ellipse to it. To get it, you just cast the *Fill* of the underlying ellipse to a *SolidColor-Brush* and return it. All very straightforward!

Now that you have your control, you'll want to implement it on your application. If you recall from Chapter 3, the default template sets Page.xaml as the default UI for the application, so let's add it there.

The first thing you'll need to do is to add a reference to the namespace containing the control. In this case, your project is called CircleControl, and it has the same namespace. Check the project properties for details on the namespace—to do this, right-click the project and then select Properties to open the Project Properties dialog box. This is discussed in more detail in Chapter 3.

Your initial *UserControl* declaration in Page.xaml should look similar to the following code.

> **Note** Some versions of Visual Studio Tools will have a *<Grid>* control on your *<UserControl>*, and some will have a *<Canvas>*. For the sake of this demonstration, *<Canvas>* is being used, but you will have no problems if you use a *<Grid>* because they are both container controls.

```
<UserControl x:Class="CircleControl.Page"
  xmlns="http://schemas.microsoft.com/client/2007"
  xmlns:x="http://schemas.microsoft.com/winfx/2006/xaml"
  xmlns:circ="clr-namespace:CircleControl"
  Width="640"
  Height="480">
    <Canvas x:Name="LayoutRoot">

    </Canvas>
</UserControl>
```

Now that you have declared the namespace, you can add the reference to the control. Note that the XML prefix is declared as *circ*, so when you start typing this in the editor, the IntelliSense feature will show this tag. You can see this in Figure 9-4, where the namespace has been identified.

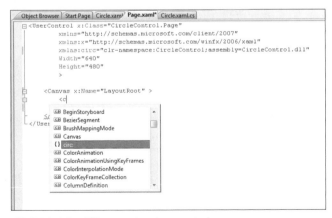

FIGURE 9-4 IntelliSense and custom control namespaces.

The IntelliSense feature will also pick up the control name and the properties available to the control, which in this case is everything on a user control plus *Fill* and *Radius*, as defined earlier. Figure 9-5 shows the *Radius* property in IntelliSense.

FIGURE 9-5 IntelliSense and custom control properties.

Here's an example of Page.xaml with the namespace declaration and two circles defined:

```
<UserControl x:Class="CircleControl.Page"
        xmlns="http://schemas.microsoft.com/client/2007"
        xmlns:x="http://schemas.microsoft.com/winfx/2006/xaml"
        xmlns:circ="clr-namespace:CircleControl"
        Width="640"
        Height="480"
        >
    <Canvas x:Name="LayoutRoot">
        <circ:Circle Fill="Black" Radius="100"
            Canvas.Left="0" Canvas.Top="50"></circ:Circle>
        <circ:Circle Fill="Red" Radius="50"
            Canvas.Left="0" Canvas.Top="50"></circ:Circle>
    </Canvas>
</UserControl>
```

You can see how this will appear on screen in Figure 9-6.

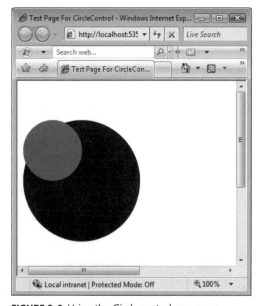

FIGURE 9-6 Using the *Circle* control on a page.

In this case, you had an existing project to which you added a control template, and then you built and used a circle control from that. This is all very nice, but it limits your flexibility in re-using the control. That's where Silverlight class library projects are useful, and we'll look at them in the next section.

Building Silverlight Class Libraries

The Visual Studio templates for Silverlight 2 include a template that allows you to build a class library that is easily reusable in other projects. This class library can contain Silverlight controls, and in this section you'll see how to add controls to the library, using a simple example of building a *Square* control.

First, open Visual Studio, and select New Project from the File menu. The New Project dialog box will appear. Use this to create a new Silverlight class library project and give it an appropriate name. You can see an example of this in Figure 9-7.

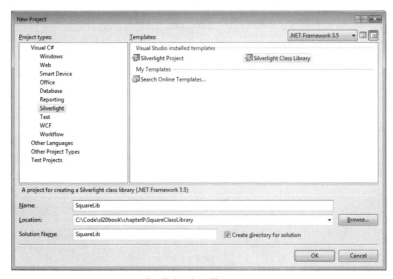

FIGURE 9-7 Creating a new Silverlight class library.

This will create a class library project, as shown in Figure 9-8. This is a typical Visual Studio–based class library project, so if you're familiar with building in C#, your skills will transfer right over into Silverlight 2.

To add a new Silverlight control, right-click on the project, select Add, and then select New Item, as you did earlier (if you need to refresh your memory, look back to Figure 9-3), and call it *SquareControl*.

You can now follow the same steps as earlier to edit the XAML and code for your control. Here's an example of the XAML for the *Square* control:

Note   Some versions of Visual Studio Tools will create a *Grid* instead of a *Canvas* called *LayoutRoot*. In this section, *Canvas* is being used, but the code is interchangeable.

```xml
<UserControl x:Class="SquareLib.SquareControl"
        xmlns="http://schemas.microsoft.com/client/2007"
        xmlns:x="http://schemas.microsoft.com/winfx/2006/xaml"
        Width="640"
        Height="480"
        >

    <Canvas x:Name="LayoutRoot" >
        <Rectangle x:Name="rootControl"></Rectangle>
    </Canvas>
</UserControl>
```

FIGURE 9-8 Visual Studio with a class library project.

Similar to the *Circle* control that we saw earlier, the *Square* control is based on an underlying XAML control, in this case a *Rectangle* control that we call *rootControl*. Here's the C# code that implements the *Square* control:

```csharp
using System;
using System.Collections.Generic;
using System.Linq;
```

```
using System.Windows;
using System.Windows.Controls;
using System.Windows.Documents;
using System.Windows.Input;
using System.Windows.Media;
using System.Windows.Media.Animation;
using System.Windows.Shapes;

namespace SquareLib
{
    public partial class SquareControl : UserControl
    {
        public SquareControl()
        {
            // Required to initialize variables
            InitializeComponent();
        }
        public double Size
        {
            get
            {
                return rootControl.Width;
            }
            set
            {
                rootControl.Width = value;
                rootControl.Height = value;
            }
        }
        public SolidColorBrush Fill
        {
            get
            {
                return (SolidColorBrush)rootControl.Fill;
            }
            set
            {
                rootControl.Fill = (SolidColorBrush)value;
            }
        }
    }
}
```

Compiling this solution will give you a class library DLL that can now be included in other projects.

To use this class library, you can create a new project and reference it. To do this, create a new Silverlight project using the New Project dialog box (File, New Project), and select the Silverlight Project template.

The default template creates two projects in a solution, a Silverlight control and an ASP.NET Web site to host it.

The Silverlight Control project allows you to add a reference by right-clicking on the References folder and then selecting Add Reference (see Figure 9-9).

FIGURE 9-9 Adding a reference to your Silverlight project.

From here, you can browse to the directory containing the compiled DLL from your class library project. It should be in the ClientBin subdirectory. Add the reference, and then you'll see it listed in the references list. If your class library has any dependencies, they will be listed there, too. Figure 9-10 shows the reference to the *SquareLib* assembly after it's correctly made.

FIGURE 9-10 Using your custom reference.

Now, you can return to your Page.xaml and add the namespace reference that will allow you to use the controls within this assembly. The Visual Studio IntelliSense feature will help you greatly here. At the top of the XAML file, add a new *xmlns* tag where you define the namespaces and give it a prefix (for example, sq, as in Figure 9-11). IntelliSense will provide a list of possible assemblies or schemas. You simply have to pick the name of the assembly you want to reference. In this case, it is *SquareLib*, so select it. Note that your list of assemblies may appear different from that shown in Figure 9-11.

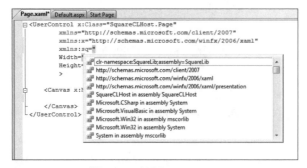

FIGURE 9-11 IntelliSense and XML namespaces.

When you are finished, the reference will be made to the correct namespace and assembly. You can see them here:

```
<UserControl x:Class="SquareCLHost.Page"
      xmlns="http://schemas.microsoft.com/client/2007"
      xmlns:x="http://schemas.microsoft.com/winfx/2006/xaml"
      xmlns:sq="clr-namespace:SquareLib;assembly=SquareLib"
      Width="640"
      Height="480"
      >

   <Canvas x:Name="LayoutRoot">

   </Canvas>
</UserControl>
```

Because you defined the sq prefix to reference this space, you can now add controls from it with the IntelliSense feature simply by using this prefix.

So, for example, if you go to the *LayoutRoot* canvas and type a < character to open an XML node, you'll see sq: as one of the options in the pop-up list. If you fill this out, you will then get a list of available classes, as shown in Figure 9-12.

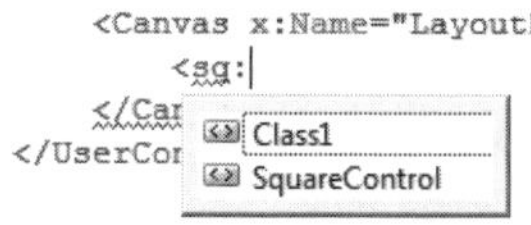

FIGURE 9-12 IntelliSense for your custom control class library.

Finally, here's an example of a XAML with several instances of the *SquareControl:*

```
<UserControl x:Class="SquareCLHost.Page"
      xmlns="http://schemas.microsoft.com/client/2007"
      xmlns:x="http://schemas.microsoft.com/winfx/2006/xaml"
      xmlns:sq="clr-namespace:SquareLib;assembly=SquareLib"
      Width="640"
      Height="480"
      >

   <Canvas x:Name="LayoutRoot" >
      <sq:SquareControl Size="10" Canvas.Top="10"
         Canvas.Left="10" Fill="Red"></sq:SquareControl>
      <sq:SquareControl Size="10" Canvas.Top="20"
         Canvas.Left="20" Fill="Green"></sq:SquareControl>
      <sq:SquareControl Size="10" Canvas.Top="30"
         Canvas.Left="30" Fill="Yellow"></sq:SquareControl>
      <sq:SquareControl Size="10" Canvas.Top="40"
         Canvas.Left="40" Fill="Blue"></sq:SquareControl>
   </Canvas>
</UserControl>
```

Summary

In this chapter, you saw the flexible extensibility model that Silverlight 2 offers. You learned how controls can be added to applications and how functionality can be encapsulated within a control for easy reuse. You also saw how the Silverlight class library template allows you to build controls that are compiled into .NET assemblies for easy reference and reuse within a project.

Using this as a platform, you can now start building your own controls or adding on to the ones that you learned about in Chapters 7 and 8.

In Chapter 10, "Building Connected Applications with Silverlight," we'll be shifting gears a little to take a look at how networking and communication work in Silverlight 2.

Chapter 10
Building Connected Applications with Silverlight

In this chapter, you'll take a look at how to build *connected* applications using Silverlight. The chapter is divided into three main sections. First, we'll look at an outline of the Silverlight architecture, and you will be able to see how it decouples the design from the implementation, allowing you to build services in Personal Hypertext Processor (PHP) or Java and have them generate XAML that you can render with your Silverlight applications. The next section examines the browser itself and how it can be used to connect to distant services using AJAX technology. The final section introduces some of the classes available in .NET, including the *WebClient* and *WebRequest* classes, and shows how you will be able to use these to consume data from servers and render it in your Silverlight application.

Connecting Applications with XAML

One of the characteristics of Silverlight that makes it such a powerful tool is that the XAML that provides the structural framework is XML and thus can be generated by a server. In the examples you've seen so far, the XAML is static, and a document is generated by a designer using a tool such as Expression Blend. However, you aren't limited to using static XAML, and you can enable a whole range of new scenarios by dynamically generating your XAML and having it sent to your users in response to application logic or state.

For example, if you want to build an application that provides weather details in XAML, you couldn't effectively do this with static XAML without having to create a complicated system to generate different XAML documents periodically for each of your users' locations so users could download the appropriate document on request. It is far easier to generate an application template and then fill in the placeholders within the application user interface (UI) using information gleaned from a server.

There are many different languages that can be used to build server applications, and in this section we'll explore PHP and Java. We'll examine how to generate XAML in each of these languages, first in a generic sense and then using the specific weather information example.

Silverlight and PHP

PHP (available for download from *http://www.php.net*) is a simple yet powerful scripting language that can be used easily to template XAML. It typically takes PHP code as its input and creates Web pages as its output. You can use the same method to generate XAML dynamically. If you aren't familiar with PHP, the following information will provide you with a basic introduction.

Your First PHP Page

PHP can be used to generate Web pages dynamically based on input parameters. So, for example, consider the page created with this simple HTML code:

```
<HTML>
<HEAD>
</HEAD>
<BODY>
<H1>Hello, World!</H1>
</BODY>
</HTML>
```

This renders a simple HTML page containing the text "Hello, World!", which you can see in Figure 10-1.

FIGURE 10-1 Simple "Hello World" Web page.

You can make this simple page dynamic using PHP. In this case, the page takes a parameter, and the PHP preprocessor fills it in. Following is the PHP code:

```
<HTML>
<HEAD>
</HEAD>
<BODY>
<H1>Hello, <?php echo($_REQUEST['name']);?>!</H1>
<BODY>
</HTML>
```

Here you can see the HTML markup code has some embedded PHP code that retrieves the URL parameter *name* and then writes it to the response stream using the *echo* command. So, if you browse to this page, passing it a value for *name*, then the PHP processor will dynamically render the page markup. The following URL parameter, for example, can be seen in the display shown in Figure 10-2:

http://localhost/phptext/Hello.php?name=Laurence

FIGURE 10-2 Dynamically rendering the page in PHP.

PHP and XAML Case Study

The same principle can apply to XAML. You can easily create an XAML template for how you would like your content to be presented using Expression Blend, and this template can then be used within a PHP page. If you need repeating functionality to present the content, as with a list, you can create that content with a PHP loop.

This is best demonstrated by example. PHP (along with Apache, MySQL, and Linux) is a core element of the famous LAMP stack, so let's take a look at how we would build a PHP/MySQL application that could run on any Web server or operating system that supports LAMP. (The acronym comes from the first letters of *Linux*, *Apache*, *MySQL*, and *PHP*.) We'll actually be building an application we'll call "Windows IIS MySQL PHP," with the unfortunate acronym WIMP!

Building the Server-Side Database

In this case, MySQL is used to build a server-side database of names and addresses. MySQL can be downloaded and installed from *http://www.mysql.com*, and there is a freely available community edition that is ideal for developers to use for experimentation.

In addition to this, a suite of GUI tools, such as the MySQL Administrator and MySQL Query Browser, is available for building and populating sample databases. Instruction in using these tools is beyond the scope of this book, but you can check out the extensive documentation on the MySQL.com Web site if you're not familiar with these tools.

Figure 10-3 shows the MySQL Table Editor and how it is used to define a simple table containing names and addresses.

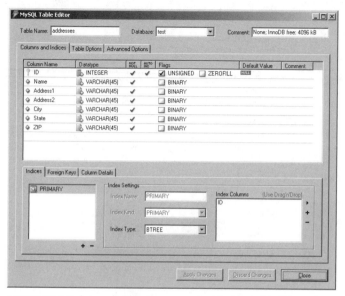

FIGURE 10-3 Defining a table of names and addresses in MySQL.

You can use the MySQL Query Browser to edit the contents of the table. Simply click the Edit button at the bottom of the application's UI (see Figure 10-4), and then you can type in sample name and address data, as shown in Figure 10-4.

FIGURE 10-4 Adding table data with the MySQL Query Browser.

With some data in your database for PHP to expose, it's time to couple the data with your XAML template. In the next section, you'll learn how to build the template using Expression Blend.

Building an XAML Template

Now that we have our data, let's think about how we're going to present it using XAML. Expression Blend is a great visual editor for XAML, and Figure 10-5 shows an example of a XAML template that we can use to provide our users with the name and address data from our table.

FIGURE 10-5 Designing an XAML template with Expression Blend.

The resulting XAML represents a collection of *Canvas*, *Rectangle*, and *TextBlock* objects. The full XAML for the template shown in Figure 10-5 is provided in Listing 10-1. Note that the XAML contains an enclosing canvas as the root node, and then another canvas contains the rest of the UI elements. It is this canvas that will be repeated for multiple records.

LISTING 10-1 XAML Address Application Template

```
<Canvas
  xmlns=http://schemas.microsoft.com/client/2007
  xmlns:x=http://schemas.microsoft.com/winfx/2006/xaml
  Width="640" Height="480"
  Background="#FF460608">
  <Canvas Width="352" Height="128" Canvas.Left="10" Canvas.Top="8" >
    <Rectangle Fill="#FF693B3D" Stroke="#FF000000" StrokeThickness="0"
      RadiusX="16" RadiusY="16" Width="352" Height="128" Canvas.Top="1"/>
    <Rectangle Stroke="#FF000000" StrokeThickness="0" RadiusX="8"
      RadiusY="8" Width="336" Height="40" Canvas.Left="8" Canvas.Top="8">
      <Rectangle.Fill>
```

```xml
                <LinearGradientBrush EndPoint="0.518,0.175"
                    StartPoint="0.515,0.825">
                  <GradientStop Color="#FF460608" Offset="0"/>
                  <GradientStop Color="#FF841316" Offset="1"/>
                </LinearGradientBrush>
            </Rectangle.Fill>
        </Rectangle>
        <TextBlock x:Name="txtName" Width="312" Height="24"
          Canvas.Left="16" Canvas.Top="16" FontFamily="Arial Unicode MS"
          FontSize="18" FontWeight="Normal" Foreground="#FFFFFFFF"
          Text="User Name" TextWrapping="Wrap"/>
        <Rectangle Stroke="#FF000000" StrokeThickness="0"
          RadiusX="8" RadiusY="8" Width="336" Height="23"
          Canvas.Left="8" Canvas.Top="48">
          <Rectangle.Fill>
                <LinearGradientBrush EndPoint="0.518,0.175"
                    StartPoint="0.515,0.825">
                  <GradientStop Color="#FF460608" Offset="0"/>
                  <GradientStop Color="#FF841316" Offset="1"/>
                </LinearGradientBrush>
            </Rectangle.Fill>
        </Rectangle>
        <TextBlock x:Name="txtAddr1" Width="312" Height="24"
          FontFamily="Arial Unicode MS" FontSize="12" FontWeight="Normal"
          Foreground="#FFFFFFFF" Text="Address1"
          TextWrapping="Wrap" Canvas.Left="14" Canvas.Top="48"/>
        <Rectangle Stroke="#FF000000" StrokeThickness="0"
          RadiusX="8" RadiusY="8" Width="336"
          Height="23" Canvas.Left="8" Canvas.Top="71">
          <Rectangle.Fill>
                <LinearGradientBrush EndPoint="0.518,0.175"
                    StartPoint="0.515,0.825">
                  <GradientStop Color="#FF460608" Offset="0"/>
                  <GradientStop Color="#FF841316" Offset="1"/>
                </LinearGradientBrush>
            </Rectangle.Fill>
        </Rectangle>
        <TextBlock x:Name="txtAddr2" Width="312" Height="24"
          FontFamily="Arial Unicode MS" FontSize="12"
          FontWeight="Normal" Foreground="#FFFFFFFF"
          Text="Address2" TextWrapping="Wrap"
          Canvas.Left="15" Canvas.Top="72"/>
        <Rectangle Stroke="#FF000000" StrokeThickness="0"
          RadiusX="8" RadiusY="8" Width="168" Height="23"
          Canvas.Left="176" Canvas.Top="94">
          <Rectangle.Fill>
                <LinearGradientBrush EndPoint="0.518,0.175"
        StartPoint="0.515,0.825">
                  <GradientStop Color="#FF460608" Offset="0"/>
                          <GradientStop Color="#FF841316" Offset="1"/>
                </LinearGradientBrush>
            </Rectangle.Fill>
        </Rectangle>
        <Rectangle Stroke="#FF000000" StrokeThickness="0"
```

```
          RadiusX="8" RadiusY="8" Width="168"
          Height="23" Canvas.Left="8" Canvas.Top="94">
        <Rectangle.Fill>
            <LinearGradientBrush EndPoint="0.518,0.175"
                StartPoint="0.515,0.825">
                <GradientStop Color="#FF460608" Offset="0"/>
                <GradientStop Color="#FF841316" Offset="1"/>
            </LinearGradientBrush>
        </Rectangle.Fill>
      </Rectangle>
      <TextBlock x:Name="txtCity" Width="144" Height="24"
        FontFamily="Arial Unicode MS" FontSize="12"
        FontWeight="Normal" Foreground="#FFFFFFFF" Text="City"
        TextWrapping="Wrap" Canvas.Left="15" Canvas.Top="96"/>
      <TextBlock x:Name="txtState" Width="144" Height="24"
        FontFamily="Arial Unicode MS" FontSize="12"
        FontWeight="Normal" Foreground="#FFFFFFFF" Text="State"
        TextWrapping="Wrap" Canvas.Left="182" Canvas.Top="96"/>
    </Canvas>
</Canvas>
```

This second canvas (hereafter called the *container*) has its *Canvas.Top* property set to 8 pixels and its *Height* is set to 128 pixels. Therefore, if we want to stack other instances of this canvas below the first, we need to locate the *Canvas.Top* for the second container at 136 (128 + 8), and then we need to locate the next container at 264 (128 + 128 + 8), and so forth.

The container canvas contains all the UI elements, but the UI elements need to have distinct names in XAML. You can see that each *TextBlock* has been named, using the *x:Name* attribute in this XAML example. When we clone the container, we'll need to edit this XAML so that it has distinct names for these nodes. The naming algorithm will be simple—we will use an index appended to the end of the name. So, for example, the *x:Name* value *txtState* recorded in the template will become *txtState1* for the first database row, and then it will be *txtState2* for the next database row, and so forth.

Cloning these elements in PHP is very straightforward, as you'll see in the next section.

Generating XAML from PHP and MySQL

MySQL implements page parsing, which means that when the server is instructed to return the page, MySQL will write formatted data to the response buffer. When MySQL encounters a special opening tag (*<?php*), it passes the processing over to the PHP parser, which then executes the code the PHP processor finds there until it encounters a closing tag (*?>*). This makes the combination of MySQL and PHP ideally suited for rendering templated content. You simply put the template for the content that you want to generate into a file with the .php extension, and any place in the file where you need to fill in some data-bound placeholders, you place the necessary PHP logic within the PHP opening and closing tags (*<?php* and *?>*, respectively).

PHP logic can contain loops, and if you have a loop statement followed by some content, then you'll find the content will be written many times. The loop can traverse open-close couplets—so, for example, you can do the following:

```
<?php
for($i=0; $i<100; $i++)
{ // Loop opening brace
// Exiting PHP, though we haven't closed our loop yet!
?>
<H1>My Text Line is <?php echo $i; ?></H1>
<?php
} // Now we close our loop
?>
```

This will repeat the HTML content (the text within and including the *<H1>* tag) 100 times. You can see that the *<?php ... ?>* couplets do not need to completely surround the text, which is useful when you couple PHP and XAML.

With XAML, our enclosing canvas can be contained within a loop, like this:

```
<?php
for($i=0; $i<100; $i++)
{ // Loop opening brace
// Exiting PHP, though we haven't closed our loop yet!
?>
<Canvas>
...
</Canvas>
<?php
} // Now we close our loop
?>
```

With this code, the XAML will be written 100 times! This makes PHP a powerful templating language for Silverlight.

To return to our example, let's take a look at what it takes to connect to the database, run a query against it, and write the appropriate number of XAML *Canvas* elements, based on the number of returned results. We'll also edit the contents of the *TextBlock* elements within the canvas to display the information from the database as well as adjust the *TextBlock* name so that they are unique.

Ultimately, you will build a PHP page that generates XAML for you. This will then be used as the source for the Silverlight control, which will render the XAML. However, to make it a little more interesting, we'll modify the generator to accept a parameter (a *state* value for our example) so that it returns information only for the people with an address in that state. This will make it a truly dynamic XAML generator.

First, we'll need to have Silverlight recognize the output from PHP as XML. To do that, you have to set the *MIME* type of the output content. This is done in PHP with the *header* command like this:

```
header('Content-type: text/xml');
```

To retrieve a request string parameter (i.e., *http://server/script.php?param=value*) using PHP, you use the *$_REQUEST* array. So, if we want to read the value of the parameter *State*, we'll use code like the following:

```
$State=$_REQUEST['State'];
```

Versions 4.x of PHP have the MySQL command set built in. Versions 5.x and greater require you to specify the MySQL command set as an extension. Regardless of which you use, the PHP syntax is the same.

To connect to the *localhost* server with the user name *user* and the password *password*, you use the *mysql_connect* command:

```
$con = mysql_connect("localhost", "user", "password");
```

The server can contain more than one database, so you select the database you want to work with using the *mysql_select_db* command:

```
mysql_select_db("test", $con); // "test" is the database name
```

Then, to run a query against this database, you use the *mysql_query* command and pass it a string containing the actual SQL query. The result set will be returned as an array of arrays of values. Following is an example:

```
$sqlString = "SELECT * from addresses";
$result = mysql_query($sqlString);
```

The *mysql_fetch_array* then splits this into rows, and you can use a *while* loop to cycle through each row, as shown in the following example:

```
while($row = mysql_fetch_array($result))
{
...
}
```

Therefore, given this scenario, following is the algorithm we want to follow:

1. Set the *MIME* type to text/xml.

2. Get the input parameter (the state).

3. Write out the "root" *Canvas* starting tag.

4. Use the input parameter to build a query.

5. Run the query and get the result set.

6. For each row in the result set:

   a. Write out the XAML of the container XAML.

b.   Fill *Text* attributes of *TextBlock*s with relevant data from a database field.

c.   Fill *x:Name* attributes with unique ID based on row count.

7.   Close the "root" *Canvas* tag.

The full PHP page to accomplish this is shown in Listing 10-2. The PHP markup within the XAML block is shown in bold type.

LISTING 10-2 PHP Code to Generate XAML

```php
<?php
header('Content-type: text/xml');
$State=$_REQUEST['State'];
?>
<Canvas
  xmlns="http://schemas.microsoft.com/client/2007"
  xmlns:x="http://schemas.microsoft.com/winfx/2006/xaml"
  Width="640" Height="480"
  Background="#FF460608"
  >
<?php
$height=128;
$top=8;
$i=0;
$con = mysql_connect("localhost", "root", "root");
mysql_select_db("test",$con);
$sqlString = "SELECT * from addresses";
if($State!="")
{
    $sqlString = $sqlString . " WHERE State = '" . $State . "'";
}
$result = mysql_query($sqlString);
while($row = mysql_fetch_array($result))
{
?>
    <Canvas Width="352" Height="128" Canvas.Left="10"
        Canvas.Top="<?php echo($top + ($height*$i)); ?>" >
      <Rectangle Fill="#FF693B3D" Stroke="#FF000000"
        StrokeThickness="0" RadiusX="16" RadiusY="16"
        Width="352" Height="128" Canvas.Top="1"/>
      <Rectangle Stroke="#FF000000" StrokeThickness="0"
        RadiusX="8" RadiusY="8" Width="336" Height="40"
        Canvas.Left="8" Canvas.Top="8">
        <Rectangle.Fill>
          <LinearGradientBrush EndPoint="0.518,0.175" StartPoint="0.515,0.825">
            <GradientStop Color="#FF460608" Offset="0"/>
            <GradientStop Color="#FF841316" Offset="1"/>
          </LinearGradientBrush>
        </Rectangle.Fill>
      </Rectangle>
      <TextBlock x:Name="txtName<?php echo $i; ?>" Width="312" Height="24"
        Canvas.Left="16" Canvas.Top="16"
        FontFamily="Arial Unicode MS" FontSize="18"
        FontWeight="Normal" Foreground="#FFFFFFFF"
```

```
      Text="<?php echo($row['Name']); ?>"
      TextWrapping="Wrap"/>
  <Rectangle Stroke="#FF000000" StrokeThickness="0"
    RadiusX="8" RadiusY="8" Width="336"
    Height="23" Canvas.Left="8" Canvas.Top="48">
  <Rectangle.Fill>
    <LinearGradientBrush EndPoint="0.518,0.175" StartPoint="0.515,0.825">
      <GradientStop Color="#FF460608" Offset="0"/>
      <GradientStop Color="#FF841316" Offset="1"/>
    </LinearGradientBrush>
  </Rectangle.Fill>
  </Rectangle>
<TextBlock x:Name="txtAddr1<?php echo $i; ?>" Width="312"
    Height="24" FontFamily="Arial Unicode MS" FontSize="12"
    FontWeight="Normal" Foreground="#FFFFFFFF"
    Text="<?php echo($row['Address1']); ?>" TextWrapping="Wrap"
    Canvas.Left="14" Canvas.Top="48"/>
<Rectangle Stroke="#FF000000" StrokeThickness="0"
    RadiusX="8" RadiusY="8" Width="336" Height="23"
    Canvas.Left="8" Canvas.Top="71">
    <Rectangle.Fill>
      <LinearGradientBrush EndPoint="0.518,0.175" StartPoint="0.515,0.825">
        <GradientStop Color="#FF460608" Offset="0"/>
        <GradientStop Color="#FF841316" Offset="1"/>
      </LinearGradientBrush>
    </Rectangle.Fill>
  </Rectangle>
  <TextBlock x:Name="txtAddr2<?php echo $i; ?>" Width="312"
    Height="24" FontFamily="Arial Unicode MS"
    FontSize="12" FontWeight="Normal"
    Foreground="#FFFFFFFF"
    Text="<?php echo($row['Address2']); ?>" TextWrapping="Wrap"
    Canvas.Left="15" Canvas.Top="72"/>
  <Rectangle Stroke="#FF000000" StrokeThickness="0"
    RadiusX="8" RadiusY="8" Width="168" Height="23"
    Canvas.Left="176" Canvas.Top="94">
    <Rectangle.Fill>
      <LinearGradientBrush EndPoint="0.518,0.175" StartPoint="0.515,0.825">
        <GradientStop Color="#FF460608" Offset="0"/>
        <GradientStop Color="#FF841316" Offset="1"/>
      </LinearGradientBrush>
    </Rectangle.Fill>
  </Rectangle>
  <Rectangle Stroke="#FF000000" StrokeThickness="0"
    RadiusX="8" RadiusY="8" Width="168"
    Height="23" Canvas.Left="8" Canvas.Top="94">
    <Rectangle.Fill>
      <LinearGradientBrush EndPoint="0.518,0.175" StartPoint="0.515,0.825">
        <GradientStop Color="#FF460608" Offset="0"/>
        <GradientStop Color="#FF841316" Offset="1"/>
      </LinearGradientBrush>
    </Rectangle.Fill>
  </Rectangle>
  <TextBlock x:Name="txtCity<?php echo $i; ?>" Width="144"
```

```
          Height="24" FontFamily="Arial Unicode MS"
          FontSize="12" FontWeight="Normal" Foreground="#FFFFFFFF"
          Text="<?php echo($row['City']); ?>" TextWrapping="Wrap"
          Canvas.Left="15" Canvas.Top="96"/>
        <TextBlock x:Name="txtState<?php echo $i; ?>" Width="144"
          Height="24" FontFamily="Arial Unicode MS" FontSize="12"
          FontWeight="Normal" Foreground="#FFFFFFFF"
          Text="<?php echo($row['State']); ?>"
          TextWrapping="Wrap" Canvas.Left="182" Canvas.Top="96"/>
    </Canvas>
<?php
$i++;
}
?>
</Canvas>
```

Building a PHP Page to Deliver Silverlight

As you saw in the previous section, when you use PHP, the server outputs content directly until it sees the opening tag (<*?php*), at which point it references the PHP interpreter, which then runs the code contained within opening and the closing tag (*?>*).

The PHP code typically is used to activate HTML code, and because Silverlight is delivered from HTML, it is a straightforward process to edit an HTML page to add these tags and rename the page with a .php file extension. So, to deliver Silverlight using PHP, you want a page that includes Silverlight.js and createSilverlight.js in the usual way, calling *createSilverlight* to instantiate the Silverlight control.

Because we want this page to accept a parameter for a particular state so that the user can access the names and addresses in the database by state, this page must be designed to accept a parameter and then use the parameter to create Silverlight content using the XAML source PHP that you saw in the previous step, which, fortunately, is quite simple in PHP. To display the rendered XAML, all you need to do is set the *content* property of the Silverlight control to your application's Uniform Resource Indicator (URI), and Silverlight will contact the server at that URI, accept the resulting XAML, and render it.

Following is an example of a complete PHP page that generates HTML:

```
<html xmlns="http://www.w3.org/1999/xhtml">
<head>
<title>SilverlightJSApplication2</title>

<script type="text/javascript" src="Silverlight.js"></script>
<script type="text/javascript" src="createSilverlight.js"></script>
<script type="text/javascript">
  function handleLoad(control, userContext, rootElement)
  {
<?php
  if(!isset($_REQUEST['State']))
    $State="";
```

```
    else
      $State=$_REQUEST['State'];
?>
  control.source = "http://localhost/phptest/xaml.php?State=<?php echo($State) ?>";
  }
</script>
</head>
<body>
   <div id="SilverlightControlHost">
      <script type="text/javascript">
         createSilverlight();
      </script>
   </div>
</body>
</html>
```

Figures 10-6 and 10-7 show how this PHP page is rendered in the browser, using Silverlight, for addresses in New York (NY in the database) and Washington (WA).

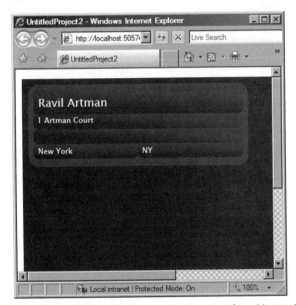

FIGURE 10-6 PHP application-rendered content for addresses in New York.

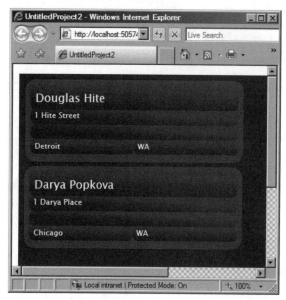

FIGURE 10-7 PHP application-rendered content for addresses in Washington.

Silverlight and Java

The Java language is compiled into byte code that is either interpreted or Just-In-Time (JIT) compiled and then executed at run time on a virtual machine. This makes it ideal for server environments, particularly where diverse operating systems are present in the data center. Java is supported on nearly every major operating system.

There are many ways to build server applications in Java and its associated Enterprise edition, commonly called *J2EE* or just *JEE*. One method is to use Java Server Pages (JSP), which are similar in concept to PHP, in which the desired output is marked up with code that will execute at run time. So, to produce browsable HTML, you use standard HTML markup but activate it by placing JSP tags within it that will execute as the page is being rendered. Another way is to use the Java *Servlet*, which is an application that runs on a server and accepts parameters via HTTP.

The openness of Silverlight makes it easy to build applications incorporating both Silverlight and Java. You can use JSP technology to build pages that contain Silverlight content, and server-based technologies such as servlets are ideal for generating the XAML that is rendered by the browser.

To demonstrate how to build Silverlight applications in a Java-based infrastructure, we will use both of these technologies. First we will investigate how to build a JSP page to deliver the Silverlight control, and then we will build a servlet to generate XAML that the Silverlight control renders.

Building an XAML Source Servlet

A *servlet* is an application that extends the *HttpServlet* class in the *javax.servlet* namespace. It exposes two functions, *doGet* and *doPost*, that are used to capture *HTTP-GET* and *HTTP-POST* commands, respectively. Each of these functions takes an *HTTPRequest* and *HTTPResponse* object. The former is used to capture the details of the request; the latter controls the response. Typically, you'll read parameters from the *HTTPRequest* object and write output to the *HTTPResponse* object. Following is an example of these functions:

```
protected void doGet(HttpServletRequest request, HttpServletResponse response)
    throws ServletException, IOException {
        // Handle GET
    }

protected void doPost(HttpServletRequest request, HttpServletResponse response)
    throws ServletException, IOException {
        // Handle POST
    }
```

In a typical design pattern, you would write a helper function that accepts the request and response objects, and then the *doGet* and *doPost* methods call that function. In this manner, regardless of how the servlet is invoked, you'll run the same code.

For this example, the servlet will take an XAML document as a template and then use the XML application programming interfaces (APIs) in Java to manipulate the document, filling in its contents with the results of a database query.

Following is an example of the simple XAML document that is used in this case study:

```
<Canvas
  xmlns="http://schemas.microsoft.com/winfx/2006/xaml/presentation"
  xmlns:x="http://schemas.microsoft.com/winfx/2006/xaml"
  Width="200" Height="80"
  Background="#FF000000">
  <TextBlock x:Name="txtName" Width="200" Height="24"
      Canvas.Left="24" Canvas.Top="8" Foreground="#FFEFB9B9"
      Text="Name" TextWrapping="Wrap"/>
  <TextBlock x:Name="txtCity" Width="200" Height="24"
      Canvas.Left="24" Canvas.Top="40" Foreground="#FFEFB9B9"
      Text="City" TextWrapping="Wrap"/>
  <TextBlock x:Name="txtCountry" Width="200" Height="24"
      Canvas.Left="24" Canvas.Top="72" Foreground="#FFEFB9B9"
      Text="Country" TextWrapping="Wrap"/>
</Canvas>
```

This XAML contains three *TextBlock* elements. The servlet will query the *Customers* database in the *Northwind* database and fill these *TextBlock* elements with the results. The query takes the customer ID as a parameter and uses it to pull the relevant customer record. The customer record data of interest include the customer's name, city, and country.

If you don't already have the *Northwind* database used in this example, you can download it from the Microsoft Developer Network (MSDN). The *Northwind Traders* database is a free sample database offered by Microsoft for SQL Server. It contains a full database of information for a ficticious online store that provides a useful source of sample data for examples like the one presented here.

To fill the *TextBlock* elements, we'll need to locate them in the XAML document. When you use the Java XML APIs to find nodes based on an XPath, you will need to define a namespace prefix for elements in the default namespace, so you will notice later that elements in the default namespace (i.e., *<TextBlock>*) will be referred to using a run-time–added default namespace prefix (i.e., *<d:TextBlock>*).

So, in Java, we will use the XML APIs to find the node that we want to edit based on their name—for example, the *TextBlock* that contains the country is called *txtCountry*, and when we have it, we'll change its value. So, to generate our application's XAML, the helper function will perform the following steps:

1.   Get the input parameter. If it is *null*, set it to a default.

2.   Set the output *MIME* type to text/xml.

3.   Create an XML document, and load the template XAML file. In this example, the XAML is saved into a document called Template.xml.

4.   Open the SQL Server database, and query the Northwind Customers table for a customer matching the input parameter.

5.   There will be a maximum of one record to be read, so read it.

6.   Use the XPath of the *ContactName* node to find it, and then replace its contents with the value of the *ContactName* field read from the database.

7.   Use the XPath of the *City* node to find it, and then replace its contents with the value of the *City* field read from the database.

8.   Use the XPath of the *Country* node to find it, and then replace its contents with the value of the *Country* field read from the DB.

9.   Write the XML to the response stream.

Keep this algorithm in mind as you look at Listing 10-3, which shows the helper function code the servlet uses to generate XAML.

LISTING 10-3 Java Code to Generate XAML

```
protected void processRequest(HttpServletRequest request,
        HttpServletResponse response)
    throws ServletException, IOException {
    try
        {
```

```
String strID = request.getParameter("ID");
if(strID==null)
    strID="ALFKI";
DocumentBuilderFactory factory =
        DocumentBuilderFactory.newInstance();
factory.setNamespaceAware(true);
response.setContentType("text/xml");
PrintWriter out = response.getWriter();
DocumentBuilder builder = factory.newDocumentBuilder();
String uri = getServletContext().getRealPath("template.xml");
Document doc = builder.parse(uri);
DOMSource domSource = new DOMSource(doc);
StreamResult streamResult = new StreamResult(out);
TransformerFactory tf = TransformerFactory.newInstance();
Transformer serializer = tf.newTransformer();
XPathFactory xpFactory = XPathFactory.newInstance();
XPath xpath = xpFactory.newXPath();
xpath.setNamespaceContext(new DefaultNameSpaceContext());
String strContactName="";
String strCity="";
String strCountry="";
java.lang.Class.forName
  ("com.microsoft.sqlserver.jdbc.SQLServerDriver");
Connection c = java.sql.DriverManager.getConnection
  ("jdbc:sqlserver://localhost\\SQLEXPRESS;databasename=Northwind;
    user=javauser;password=javauser;");
String SQL =
    "Select ContactName, City, Country
    from Customers where CustomerID = ?";
PreparedStatement pstmt = c.prepareStatement(SQL);
pstmt.setString(1, strID);
ResultSet rs = pstmt.executeQuery();
while (rs.next()) {
    strContactName = rs.getString("ContactName");
    strCity=rs.getString("City");
    strCountry=rs.getString("Country");
    String strXPath = "//d:TextBlock[@x:Name='txtName']";
    XPathExpression expr = xpath.compile(strXPath);
    Object result = expr.evaluate(doc,XPathConstants.NODESET);
    NodeList nodes = (NodeList) result;
    Node ndeT1 =
      nodes.item(0).getAttributes().getNamedItem("Text");
    ndeT1.setNodeValue(strContactName);
    strXPath = "//d:TextBlock[@x:Name='txtCity']";
    expr = xpath.compile(strXPath);
    result = expr.evaluate(doc,XPathConstants.NODESET);
    nodes = (NodeList) result;
    ndeT1 =
      nodes.item(0).getAttributes().getNamedItem("Text");
    ndeT1.setNodeValue(strCity);
    strXPath = "//d:TextBlock[@x:Name='txtCountry']";
    expr = xpath.compile(strXPath);
    result = expr.evaluate(doc,XPathConstants.NODESET);
    nodes = (NodeList) result;
```

```
        ndeT1 =
          nodes.item(0).getAttributes().getNamedItem("Text");
        ndeT1.setNodeValue(strCountry);
        }
        rs.close();
        pstmt.close();
        serializer.transform(domSource, streamResult);
            out.close();
    }
    catch(Exception ex)
    {
        ex.printStackTrace();
    }

}
```

You can see the results of running this servlet (in the Tomcat application server) in Figure 10-8.

FIGURE 10-8 Generating XAML from a servlet.

Delivering Silverlight from JSP

To build a JSP page, you build an HTML page and then edit it with JSP markup for the parts where you want to execute page logic. In this case, you want to deliver a Silverlight solution, and you typically would do this by importing the Silverlight.js and createSilverlight.js script libraries and then calling *createSilverlight* within a named DIV.

However, this JSP page is going to do a little more—it is going to accept a parameter, and then it is going to use this parameter to build the XAML source element that you created earlier. To do this, you write Java code and embed it using the JSP <% and %> tags. You can see the full JSP page code in Listing 10-4.

LISTING 10-4 JSP Code to Deliver Silverlight Content

```
<%@page contentType="text/html"%>
<%@page pageEncoding="UTF-8"%>
<!DOCTYPE HTML PUBLIC "-//W3C//DTD HTML 4.01 Transitional//EN"
```

```
                "http://www.w3.org/TR/html4/loose.dtd">

<html>
    <head>
        <meta http-equiv="Content-Type" content="text/html; charset=UTF-8">
        <script type="text/javascript" src="js/silverlight.js"></script>
        <script type="text/javascript"
            src="js/createSilverlight.js"></script>
        <script type="text/javascript">
            function handleLoad(control, userContext, rootElement)
            {
                <%
                    String strValue="";
                    if (request.getParameter("ID") == null) {
                        strValue = "ALFKI";
                    } else {
                        strValue = request.getParameter("ID");
                    }
                %>
                control.source = "http://localhost:8084/ScreenCast2/XamlSource?ID=<%
out.print(strValue); %>";
            }
        </script>
        <title>JSP Page</title>
    </head>
    <body>

    <h1>Silverlight JSP Page</h1>

    <div id="slContent">
        <script type="text/javascript">
            createSilverlight();
        </script>
    </div>
    </body>
</html>
```

Figures 10-9 and 10-10 show how this page looks. Note that the parameter *AROUT* is passed to the JSP page in the first page's query string, whereas *ALFKI* is passed to the second page.

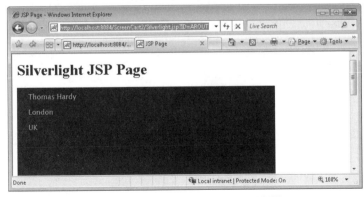

FIGURE 10-9 Running the JSP with the ID parameter *AROUT*.

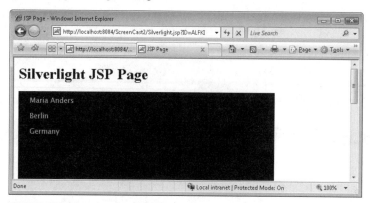

FIGURE 10-10 Running the JSP with the ID parameter *ALFKI*.

Building Connectivity Using JavaScript

Because Silverlight is a browser-based technology, JavaScript, and in particular AJAX, can be used to create connected applications. In this section we'll explore the methods that can be used to achieve this, including capturing data from a server application using AJAX and adding it to our Silverlight application, as well as using ASP.NET AJAX to communicate with a Web Service, taking the raw data from the server, and rendering it from Silverlight.

Using AJAX

We're going to build a simple application that emits data, which will then be captured by an AJAX call and passed to Silverlight so that it can be rendered. To do this, we first need to build a time server application, which will return the current time, as understood by the server, when it is called.

Building the Time Server

To get started, create a new ASP.NET Web Application. Add a new generic handler called *ServerTime.ashx* to this application. You'll then edit the code for this handler so that it writes out the current system time as straight text. Here's the full code for the ASHX:

```
using System;
using System.Collections;
using System.Data;
using System.Linq;
using System.Web;
using System.Web.Services;
using System.Web.Services.Protocols;
using System.Xml.Linq;

namespace AJAXSample
{
[WebService(Namespace = "http://tempuri.org/")]
```

```
[WebServiceBinding(ConformsTo = WsiProfiles.BasicProfile1_1)]
public class ServerTime : IHttpHandler
{
  public void ProcessRequest(HttpContext context)
  {
    context.Response.ContentType = "text/plain";
    context.Response.Write(System.DateTime.Now.ToShortTimeString());
  }

  public bool IsReusable
  {
    get
    {
      return false;
    }
  }
 }
}
```

When you run this ASHX, it will report the current system time to the browser, as shown in Figure 10-11.

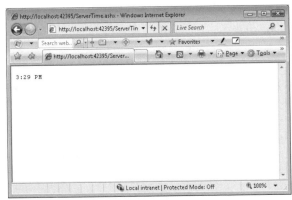

FIGURE 10-11 Running the *ServerTime* handler.

Now, let's take a look at how we can get this data and render it in Silverlight.

Building the Time Client

If you use Microsoft Visual Studio to create a new Silverlight script application, it creates an application with a simple button on it that looks like the one shown in Figure 10-12. We're going to amend this application so that, when the page loads, it calls the Server to get the time via the ASHX handler we just built, and then it sets the caption of the button to this time.

FIGURE 10-12 Basic Silverlight application.

It is very simple to add AJAX to this. Within a script block, add the following code:

```
var xmlHttp;

function getLatestTime()
{
  xmlHttp = new XMLHttpRequest();
  xmlHttp.open("GET","http://localhost:42395/ServerTime.ashx",true);
  xmlHttp.onreadystatechange = handleAJAXCallback;
  xmlHttp.send(null);
}
```

If you aren't familiar with AJAX, don't worry—this is fairly straightforward. The first line creates a new *XMLHttpRequest* object that is at the core of what AJAX does. Note that we are keeping this code simple, so for older browsers, instantiating *xmlHttp* will have a different syntax. It then opens the URI of the *ServerTime* generic handler that you created earlier.

> **Tip** Be sure to replace the URL in the previous code with the appropriate URL to make this work on your computer.

The next thing it does is to declare an event handler function for whenever the *readyState* property of the *AJAX* object changes. The event in this case is *onreadystatechange* (note the case sensitivity; it should be all lowercase), and the event handler will be in a function called *handleAJAXCallback*, which you will see in a moment. Finally, it calls the *send()* function on the *xmlHttp* object to start the network communication.

The *handleAJAXCallback* function is then called whenever the *readyState* property of the *xmlHttp* object changes. It has five different states:

- 0—The request has not yet initialized.
- 1—The request has been set up.

- 2—The request has been sent.

- 3—The request is being processed.

- 4—The request is complete.

We are interested in the state that indicates the request is complete, so we check for state 4. Here's the code:

```
function handleAJAXCallback()
{
  if((xmlHttp.readyState == 4) && (xmlHttp.status ==200))
  {
    var SL = document.getElementById("silverlightPlugIn");
    SL.content.findName("txt").Text = xmlHttp.responseText;
  }
}
```

This code checks that the *readyState* property is equal to 4 and the HTTP status code (in the *status* property) is equal to 200 (i.e., the communication was successful), and if so, the application finds the element called *txt* in the XAML and sets it to the value of the response text. Note that if you are using the basic template XAML, the *TextBlock* with the button caption does not have a name, so be sure to set its name to *txt* to ensure that this code will work. The *responseText* property of the *xmlHttp* object will contain the data returned from the server, which in this case is the current server time.

One final thing to remember is that you need to ensure that the script gets called when the page is loaded. You can do this by specifying the *onLoad* script in the *<BODY>* tag of the page. Here's an example:

```
<body onload="getLatestTime();">
```

You can see how all this will look in Figure 10-13.

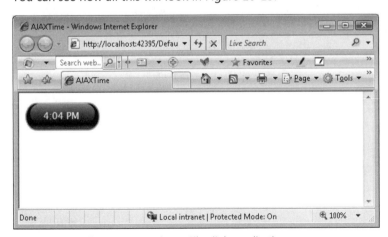

FIGURE 10-13 Using AJAX to update a Silverlight application.

This is a useful technique for creating highly dynamic Silverlight sites using standards-oriented technologies. It also shows that Silverlight is decoupled from the Microsoft server infrastructure and can be hosted and updated from any server.

In the next section, we'll look at ASP.NET Web Services and how ASP.NET AJAX can be used to manage interaction between them and Silverlight.

Using ASP.NET AJAX and Web Services

When you create a Web Service using ASP.NET, you can mark the Web Service to be scriptable, meaning that a JavaScript-based proxy can be automatically generated for you by the Web Service. This proxy uses JavaScript Object Notation (JSON) to allow you to pass complex data types across the wire easily and without interoperability issues. So, let's go ahead and build one, and then we will see how we can use JavaScript to pull data from it and put it into Silverlight.

Using Visual Studio, create a new application and add an ASMX Web Service to it. We will use this Web Service to create the current time in both short and long formats. To do this, let's create a class that contains two strings, effectively giving us a structured object that contains the data. Here's what it looks like:

```
public class DateData
{
    public string strShortTime;
    public string strLongTime;
}
```

Now, here's the code for the Web Service class that will expose the current time in both short and long formats using this class to return the data. Note that the class is attributed as a *System.Web.Script.Services.ScriptService*. This instructs the ASP.NET infrastructure to tag this as a scriptable service:

```
using System;
using System.Linq;
using System.Web;
using System.Web.Services;
using System.Web.Services.Protocols;
using System.Xml.Linq;

[WebService(Namespace = "http://tempuri.org/")]
[WebServiceBinding(ConformsTo = WsiProfiles.BasicProfile1_1)]
[System.Web.Script.Services.ScriptService]
public class Service : System.Web.Services.WebService
{
    public Service () {

    }
```

```
[WebMethod]
public DateData getTime(){
    DateData dReturn = new DateData();
    dReturn.strLongTime = System.DateTime.Now.ToLongTimeString();
    dReturn.strShortTime = System.DateTime.Now.ToShortTimeString();
    return dReturn;
}

}
```

When you run this service, appending /js to the end of the URI will generate the JavaScript proxy, so to consume the Web Service, you can either use an HTML page that includes this script, or you can use an ASP.NET page that has a *ScriptManager* on it that references this service. We'll use the latter method here.

Create an ASP.NET page in your solution, and add a *ScriptManager* control to it. Within this *ScriptManager,* you should then add a service reference to the Web Service that you just created. You can do this with the *<Services>* tag. Here's an example:

```
<asp:ScriptManager ID="ScriptManager1" runat="server">
  <Services>
    <asp:ServiceReference Path="~/Service.asmx" InlineScript="true" />
  </Services>
</asp:ScriptManager>
```

Next, you'll add Silverlight to the page in the usual manner. But first, here's the XAML that the Silverlight will render. I'm keeping it simple here for the purposes of demonstration:

```
<Canvas xmlns="http://schemas.microsoft.com/client/2007"
        xmlns:x="http://schemas.microsoft.com/winfx/2006/xaml">
  <TextBlock Canvas.Top="0" x:Name="txtShort"></TextBlock>
  <TextBlock Canvas.Top="20" x:Name="txtLong"></TextBlock>
</Canvas>
```

This is then added to a page and instantiated in the usual way. Here's the code that can be added to the *<body>* section of your ASP.NET markup:

```
<div id="silverlightPlugInHost">
  <script type="text/javascript">
    Silverlight.createObjectEx({
      source: 'Scene.xaml',
      parentElement: document.getElementById('silverlightPlugInHost'),
      id: 'silverlightPlugIn',
      properties: {
        width: '100%',
        height: '100%',
        background:'white',
        version: '1.0'
      },
      events: {
        onLoad: handleLoad
      },
```

```
        context: null

    });
</script>
```

Do note a couple of things in this code. First, the source is specified as being *Scene.xaml*, so be sure to call your XAML file by this name. Next, the *handleLoad* event is defined as the event to fire when the Silverlight content is loaded and rendered.

So, let's take a look at this *handleLoad* event:

```
function handleLoad()
{
    Service.getTime(onSuccess, onFailed,"");
}
```

The Web Service was called *Service*, and as such, the JavaScript proxy takes its name. So the JavaScript proxy can be called using the *ClassName.WebMethod* syntax. Because our Web method was called *getTime*, we simply call *Service.getTime*. The JavaScript proxy then uses AJAX to talk to the Web Service, and because AJAX uses a callback mechanism, you specify the callback functions for success and failure (or timeout) conditions. So, in this case, you are specifying that the callbacks for these conditions are *onSuccess* and *onFailed*, respectively. The third parameter is a context parameter which can be blank.

Here are the *onSuccess* and *onFailed* functions:

```
function onSuccess(result)
{
    var sl = document.getElementById("silverlightPlugIn");
    sl.content.findName("txtShort").Text = result.strShortTime;
    sl.content.findName("txtLong").Text = result.strLongTime;
}

function onFailed(result)
{
    alert("Timed out");
}
```

These functions accept the returned value in the *result* parameter. Because we are using JSON, this is a structured class, so the *result.strShortTime* and *result.strLongTime* values will contain the short and long time format strings, respectively. All we have to do in that case is to find the *TextBlocks* using their names and set their values accordingly.

Connectivity and Data in .NET

When using .NET in Silverlight 2, there are two main classes that can be used for connectivity to services: *WebClient* and *WebRequest*. These provide a flexible means to access data, as you will see shortly. In addition, you'll also see how the Windows Communication Foundation classes and ADO.NET Data Services can be consumed using Silverlight.

The *WebClient* Class

The *WebClient* class provides the simplest remote communication class to use in Silverlight. To use it, you need to provide it with the *Uri* of the content that you want to access and then call either the *DownloadStringAsync* or *OpenReadAsync* methods to use it to download data. The former is used to get strings, and the latter is used for all other data. When using these, you'll need a callback function to capture the results. These will be called *DownloadStringCompleted* or *OpenReadCompleted*, respectively.

To try this out, create a new Silverlight application and, as earlier, add a generic handler to the Web application and use it to write back the current server time. To do this, just change the *ProcessRequest* in the code to this:

```
public void ProcessRequest (HttpContext context) {
   context.Response.ContentType = "text/plain";
   context.Response.Write(System.DateTime.Now.ToLongTimeString());
}
```

Now, within your Page.xaml.cs, you can use the *WebClient* class to talk to this service. To use the *WebClient* class, make sure that the *System.Net* classes are referenced by adding this line to the top of your code:

```
using System.Net;
```

Then, to use the *WebClient* class, you'll simply use the following code. Note that when I was coding this application, I was using Cassini, so you'll see that the port *65144* is being used. You may have a different port when you run the application, so be sure to use that port here, or configure Cassini for a static port.

```
public Page()
{
   InitializeComponent();
   WebClient cl = new WebClient();
   Uri uri = new Uri("http://localhost:65144/WebClientTest_Web/Time.ashx");
   cl.DownloadStringCompleted +=
      new DownloadStringCompletedEventHandler(cl_DownloadStringCompleted);
   cl.DownloadStringAsync(uri);
}
```

The *DownloadStringCompleted* event is declared as being handled by the *cl_DownloadStringCompleted* function, so when the data transfer is complete, this function will be called. Let's take a look at it:

```
void cl_DownloadStringCompleted(object sender,
      DownloadStringCompletedEventArgs e)
{
   txtTime.Text = e.Result;
}
```

As you can see, the function receives an arguments object (in the form of a *DownloadString-*

CompletedEventArgs class), which contains a *Result* property, which contains the returned string.

Other useful attributes of *WebClient* are the *IsBusy* property, which will return *true* if you are in the midst of an asynchronous transfer, and the *CancelAsync* method, which you can use to cancel ongoing asynchronous transactions. If this happens, the appropriate completed handler (*DownloadStringCompleted* or *OpenReadCompleted*) has an event argument that has the *Cancelled* property set to *true*.

The *WebRequest* Class

For a little more control, including the facility to use Silverlight as the front end for a standard HTTP forms template (using *HTTP-POST*), you can use the *WebRequest* class. This is really useful from an interoperability perspective because the *HTTP-POST* methodology is commonly used across all server technologies, so you can replace an HTML front end to these with a Silverlight one without having to change your server code.

So, for example, let's put together a server component that receives an HTTP post of three text fields, called *t1*, *t2* and *t3*. First, create a Silverlight application, and add a generic handler to the Web project. Edit the handler's *ProcessRequest* method to accept a form submission. Here's how to do it to accept three strings from an *HTTP-POST* request:

```
public void ProcessRequest (HttpContext context) {
  string str1 = "";
  string str2 = "";
  string str3 = "";
  if (context.Request.HttpMethod == "POST")
  {
    str1 = context.Request.Form["t1"];
    str2 = context.Request.Form["t2"];
    str3 = context.Request.Form["t3"];
  }
  context.Response.ContentType = "text/plain";
  context.Response.Write("OK");
}
```

Typically, you would use an HTML form with three *TextField* controls named *t1*, *t2*, and *t3* and a Submit button to pass this data. It is simple to do the same thing in Silverlight. Here's the XAML for a simple data entry form:

```
<UserControl x:Class="WebRequestTest.Page"
  xmlns="http://schemas.microsoft.com/client/2007"
  xmlns:x="http://schemas.microsoft.com/winfx/2006/xaml"
  Width="400" Height="300">
  <Grid x:Name="LayoutRoot" Background="White">
    <Grid.ColumnDefinitions>
      <ColumnDefinition Width="0.265*"/>
      <ColumnDefinition Width="0.735*"/>
    </Grid.ColumnDefinitions>
```

```
    <Grid.RowDefinitions>
      <RowDefinition Height="0.037*"/>
      <RowDefinition Height="0.1*"/>
      <RowDefinition Height="0.05*"/>
      <RowDefinition Height="0.106*"/>
      <RowDefinition Height="0.054*"/>
      <RowDefinition Height="0.09*"/>
      <RowDefinition Height="0.563*"/>
    </Grid.RowDefinitions>
    <WatermarkedTextBox Margin="0,0,25,0" Grid.Column="1"
        Grid.Row="1" x:Name="t1"
        Watermark="Enter Field 1 Text Here"/>
    <WatermarkedTextBox Margin="0,0,25,0" Grid.Column="1"
        Grid.Row="3" x:Name="t2"
        Watermark="Enter Field 2 Text Here"/>
    <WatermarkedTextBox Margin="0,0,25,0" Grid.Column="1"
        Grid.Row="5" x:Name="t3"
        Watermark="Enter Field 3 Text Here"/>
<TextBlock Margin="8,0,0,0" Grid.Row="1"
    Text="Field 1" TextWrapping="Wrap"/>
<TextBlock Margin="8,0,8,0" Grid.Row="3"
    Text="Field 2" TextWrapping="Wrap"/>
<TextBlock Margin="8,0,8,0" Grid.Row="5"
    Text="Field 3" TextWrapping="Wrap"/>
    <Button Height="36" HorizontalAlignment="Left"
        Margin="0,26.9,0,0" VerticalAlignment="Top"
        Width="77" Grid.Column="1" Grid.Row="6"
        Content="Submit" x:Name="b" Click="b_Click"  />
  </Grid>
</UserControl>
```

You can see how this form will appear in Figure 10-14.

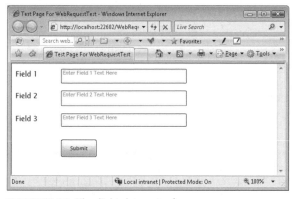

FIGURE 10-14 Silverlight data entry form.

The user types text in the three fields and then presses the Submit button. This fires the
b_Click event. You can see the code here:

```
private void b_Click(object sender, RoutedEventArgs e)
{
  Uri uri = new Uri(
    "http://localhost:22602/WebRequestTest_Web/SubmitForm.ashx");
  WebRequest rq = WebRequest.Create(uri);
  rq.Method = "POST";
  rq.ContentType = "application/x-www-form-urlencoded";
  rq.BeginGetRequestStream(new AsyncCallback(RequestReady), rq);
  rq.BeginGetResponse(new AsyncCallback(ResponseReady), rq);
}
```

When using the *WebResponse* class, you need to first set up the URI that you are going to be calling. This is done using a *Uri* object that you point at the site containing the forms processor. You then pass this URI to the *Create* method of the *WebRequest* in order to set up the communication. You'll also specify the *Method* that you need to use. This method is an *HTTP-Verb* such as *POST* or *GET*. In this case, you're sending form data, so you'll need to use *POST*.

The next thing necessary is to set the content type. Again, because you are using a form, you use the appropriate type, which is *application/x-www-form-urlencoded*. All of this information is based on Web standards, so check any good Web reference book and you'll see the various options.

Finally, you need to set up the request stream. It is a stream because you are going to be writing data to the request. This requires you to specify an asynchronous callback that will fire when the *Request* is ready to go, as well as a reference to the request object itself. Additionally, you'll need to catch the response from the form, so you call the *BeginGetResponse* to start setting up the stream and specify a callback that will be fired when the response stream is ready.

On the request callback (fired when the request stream is ready to go), you can then write to the stream using a *StreamWriter* object. In this case, you are writing multiple parameters, and the HTTP protocol requires these to be separated with & characters, like this: *t1=value1&t2=value2&t3=value3*.

So, all we have to do now is write the parameter name followed by the *Text* property of the entry fields:

```
void RequestReady(IAsyncResult aR){
  WebRequest rq = aR.AsyncState as WebRequest;
  Stream rqStream = rq.EndGetRequestStream(aR);
  StreamWriter w = new StreamWriter(rqStream);
  w.Write("t1=" + t1.Text + "&");
  w.Write("t2=" + t2.Text + "&");
  w.Write("t3=" + t3.Text );
  w.Flush();
}
```

As you saw earlier in the generic handler, after the server catches the data, it writes back OK as a status report. When the response has finished writing, the *ResponseReady* callback will fire.

```
void ResponseReady(IAsyncResult aR)
{
  WebRequest rq = aR.AsyncState as WebRequest;
  using(WebResponse rs = rq.EndGetResponse(aR))
  using (Stream rpStream = rs.GetResponseStream())
  {
    StreamReader rdr = new StreamReader(rpStream);
    string postStatus = rdr.ReadToEnd();
  }
}
```

This simply pulls the response stream from the asynchronous result and reads the stream to its end. In this case, it's a simple status, but this could also be used to pull responses from the server for each of the individual fields.

Using this methodology, you can see it's pretty easy and straightforward to create Silverlight applications that front HTTP forms!

Using *SyndicatedFeed* to Access RSS and ATOM

Two of the more popular types of data available on the Internet are RSS and ATOM feeds, typically used in blogs or news sites. Silverlight offers a class called *SyndicatedFeed* that allows you to access these easily.

SyndicatedFeed is very straightforward to use. Let's take a look at it by example. But before continuing, let's take a moment to talk about cross-domain access in Silverlight. When accessing content from sites other than the one that serves the Silverlight content, the .NET classes look for a file called Crossdomain.xml on the server. If they find it, they parse the cross-domain rules to see if they are allowed to access the content. If they are not, they will throw an error, so, before using *SyndicatedFeed* to access the data, be aware of this, or you might encounter some problems. There is a lot of information on the Web about Crossdomain.xml because it is a de facto, standard, cross-technology way of providing cross-domain access.

For this example, however, we will simply use a static XML document stored on the server as *Doc.rss*.

Before writing any code, make sure that you have the correct references to be able to use *SyndicatedFeed*, streaming, and XML.

```
using System.Net;
using System.Xml;
using System.IO;
using System.ServiceModel.Syndication;
```

You will probably have to add a reference to *System.ServiceModel.Syndication* to be able to create this reference.

The next thing to do—before writing any code—is to put together a presentation for the data in XAML.

```
<UserControl x:Class="RSSClient.Page"
    xmlns="http://schemas.microsoft.com/client/2007"
    xmlns:x="http://schemas.microsoft.com/winfx/2006/xaml"
    Width="400" Height="300">
<Canvas x:Name="LayoutRoot" Width="400"
  Height="300" Background="White">
        <ItemsControl x:Name="_rssTitles">
            <ItemsControl.ItemTemplate>
                <DataTemplate>
                    <StackPanel Orientation="Vertical">
                        <TextBlock FontWeight="Bold"
                          Text="{Binding Title.Text}" />
                    </StackPanel>
                </DataTemplate>
            </ItemsControl.ItemTemplate>
        </ItemsControl>
    </Canvas>
</UserControl>
```

This will use an *ItemsControl* object in XAML which, when used in conjunction with an *Item-Template*, will provide a basic repeater function. This is bound to data using a *DataTemplate* specifying that a *TextBlock* control is bound to data within the RSS feed based on its *Title*.

Going back to our C# code, we can now create a *WebClient* object to read the RSS document, and when it has downloaded, we can read it with a *SyndicatedFeed* control. Here's the code to create the *WebClient* that accesses the RSS document:

```
public Page()
{
  InitializeComponent();
  WebClient client = new WebClient();
  Uri uri = new Uri("doc.rss",UriKind.Relative);
  client.OpenReadCompleted +=
    new OpenReadCompletedEventHandler(client_OpenReadCompleted);
  client.OpenReadAsync(uri);
}
```

This sets up a callback function (*client_OpenReadCompleted*) that fires when the download is complete. Here's the code for this callback:

```
void client_OpenReadCompleted(object sender,
    OpenReadCompletedEventArgs e)
{
  XmlReader r = XmlReader.Create(e.Result);
  SyndicationFeed feed = SyndicationFeed.Load(r);
  _rssTitles.ItemsSource = feed.Items;
}
```

This creates an *XmlReader* that reads the result of the callback and then passes it to the *SyndicationFeed*. This then contains the appropriate collections for each item within the *SyndicationFeed*, including the *Items* collection. This collection contains the *Title* (among other things) for the RSS item, so by setting the *ItemsSource* property of the *_rssTitles ItemsControl*, we bind the data, and the titles will be rendered by Silverlight. You can see the results in Figure 10-15.

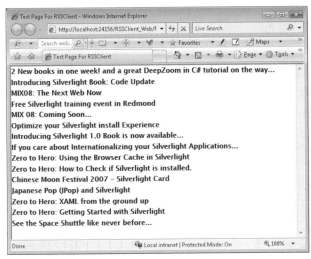

FIGURE 10-15 Viewing RSS data using *SyndicationFeed* and data binding.

Going beyond simple feeds such as RSS and ATOM, Silverlight provides the facility to consume more advanced services such as ASMX and WCF Web Services. You'll explore these in the next section.

Silverlight and WCF

The *System.ServiceModel* namespace contains classes that Silverlight can use to consume Web Services from different sources. Now, let's step through building a simple service in WCF and how to consume it in Silverlight.

Create a new Silverlight application, and in the Web project, add a new class. Call it *Person*, and you'll have a *Person.cs* class created for you. This will be used to pass data between the service and the client. To do so, you need to attribute the class as a *DataContract* between WCF and Silverlight, and make each element within the class that you want to be exposed to Silverlight a *DataMember*.

Note that you will need to include *System.Runtime.Serialization*. Here's the code:

```
[DataContract]
public class Person
{
    public Person(string strName, string strAge)
```

```
        {
            Name = strName;
            Age = strAge;
        }
        [DataMember]
        public string Name { get; set; }
        [DataMember]
        public string Age { get; set; }
    }
```

This also includes a constructor that is used to initialize the name and age properties.

Next, you should add a WCF Service template to your project. Naming it *PersonService* will create the PersonService.cs and IPersonService.cs files for you. The IPersonService.cs file will create the interface that defines the service contract. You will need to modify this to define a service method that returns a list of people. This is straightforward—simply attribute the interface as a *ServiceContract* and the method that is available to service callers as an *Operation-Contract*.

```
[ServiceContract]
public interface IPersonService
{
    [OperationContract]
    Person[] getPeople();
}
```

The service implementation is in the *PersonService.cs* class. This should implement *at least* the methods that you defined using *OperationContract*. Here's an example:

```
public class PersonService : IPersonService
{
    public Person[] getPeople()
    {
        Person[] people = {
            new Person("Derek Snyder","32"),
            new Person("Yoshi Latimer","19"),
            new Person("Mark  Steel","31")

                    };
        return people;
    }
}
```

This creates an array of *Person* objects called *people* and returns it to the caller. This will provide a *Collection* of items to which Silverlight can bind. Before continuing, you'll need to ensure that WCF has been configured properly for basic HTTP binding, which the Silverlight client will use. You do this within the Web.config file. Within the *<serviceModel>* node, find the following code and make sure that the binding is set to *basicHttpBinding*, as shown:

```
<service behaviorConfiguration="PersonServiceBehavior"
        name="PersonService">
<endpoint address=""
          binding="basicHttpBinding"
          contract="IPersonService">
   <identity>
     <dns value="localhost"/>
   </identity>
  </endpoint>
  <endpoint address="mex" binding="mexHttpBinding" contract="IMetadataExchange"/>
</service>
```

Test the Service to see if it works by right-clicking the PersonService.svc file and then selecting View In Browser from the shortcut menu. If all goes well, you'll see something like the output shown in Figure 10-16 on your screen.

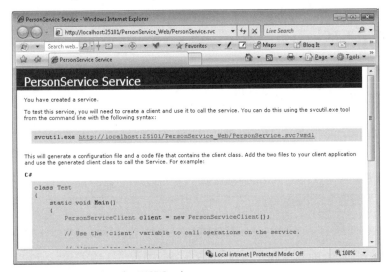

FIGURE 10-16 Running the WCF Service.

If your service is working properly, you can now add a reference to it from within the Silverlight project. Again, this is straightforward—right-click the *References* node in Solution Explorer, and select Add Service Reference from the shortcut menu. The Add Service Reference dialog box will open, as shown in Figure 10-17. Enter the address of the service, and click the Go button. This will create a service proxy.

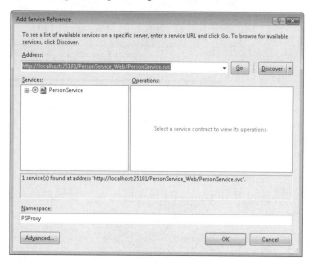

FIGURE 10-17 Adding a service reference.

The proxy will be created in the namespace specified in the dialog box. In this case, the name *PSProxy* is being used, which you'll see in the code in a moment.

First, you'll need some XAML to define the presentation tier. This is data-bound XAML that you'll bind to the results of the call to the service:

```
<ItemsControl x:Name="_itemTitles">
  <ItemsControl.ItemTemplate>
    <DataTemplate>
      <StackPanel Orientation="Vertical">
        <StackPanel Orientation="Horizontal">
          <TextBlock FontWeight="Bold" Text="{Binding Name}" />
          <TextBlock Text=" : "></TextBlock>
          <TextBlock FontWeight="Bold" Text="{Binding Age}" />
        </StackPanel>
      </StackPanel>
    </DataTemplate>
  </ItemsControl.ItemTemplate>
</ItemsControl>
```

As you can see, there are two *TextBlocks*, bound to the values of *Name* and *Age*. Let's take a look at the service call and how this is used to get the data into this Silverlight content:

```
Binding binding = new BasicHttpBinding();
EndpointAddress endPoint = new EndpointAddress
    ("http://localhost:25101/PersonService_Web/PersonService.svc");

PSProxy.PersonServiceClient client = new
    PSProxy.PersonServiceClient(binding, endPoint);

client.getPeopleCompleted += new
  EventHandler<PersonService.PSProxy.getPeopleCompletedEventArgs>
```

```
(client_getPeopleCompleted);

client.getPeopleAsync();
```

This creates a new *BasicHttpBinding* class called *binding* (which matches what you set up in Web.config for the service) and an *EndpointAddress* that points at the service itself. It then creates a new instance of a service client (which was generated for you when you created the service reference) and sets up its callback function. Finally, it calls the *getPeopleAsync* function, which calls the service method asynchronously. When the service method finishes, the callback function will run.

The callback will get arguments containing the array of *Person* objects that the service method generated. This is a collection that can be bindable to the *ItemsControl* that you saw earlier. Here's the code:

```
void client_getPeopleCompleted(object sender,
    PersonService.PSProxy.getPeopleCompletedEventArgs e)
{
  _itemTitles.ItemsSource = e.Result;
}
```

You can see the results of this in Figure 10-18.

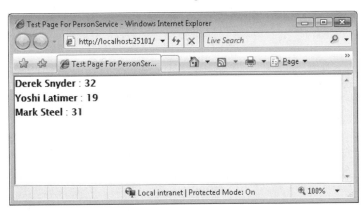

FIGURE 10-18 Silverlight WCF client.

Although these samples are trivial, I hope they help illustrate the different scenarios that are available for you to build connected applications and that they will provide a basis for the real-world code that you will build in Silverlight!

Summary

In this chapter, you looked at various strategies for building connected applications with Silverlight. You saw how XAML could be used as a communications tool from servers built on PHP and Java and how Silverlight could be used to communicate with these servers. You then looked at AJAX and discovered how AJAX and JavaScript techniques could be used to consume data from server applications and how the open nature of the Silverlight render tree allows you to pass this data to the Silverlight control for it to render. Finally, you looked at some of the new classes available in Silverlight 2 for networking and connectivity. You saw the *WebClient* and *WebRequest* classes, and you also learned how to create an application to consume WCF-based services through a proxy.

In the next chapter, you'll learn about some of the consumer-oriented technology that is available to you in Silverlight 2, including controls for media content, a control that allows pen-based computers to interact with your application, and a new control that provides deep zooming functionality for your Silverlight applications.

Chapter 11
Media, Ink, and Deep Zoom

You were introduced to general controls for building rich interactive Internet applications in previous chapters. In this chapter, you'll take a look at three controls that provide special functionality beyond the basics. First, you'll learn in some detail about the *MediaElement* control, which provides an API that gives you control over audio and video in your application, allowing you to build great media applications. Then, you'll look at the *InkPresenter* control, which allows pen-based computers to interact with your application so that handwritten or drawn content can be added using Ink annotation. Finally, you'll find out more about a new control in Silverlight 2, the *MultiScaleImage* control, which can give a new dimension to your applications, one with deep-zooming capability.

The *MediaElement* Control

One of the most important uses for Silverlight on the Web is to enable cross-platform, next-generation media. To accomplish this, Silverlight supports the *MediaElement* control. In this section, we'll look at the *MediaElement* in detail, and you will have a chance to work through a use case to build a simple media player that allows for progressive download and playback of videos. In addition to this, you'll learn how to paint surfaces with the video brush, which allows you to add interesting graphical effects. The *MediaElement* control supports the following formats:

Video

- WMV1: Windows Media Video 7
- WMV2: Windows Media Video 8
- WMV3: Windows Media Video 9
- WMVA: Windows Media Video Advanced Profile, non–VC-1
- WMVC1: Windows Media Video Advanced Profile, VC-1

Audio

- WMA7: Windows Media Audio 7
- WMA8: Windows Media Audio 8
- WMA9: Windows Media Audio 9
- MP3: ISO/MPEG Layer 3
- Mono or stereo

- Sampling frequencies from 8 to 48 KHz

- Bit rates from 8 to 320 KBps

- Variable bit rate

In addition to these formats, the *MediaElement* control also supports ASX playlists, as well as the http, https, and mms protocols.

When it comes to streaming video and/or audio, *MediaElement* supports live and on-demand streaming from a Windows Media Server. If the URI specifies the mms protocol, streaming is enabled; otherwise, the file will be downloaded and played back with progressive download, which involves downloading enough of the file to fill a playback buffer, at which point the buffered video is played back while the rest of the file is being downloaded.

If the protocol specifies the http or https protocols, then the reverse happens. *MediaElement* tries to progressively download first, and if this fails, the *MediaElement* control will attempt to stream the file.

Using the *MediaElement* Control

The *MediaElement* control is easy to get up and running in a basic setting, but it has many advanced features that can provide you with some pretty compelling scenarios when you have learned how to use them. But, let's walk before we try to run and first step through how to do the most common tasks with the *MediaElement*.

Simple Video Playback with the *MediaElement* Control

To get started with the *MediaElement* control, add it to your page and set its *Source* attribute to the URL of the video that you want to play back. Following is an example:

```
<Canvas
  xmlns="http://schemas.microsoft.com/client/2007"
  xmlns:x="http://schemas.microsoft.com/winfx/2006/xaml"
  Background="White"
  >
  <MediaElement Source="balls.wmv"/>
</Canvas>
```

This will load and play back the media automatically. The *size* of the media is determined by the following rules:

- If the *MediaElement Height* and *Width* properties are specified, then the *MediaElement* control will use them.

- If one of them is used, the *MediaElement* control will stretch the media to maintain the aspect ratio of the video.

- If neither *Height* nor *Width* is set, the *MediaElement* control will play back the video at its default size. If this is bigger than the Silverlight control's allotted viewing area, then the *MediaElement* control will crop the video to fit the allotted viewing area.

Let's look at an example. The balls.wmv video used in this chapter (and available to download from the companion Web site) is a 480 × 360 video. If you instruct the *MediaElement* to show this video and do not set the *Height* and *Width* of the *MediaElement*, then the video will play back at 480 × 360. If your Silverlight component is 200 × 200, then you will see the pixels in the upper-left 200 pixels of the video. You can see the portion of the video cropped in this way in Figure 11-1.

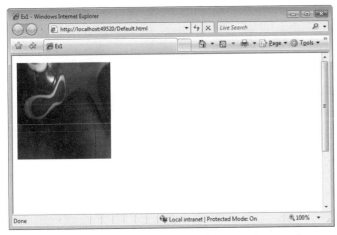

FIGURE 11-1 Video cropped to the size of the Silverlight control.

Controlling the Size of the *MediaElement* Control

As you saw in the previous section, the size of the *MediaElement* is important when determining how the video plays back. If the control does not have its size defined and the video resolution is larger than the dimensions of the Silverlight control, it will be cropped.

To control the height and width of the *MediaElement* itself, you can use its *Height* and *Width* properties. When the control is rendered, the media will be stretched (or shrunk) to fit the media control. If the defined size of the media control is larger than the Silverlight control, then the media will be cropped to the size of the Silverlight control.

Following is an example of the *MediaElement* control set to 200 × 200, and Figure 11-2 shows how the video is rendered as a result:

```
<MediaElement Source="balls.wmv" Height="200" Width="200" />
```

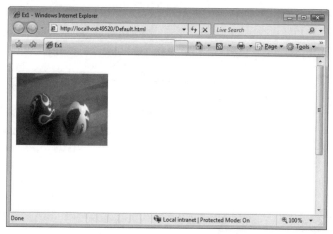

FIGURE 11-2 Video display after sizing the *MediaElement*.

Controlling How the Media Is Stretched

In the preceding example, the video has been stretched to fit the 200 × 200 *MediaElement*. As you can see in Figure 11-2, the video (which, as you recall, has a 480 × 360 pixel native resolution) is stretched to fit the dimensions while maintaining its aspect ratio. This can yield black bars at the top and bottom of the video, giving the video a "letterbox" effect. You can override this behavior using the *Stretch* property of the *MediaElement*. This property can take four different values:

- **None**   No stretching takes place. If the *MediaElement* is larger than the video, the video will be centered within it. If it is smaller, the center portion of the video will be shown. For example, the video is 480 × 360. If the *MediaElement* is 200 × 200 and *Stretch* is set to *None*, the center 200 × 200 area of the video will be displayed, as shown in Figure 11-3.

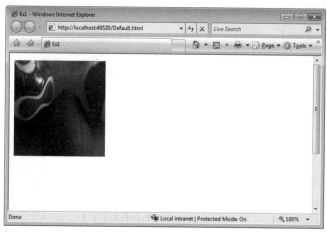

FIGURE 11-3 Setting the *Stretch* property to *None*.

- **Uniform** This is the default stretching mode, and it maintains the video's aspect ratio and adds bars at the top, bottom, or sides to maintain it.

- **UniformToFill** This stretches the video, maintaining the aspect ratio but cropping the video to fit the window. So, for example, if the video is wider than it is high (e.g., 480 × 360) and is stretched to accommodate a 200 × 200 window, the sides of the video will be cropped to fit the allotted viewing window (a smaller square, in this case). You can see how this affects the video display in Figure 11-4. If you compare the image in Figure 11-4 to the same frame of video shown in Figure 11-2, you can see how it is cropped on both sides.

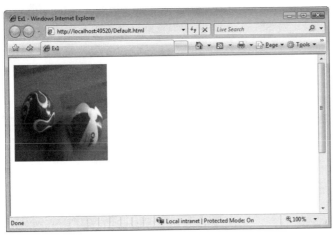

FIGURE 11-4 Using *UniformToFill* stretch mode.

- **Fill** This stretch mode fills the *MediaElement* with the video, distorting the aspect ratio if necessary. Figure 11-5 shows the video when *Stretch* is set to *Fill*. As you can see in this case, the video has been stretched vertically to fill the paint area.

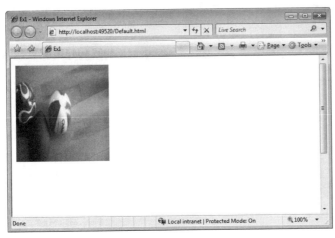

FIGURE 11-5 Using *Stretch* set to *Fill*.

Controlling Video Opacity

You can control the opacity of the *MediaElement* by using the *Opacity* property. This contains a normalized value, with 0 equal to totally invisible, 1 equal to completely visible, and everything in between representing different levels of opacity. The video will be rendered with this opacity, and items behind the media element will become visible.

Following is an example of some XAML with a red rectangle and a *MediaElement*. The *MediaElement* is set to 0.5 opacity, which will make the video appear semitransparent. Because the *MediaElement* is rendered second, it is placed higher in the Z-order, and thus it is rendered on top of the rectangle. Figure 11-6 shows the result of this example on the video display.

```
<Rectangle Fill="Red" Height="100" Width="200" />
<MediaElement Source="balls.wmv" Height="200"
        Width="200" Stretch="Fill" Opacity="0.5" />
```

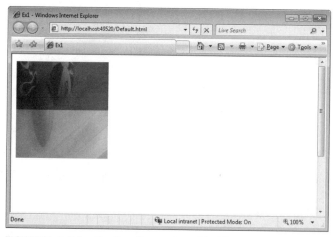

FIGURE 11-6 Using the *Opacity* property with video.

Using Transformations with the *MediaElement* Control

Chapter 5, "XAML Transformation and Animation," described transformations in detail, but one of the nice things about the *MediaElement* is that you can use it to perform transformations, and the video that you are rendering will also be transformed. This can lead to some very nice effects. For example, the following is a *MediaElement* with a skew transform applied:

```
<MediaElement Source="balls.wmv" Height="200" Width="200" Stretch="Fill" >
    <MediaElement.RenderTransform>
        <SkewTransform AngleX="45"/>
    </MediaElement.RenderTransform>
</MediaElement>
```

You can see how this appears in Figure 11-7.

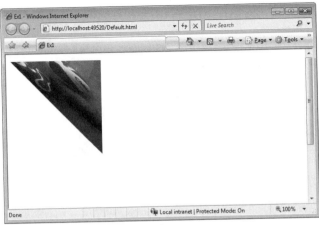

FIGURE 11-7 Skewing video with *SkewTransform*.

Writing Content on Video

Silverlight allows you to place content, including text and graphics, on top of video with ease. You can either place it using *ZOrder* properties on user interface (UI) elements (see Chapter 1, "Introducing Silverlight 2"), or you can simply place UI elements in the same space as the media element and declare them later in the XAML. Following is an example of a *MediaElement* that has a *Canvas* containing a rectangle and text block that overlays the video:

```
<MediaElement Source="balls.wmv" Height="200" Width="200" Stretch="Fill" />
<Canvas Canvas.Top="140" Canvas.Left="20">
    <Rectangle Fill="Red" Height="40" Width="160" />
    <TextBlock>Subtitle on Video</TextBlock>
</Canvas>
```

Figure 11-8 shows how this will be rendered.

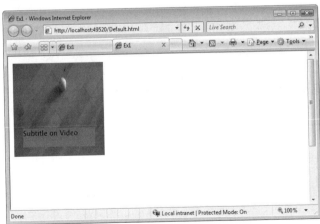

FIGURE 11-8 Rendering content on top of video.

Clipping Media with Geometries

Chapter 4, "XAML Basics," introduced you to clipping and geometries. These features can also be applied to a *MediaElement*, where you can define a geometry using shapes or paths and set this to be the clipping geometry for the *MediaElement* you're working with. For example, the following XAML defines an ellipse as the clip region for our *MediaElement*:

```
<MediaElement Source="balls.wmv" Height="200" Width="200" Stretch="Fill" >
    <MediaElement.Clip>
        <EllipseGeometry RadiusX="100" RadiusY="75" Center="100,75"/>
    </MediaElement.Clip>
</MediaElement>
```

You can see the results of this in Figure 11-9.

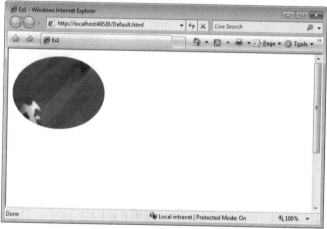

FIGURE 11-9 Clipping media with geometries.

Determining Automatic Playback Behavior

The default behavior for the *MediaElement* after its source is set is to have the media play back automatically. This can be controlled using the *AutoPlay* property. This defaults to *true*, but you can override this by setting it to *false*. You can play back the media later using its *Play* method. This and the other methods and events that you can use in programming the media element are shown in the next section.

Controlling Audio

You can use the *MediaElement* control's *IsMuted* property to set the audio to accompany the playback or not. This property is a Boolean value, and if you set it to *true*, no audio will be heard.

Additionally, you can control the volume of the audio using the *Volume* property. This is a normalized value with 0 equal to no audio, 1 equal to full volume, and values in between representing the relative volume. So, for example, 0.43 would set the volume to play at 43 percent of its full capacity.

Finally, the balance of the audio can be controlled with the *Balance* property. This is set with a value between –1 and +1. A value of –1 will cause the audio to be panned all the way to the left—that is, the left speaker will play the audio at 100 percent volume, and the right speaker will play no audio, or 0 percent volume. A value of +1 will cause just the opposite to happen—the audio will be panned all the way to the right, with the right speaker playing the audio at 100 percent volume. A value of 0 causes the volume to be distributed evenly between the two speakers.

As an example, if the *Balance* property is set to a value of 0.8, then the right speaker will play the audio at 80 percent volume and the left speaker will play it at 20 percent volume. If the value –0.8 is used, the left speaker will play the audio at 80 percent volume and the right speaker will play the audio at 20 percent volume.

Following is some XAML specifying that the audio is not muted, that the master volume is at 50 percent, and that the audio is balanced toward the right speaker:

```
<MediaElement x:Name="vid" Source="balls.wmv" Height="200" Width="200"
        Stretch="Fill" IsMuted="False" Volume="0.5" Balance="0.8" />
```

Programming the *MediaElement*

The *MediaElement* offers a rich programming model that allows you to control playback with play, stop, and pause methods. It also allows you to respond to the video, capturing the buffering and download progress as well as responding to markers placed within the video. You also can specify events to trap, such as mouse behavior.

Providing Basic Video Controls

The basic video control methods available are *Play*, *Stop*, and *Pause*. When you set the *Auto-Play* property of the *MediaElement* to *false*, then these controls are necessary to start playing the video. Even if *AutoPlay* is set to *true* and the video starts playing, then you can stop or pause it with these methods. Following is an example of a XAML containing a media element and three simple video playback controls, implemented as *TextBlock* elements:

```
<MediaElement x:Name="vid" Source="balls.wmv" Height="200" Width="200" Stretch="Fill" />
<Canvas Canvas.Top="160">
    <Rectangle Fill="Black" Width="200" Height="24" Opacity="0.7"/>
    <TextBlock Foreground="White" Canvas.Left="20">Play</TextBlock>
    <TextBlock Foreground="White" Canvas.Left="80">Stop</TextBlock>
    <TextBlock Foreground="White" Canvas.Left="140">Pause</TextBlock>
</Canvas>
```

Figure 11-10 shows how the controls will appear on the video.

FIGURE 11-10 Adding controls to the video.

To create the controls, you specify the name of the code function that should run in response to a mouse event using an attribute of the video control element itself. You'll find much more detail about handling Silverlight events with JavaScript in Chapter 6, "The Silverlight Browser Control." However, in this case, we simply want the video to start, stop, or pause when the user clicks on the appropriate text block. This is achieved by handling the *MouseLeftButtonDown* event, exhibited by the text block, that is hooked to functions that will play, pause, or stop the media element.

When programming in JavaScript, these functions need to be accessible from the page hosting the Silverlight control. So, they can either be implemented using JavaScript elements on the page or within a .js file that is included on the page using the JavaScript element with its *Src* property set accordingly.

If you're using Expression Blend to put together your XAML content, it provides a pseudo code-behind file for Page.xaml called Page.xaml.js. This is an ideal location to implement your JavaScript functionality.

Following is the XAML that defines the same UI that was created in the previous example, but with event handler declarations added:

```
<MediaElement x:Name="vid" Source="balls.wmv"
              Height="200" Width="200" Stretch="Fill" />
<Canvas Canvas.Top="160">
   <Rectangle Fill="Black" Width="200" Height="24" Opacity="0.7"/>
   <TextBlock MouseLeftButtonDown="doPlay"
           Foreground="White"
           Canvas.Left="20">Play</TextBlock>
   <TextBlock MouseLeftButtonDown="doStop"
           Foreground="White"
           Canvas.Left="80">Stop</TextBlock>
   <TextBlock MouseLeftButtonDown="doPause"
```

```
                Foreground="White"
                Canvas.Left="140">Pause</TextBlock>
</Canvas>
```

Now you can write JavaScript to play, stop, and pause the video. Here's the code:

```
function doPlay(sender, args)
{
  var meVid = sender.findName("vid");
  meVid.Play();
}

function doStop(sender, args)
{
  var meVid = sender.findName("vid");
  meVid.Stop();
}

function doPause(sender, args)
{
  var meVid = sender.findName("vid");
  meVid.Pause();
}
```

When you define a JavaScript function as an event handler, it should take two parameters. The first, *sender*, is an object that represents the object that raised the event. The second, *args*, contains arguments that are included as part of the event.

Now, within this JavaScript function, you'll have to get a reference to the *MediaElement* object that you are controlling. You do this using the *findName* method on the sender. Although the sender is the text block that the user clicked, executing its *findName* method will still search through the entire XAML document until it finds an element called *vid* (which we established using the *x:Name* attribute as applied to our *MediaElement* object). If you look back to the XAML, you'll see that the *MediaElement* had an *x:Name* value of *vid*, so this should succeed. You'll be given a reference to the corresponding *MediaElement* object in a JavaScript variable called *meVid*. You can now simply invoke the *Play*, *Stop*, or *Pause* methods on this to control the video.

When using .NET, the process is even simpler—you don't need to use *findName* to access the element, and it's already named *vid*, so your code will look like this:

```
private void doPlay(object sender, MouseButtonEventArgs e)
{
  vid.Play();
}
private void doPause(object sender, MouseButtonEventArgs e)
{
  vid.Pause();
}
```

```
private void doStop(object sender, MouseButtonEventArgs e)
{
    vid.Stop();
}
```

Managing Buffering and Download

When using progressive video download, the media infrastructure determines how much vid-eo it needs to cache before it can start playing back the video. So, depending on the band-width required to serve the video and the bandwidth available, it creates a buffer to hold enough video so that it can start playing back the video while it is downloading video to the buffer in the background.

When the buffer is 100 percent full, the video will begin playing back. Video may pause mo-mentarily as network conditions change and the buffer is refilled. Silverlight allows you to monitor this behavior with the *BufferingProgressChanged* event and the *BufferingProgress* property. You can use this to provide status to your users as to the current buffering status or to run logic to improve your user experience (UX) as a result of buffering conditions. For ex-ample, you may have a poor connection, and buffering may never improve to above 50 per-cent. You can trap this value and provide the appropriate feedback to your client.

To manage buffering, hook an event handler to your *MediaElement* that defines a function to handle the *BufferingProgressChanged* event like this:

```
<MediaElement x:Name="vid" Source="balls.wmv" Height="200" Width="200"
        Stretch="Fill" BufferingProgressChanged="doBuff"/>
<TextBlock x:Name="txtBuff"></TextBlock>
```

This specifies that a function called *doBuff* will run whenever the buffering progress changes. This event goes hand in hand with the *BufferingProgress* property. This property contains a value from 0 to 1, where 0 is an empty buffer and 1 is a full buffer. The event will fire when the buffer changes by 5 percent (i.e., 0.05) or more and when it is full.

Following is code that you can use to handle in response to this event firing that provides feedback on the current state of the buffer to your users.

First, here's the JavaScript version:

```
function doBuff(sender, args)
{
    var theText = sender.findName("txtBuff");
    var meVid = sender.findName("vid");
    var prog = meVid.BufferingProgress * 100;
    prog = "Buffering % " + prog;
    theText.Text = prog;
}
```

And here's how you would do it if you were using .NET code-behind (with C#):

```
private void doBuff(object sender, RoutedEventArgs e)
{
  double prog = vid.BufferingProgress * 100;
  txtBuff.Text = "Buffering % " + prog;
}
```

You can override the automatic buffer by setting a specific buffer time. So, if you want to control the video-buffering process so that you'll always have a 10-second buffer of video and thereby reduce your risk of paused video while buffers resynchronize in bad network conditions, you can set the *BufferingTime* property. You set this using a time span. To apply a 10-second buffer, for example, you specify the *BufferingTime* as 0:0:10, as shown in the following example:

```
<MediaElement x:Name="vid" Source="balls.wmv"
     Height="200" Width="200" Stretch="Fill"
     BufferingProgressChanged="doBuff"
     BufferingTime="0:0:10"/>
<TextBlock x:Name="txtDown"></TextBlock>
```

When progressive download isn't available or supported, the entire video file needs to be downloaded before it can be played back. In this case, the *DownloadProgressChanged* event and *DownloadProgress* property can be used to provide the status of the download. You use these in the same manner as the buffering functions. Following is XAML that defines a *DownloadProgressChanged* event:

```
<MediaElement x:Name="vid" Source="balls.wmv"
     Height="200" Width="200" Stretch="Fill"
     BufferingProgressChanged="doBuff"
     BufferingTime="0:0:10"
     DownloadProgressChanged="doDown"/>
<TextBlock x:Name="txtDown"></TextBlock>
```

And following is the code for the *doDown* function that defines the event handler—again, first take a look at the JavaScript version:

```
function doDown(sender, args)
{
   var theText = sender.findName("txtDown");
   var meVid = sender.findName("vid");
   var prog = meVid.DownloadProgress * 100;
   prog = "Downloading % " + prog;
   theText.Text = prog;
}
```

And here is the .NET version:

```
private void doDown(object sender, RoutedEventArgs e)
{
  double prog = vid.DownloadProgress * 100;
  txtBuff.Text = "Downloading % " + prog;

}
```

Managing Current Video State

Silverlight presents a *CurrentState* property and an associated *CurrentStateChanged* event that can be used to respond to changes in state of the media.

The valid states for the *CurrentState* property are as follow:

- **Buffering**   The buffer is less than 100 percent full, so the media is in a paused state while the buffer fills up.

- **Closed**   The media has been closed.

- **Error**   There is a problem downloading, buffering, or playing back the media.

- **Opening**   The media has been found, and buffering or downloading is about to begin.

- **Paused**   The media has been paused.

- **Playing**   The media is being played back.

- **Stopped**   The media has been stopped.

Here's how you specify the *MediaElement*'s *CurrentStateChanged* event in XAML:

```
<MediaElement x:Name="vid" Source="balls.wmv" Height="200" Width="200"
    Stretch="Fill" CurrentStateChanged="doState" BufferingTime="0:0:10" />
```

This specifies a *doState* function to call in response to the changing current state. Following is a sample JavaScript function that runs as a result of this, using the *CurrentState* property of the *MediaElement* in an alert string:

```
function doState(sender, args)
{
   var meVid = sender.findName("vid");
   alert(meVid.CurrentState);
}
```

If you want to do this in C#, there is no alert box, so you could display the content of the *CurrentState* property in the *TextBlock* like this:

```
private void doState(object sender, RoutedEventArgs e)
{
  txtBuff.Text = vid.CurrentState;
}
```

Managing Playback Position

You can use the *NaturalDuration* and *Position* properties of the media element to control its current playback position status. After the media's *CurrentState* property is set to *Opened*, then the *NaturalDuration* property will be set. This will report the length of the video in seconds using the *NaturalDuration.Seconds* property. You can then use code to convert this to hours, minutes, and seconds.

In this example, the *MediaElement* has its *CurrentStateChanged* event wired up to the *doState* function (from the previous example). However, the function now captures the *NaturalDuration* property. The JavaScript version uses the *convertDT* JavaScript helper function to format this as a string. Following is the JavaScript code:

```
function doState(sender, args)
{
    var meVid = sender.findName("vid");
    var txtStat = sender.findName("txtStat");
    var datetime = new Date(0, 0, 0, 0, 0, meVid.naturalDuration.Seconds)
    durationString = convertDT(datetime);
    txtStat.Text = durationString.toString();
}

function convertDT(datetime)
{
    var hours = datetime.getHours();
    var minutes = datetime.getMinutes();
    var seconds = datetime.getSeconds();
    if (seconds < 10) {
        seconds = "0" + seconds;
    }

    if (minutes < 10) {
        minutes = "0" + minutes;
    }

    var durationString;
    if (hours > 0) {
        durationString = hours.toString() + ":" + minutes + ":" + seconds;
    }
    else {
        durationString = minutes + ":" + seconds;
    }
    return durationString;
}
```

This is a great example of how the .NET framework in Silverlight 2 makes development a lot easier—you can accomplish this in C# with one line of code:

```
txtStat.Text = vid.NaturalDuration.ToString();
```

This would work with XAML that looks something like this:

```
<Canvas x:Name="sample9" Opacity="1">
  <MediaElement x:Name="vid" Height="200" Width="200"
      Stretch="Fill" CurrentStateChanged="doState"
      BufferingTime="0:0:10" />
  <TextBlock x:Name="txtStat"></TextBlock>
</Canvas>
```

You can report on the current position of the video using the *Position* property. In this example, the position is reported on the status screen when the video is paused. The JavaScript code needed would look something like this:

```
function doPause(sender, args)
{
    var meVid = sender.findName("vid");
    meVid.Pause();
    var txtStat = sender.findName("txtStat");
    var datetime = new Date(0,0,0,0,0, meVid.Position.Seconds);
    positionString = convertDT(datetime);
    txtStat.Text = positionString.toString();
}
```

And, as before, the C# equivalent is even simpler:

```
txtStat.Text = vid.Position.ToString();
```

Using Media Timeline Markers

A timeline marker is a piece of metadata that is associated with a particular point in a media timeline. These markers are usually created and encoded into the media ahead of time using software such as Expression Media, and they are often used to provide chapter stops in video.

Silverlight supports these markers so that, when it reaches a marker on the timeline as it is playing back media, it raises the *MarkerReached* event. You can catch this event and process it to trigger actions upon hitting the mark.

Following is an example of a XAML snippet that specifies the event handler for reaching a marker using the *MarkerReached* attribute. It specifies a JavaScript function called *handleMarker* as the event handler:

```
<MediaElement x:Name="vid" Source="balls.wmv" Height="200" Width="200"
MarkerReached="handleMarker" />
```

The arguments raised by this event contain a *marker* object. This contains a *TimeSpan* object containing the time of the marker. The previous section, "Managing Playback Position," provides an example showing how to format a *TimeSpan* object into a friendly string. It also contains a *Type* property for the marker, which is a string that is defined by the person performing the encoding. Finally, it contains a *Text* parameter that allows for free-format text and is usually used to describe the parameter. Following is the JavaScript to capture all three and build a string that is rendered using an alert box:

```
function handleMarker(sender, args)
{
    var strMarkerStatus = args.marker.time.seconds.toString();
    strMarkerStatus += " : ";
    strMarkerStatus += args.marker.type;
    strMarkerStatus += " : ";
    strMarkerStatus += args.marker.text;
    alert(strMarkerStatus);
}
```

The C# code is very similar; note that the args are in the format *TimeLineMarkerRouted-EventArgs*:

```
private void handleMarker(object sender,
        TimelineMarkerRoutedEventArgs e)
{
  string strMarkerStatus = e.Marker.Time.ToString();
  strMarkerStatus += "   :   ";
  strMarkerStatus += e.Marker.Type;
  strMarkerStatus += "   :   ";
  strMarkerStatus += e.Marker.Text;
}
```

You can see how this looks in Figure 11-11.

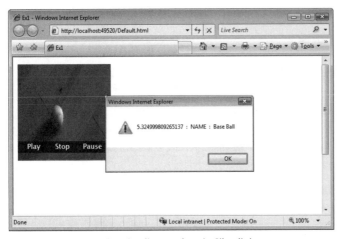

FIGURE 11-11 Capturing timeline markers in Silverlight.

You can also dynamically add timeline markers to your media file using code in Silverlight. This can be used to create chapter stops as a percentage of the length of the file, for example.

Following is an example in which the XAML for the *MediaElement* defines the function *handleOpen* to fire when the media is opened. This inserts a new timeline object into the video at the 10-second position. This element is not permanently stored in the video, and it is lost when the session ends.

```
<MediaElement x:Name="vid" Source="balls.wmv"
    Height="200" Width="200"
    MarkerReached="handleMarker"
    MediaOpened="handleOpened" />
```

The handler should then create a new timeline element in XAML and append it to the *MediaElement*'s marker collection. This sets up a timeline marker at 10 seconds, with the *Type* set to 'My Temp Marker' and the *Text* set to 'Dynamically Added Marker Marker'.

Here's how it would look if you were building it in JavaScript:

```
function handleOpened(sender, args)
{
   var marker =
   sender.getHost().content.createFromXaml(

      "<TimelineMarker Time='0:0:10'" +
      " Type='My Temp Marker' Text='Dynamically Added Marker Marker' />");
   sender.markers.add(marker);
}
```

And here's how it would look if you were building it in .NET:

```
private void handleOpened(object sender, RoutedEventArgs e)
{
  TimelineMarker t = new TimelineMarker();
  t.Time = new TimeSpan(0, 0, 0, 10);
  t.Type = "My Temp Marker";
  t.Text = "Dynamically Added Marker";
  vid.Markers.Add(t);
}
```

The *MediaElement* markers collection is made up of *TimeLineMarker* objects, so to add a new one, you simply create it and set its *Time*, *Type*, and *Text* properties and then add it to the collection. Silverlight is smart enough to know when to fire it based on the *Time* you have set, so you do not have to add new markers in time-based order.

Now, when the *MediaElement* reaches the 10-second point on the playback, the alert dialog box shown in Figure 11-12 is raised.

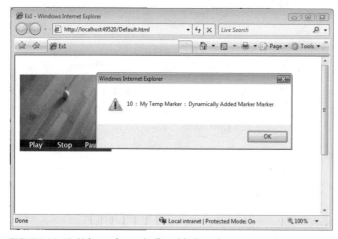

FIGURE 11-12 Using a dynamically added marker.

Painting Video Using the *VideoBrush*

A particularly exciting feature of Silverlight is its ability to paint surfaces with video using a *VideoBrush*. This is a very straightforward process. First, you'll need a media element that loads the video. This media element should be hidden and should not accept mouse events. You achieve this by setting its opacity to 0 and by setting the *IsHitTestVisible* property to *false*. You'll also have to name the media element object using the *x:Name* property. Following is an example:

```
<MediaElement x:Name="vid" Source="balls.wmv" Opacity="0" IsHitTestVisible="False" />
```

Now the *VideoBrush* object can be applied to an object in the same way any other brush is used. You need to specify the brush source as the *MediaElement* (which is why it had to be named). You can also specify the *Stretch* property to further control the visual brush effect.

For example, here's a *TextBlock* containing text that has its *Foreground* color painted using a *VideoBrush*:

```
<TextBlock FontFamily="Verdana" FontSize="80"
      FontWeight="Bold" TextWrapping="Wrap"
      Text="Video">
  <TextBlock.Foreground>
      <VideoBrush SourceName="vid"/>
  </TextBlock.Foreground>
</TextBlock>
```

Silverlight will now render the text using a *VideoBrush*, and Figure 11-13 shows how this will display.

FIGURE 11-13 Using the *VideoBrush* to paint text.

The *InkPresenter* Control

As you've seen so far in this book, Silverlight empowers the design of the next generation of Web applications by providing tools that allow you to add rich video, audio, vector graphics, animation, and other enhancements that improve the UX. Ink annotation—the creation of handwriting or drawing content using a device designed for this purpose—is another great way to make applications even more interactive and personal, and Silverlight's support for Ink-based programming brings this functionality to the Web. In this section, we'll investigate how Ink annotation is supported in Silverlight.

There are several different types of devices that can be used for Ink-based applications:

- **Pen Input**   Computers that support pen digitizers are typically Tablet PCs, but they can also be desktop computers that support external digitizers. These can take advantage of the pen input in Silverlight. They create *Ink* that can be integrated into Silverlight Web pages so that handwriting, drawing, annotation, and other input formats can be supported on the Web.

- **Touch Input**   Touch screens are very common in kiosk environments or other places where a stylus or keyboard would be unwieldy or unnecessary. Silverlight with Ink annotation supports touch screens, allowing rich Internet applications with touch-based interactivity.

- **Mouse Input**   The mouse can be used to provide digitized, penlike input similar to a Tablet PC pen. However, this Ink input will have a lower resolution than if you used a true Tablet PC pen.

An Example of Ink Annotation in Silverlight

Silverlight.net provides a great example of an application that supports Ink annotation. It is the page-turner application hosted at *http://silverlight.net/samples/1.0/Page-Turn/default.html*. You can see it in Figure 11-14.

This application demonstrates how you can download a source and browse through images and other assets using an application that mimics turning the pages of a book. It is enhanced with Ink, which allows you to annotate the images—and the annotations you add remain associated with the image. You can see an example of an annotated page in Figure 11-15.

FIGURE 11-14 Silverlight PageTurn sample.

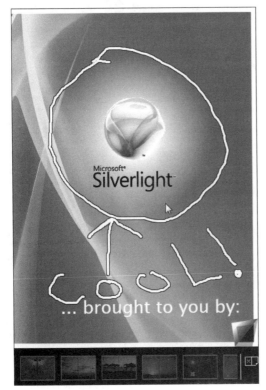

FIGURE 11-15 Annotating an image in Silverlight.

Silverlight Ink Classes for JavaScript Programmers

Support for Ink in Silverlight is very straightforward. Every time you drag the input device across the screen, you generate one or more *StylusPoint* objects. These are collected into a *StylusPointCollection*, which forms the basis of a *Stroke*. The strokes are collected into a *StrokeCollection*, which makes up the list of graphics that are used to create the Ink that the *InkPresenter* renders. So, if you consider Figure 11-15, the letter "C" in *COOL* is a stroke that is made up of a number of points collected into its *StrokeCollection*. Each letter "O," the letter "L," the line and dot in the exclamation point, and the lines that make up the arrow and the circle are all strokes. Each of these strokes is a member of the *InkPresenter*'s *StrokeCollection*, and each of them is made up of *StylusPoints* held in the relevant stroke's *StylusPointCollection*. Each of these types provides an object-oriented interface with properties and methods that allow them to be programmable.

The *StrokeCollection* Type

The *InkPresenter* object contains the *Strokes* property, which is an instance of *StrokeCollection*. This collection, in turn, contains all the metadata that is required to represent the user's Ink input.

StrokeCollection Properties

When using JavaScript to program Silverlight, the *StrokeCollection* exposes a *Count* property that can be used to return the number of strokes that are currently held within the collection.

StrokeCollection Methods

The *StrokeCollection* exposes the following methods:

- **Add**   This allows you to add a new stroke to the collection.

- **Clear**   This clears the collection of strokes, which causes an immediate re-rendering (thus clearing the Ink that was previously created).

- **GetBounds**   This returns a rectangle (in a *Rect* structure) that represents the bounding box of the strokes.

- **GetItem(index)**   This will retrieve the stroke that is stored at the specified index.

- **HitTest**   If you pass this method a *StylusPointCollection*, it will return the subset of strokes in the *StrokeCollection* that intersect with these points.

- **Insert**   This is similar to Add, except that it allows you to insert a new stroke to the collection at a specific collection index.

- **Remove**   This will remove a specific element from the *StrokeCollection*.

- **RemoveAt**   This will remove the indexed element from the *StrokeCollection*.

The *Stroke* Type

The *StrokeCollection* that you saw in the previous section is a collection of *Stroke* objects. A *Stroke* object represents a collection of points that corresponds to a stroke; the points are recorded with a single stylus action: stylus-down, stylus-move, stylus-up. These objects in turn have their own set of properties and methods.

Stroke Properties

The *Stroke* object exposes these properties:

- **DrawingAttributes**   Each stroke can have independent height, width, color, and outline color. These are set using the *DrawingAttributes* type. To use this type, you create an instance of a *DrawingAttributes* object, set these properties, and then add the new *DrawingAttributes* object to the stroke.

- **StylusPoints**   This is a *StylusPointCollection* that contains the collection of *StylusPoint* objects that make up the stroke. The *StylusPoint* is discussed in the following section.

Stroke Methods

The *Stroke* object exposes the following Ink-specific methods:

- **GetBounds**   This returns the bounding box of the *Stroke* as a *Rect* structure.

- **HitTest**   If you pass this method a *StylusPointCollection* and if any of those points intersect the *Stroke*, this method will return *true*; otherwise, it will be *false*.

The *StylusPointCollection* Type

This collection hosts a set of *StylusPoint* objects. It is used to store the stylus points for a *Stroke*, or in some cases, it can be passed to methods such as the *HitTest* method to determine whether or not strokes intersect.

StylusPointCollection Properties

The *StylusPointCollection* exposes only one property—the *Count* property, which returns a count of the stylus points that are held in this collection.

StylusPointCollection Methods

The *StylusPointCollection* object exposes these methods:

- **add**   This method allows you to add a new *StylusPoint* to the end of the collection.

- **addStylusPoints**   This method allows you to add an existing *StylusPointCollection* to the bottom of this collection.

- **clear**   This removes all *StylusPoint* objects from the collection.

- **getItem**   This gets a specific *StylusPoint* from the collection. Use it with an integer value representing the index of the item you want to reference, such as *getItem(5)*.

- **insert**   This inserts a new *StylusPoint* into the collection at the specified index.

- **remove**   This removes a specific *StylusPoint* from the collection.

- **removeAt**   This removes the *StylusPoint* at the specified index from the collection.

The *StylusPoint* Type

The *StylusPoint* type represents a single point that is collected while the user is Inking with a specific device—a pen, a mouse, or a touch screen. The point exposes a number of properties and methods for programmability.

StylusPoint Properties

The *StylusPoint* exposes the following properties:

- The *Name* property allows you to name the point. This is a unique identifier. When points are generated by user input, they are unnamed.

- The *PressureFactor* property indicates the pressure that the user puts on the pen or touch screen to generate a stroke. When using a mouse, the pressure does not change from the default. The value is a *double* between 0.0 and 1.0, with a default value of 0.5. Based on the pressure factor, you can change the height and width of the *Stroke* programmatically through its *DrawingAttributes* property to give feedback to the user.

The coordinates of the stroke are returned using the *X* and *Y* properties. These are measured in pixels.

Mouse Event Arguments and Ink

When using Ink, events raised by the input device are treated as mouse events, and arguments received by your event handlers will be *MouseEventArgs*.

The *MouseEventArgs* object contains methods that allow you to query the stylus information—to see if it is a mouse, stylus, or some other input device—and that allow you to query for the collection of *StylusPoint* objects associated with this event.

Note that this is the same *MouseEventArgs* object that is associated with the *MouseEnter*, *MouseLeave*, *MouseLeftButtonDown*, *MouseLeftButtonUp*, and *MouseMove* events.

MouseEventArgs Properties

The *MouseEventArgs* object exposes two Boolean properties called *ctrl* and *shift*. These are *true* when the user holds down the equivalent key while raising the event.

MouseEventArgs Methods

The *MouseEventArgs* object exposes three methods:

- The *GetPosition* method takes an element as its parameter and returns a *Point* that represents the x- and y-coordinates of the mouse pointer relative to that element. If nothing is passed in, then the *Point* contains the coordinates relative to the position of the control that raised the event.

- The *GetStylusInfo* method returns a *StylusInfo* object that contains information about the state of the stylus. *StylusInfo* has the following properties:

   o *IsInverted*: When a pen is inverted, it indicates that the user wants to use it to *erase* points instead of draw them. This property returns *true* in that circumstance.

   o *DeviceType*: This returns a string containing the device type—"Mouse", "Stylus", or "Touch".

- The *GetStylusPoints* method returns a clone of the stylus points that were collected since the last mouse event. This will be a *StylusPointCollection* type.

Programming for Ink in Silverlight

When programming applications with Microsoft tools, the term *Ink* generally refers to handwriting or drawing content that is created by the user with the Ink-based devices described previously, such as a digital pen, touch screen, or mouse. When they are used in a Silverlight application, these devices fill a *StrokeCollection* object with individual *Stroke* objects. In turn, a *Stroke* maintains a record of the actions of a device—such as a pen—that include, for example, the pen-down, pen-move, and pen-up actions. A *Stroke* can represent a dot, a straight line, or a curve. It does this by maintaining a *StylusPointCollection* object, which contains *StylusPoint* objects that are collected from the digitizer associated with the pen, touch screen, or mouse. Attributes of the Ink are contained in the *DrawingAttributes* class.

As mentioned, Ink is collected by Silverlight using the *InkPresenter* class. This is effectively a subclass of the *Canvas* element, which also contains a collection of strokes in a *StrokeCollection*. When strokes are added to the *StrokeCollection*, then the *InkPresenter* will automatically render them using the pertinent *DrawingAttributes*.

You'll typically add the *InkPresenter* to your XAML for your application at design time, but the *Stroke* objects within the *StrokeCollection* will be added at run time using JavaScript.

Following is an example of using *InkPresenter* on a page, overlaying an image:

```
<Canvas xmlns="http://schemas.microsoft.com/client/2007"
        xmlns:x="http://schemas.microsoft.com/winfx/2006/xaml">
    <Image Source="sushi.jpg"></Image>
    <InkPresenter
```

```
        x:Name="inkEl"
        Background="transparent"
        Width="600" Height="400"
        MouseLeftButtonDown="inkMouseDown"
        MouseMove="inkMouseMove"
        MouseLeftButtonUp="inkMouseUp"/>
</Canvas>
```

The *InkPresenter* defines event handlers for *MouseLeftButtonDown*, *MouseMove*, and *MouseUp*. We'll look how to manage these in JavaScript to build a simple inking application, and then later in this section you'll see how to create the same code in C#. The similarity is striking! These events will need event handler functions that handle the "start inking," "draw ink," and "stop inking" actions.

> **Note** Although Ink can be added with a pen, a touch screen, or a mouse, the API documentation uses the term "Mouse" throughout.

Before we look at these JavaScript event handler functions, there is a little housekeeping we need to provide that will declare the global variables necessary to support these actions:

```
var theInk;      // Reference to the ink presenter
var newStroke;   // Reference to a stroke
var theControl;  // Reference to the Silverlight control
function handleLoad(control, userContext, rootElement)
{
    // The Load event returns a reference to the control
    // But other event handlers do not. So we're going
    // to make a reference to the control here
    theControl = control;

    // Here we will create a reference to the ink element
    theInk = control.content.findName("inkEl");
}
```

The Ink actions I mentioned will be supported by functions that will use these helper variables for the *InkPresenter*, the current stroke, and the Silverlight control itself. When the Silverlight control loads, it triggers the *handleLoad* function. This takes a reference to the Silverlight control as one of its parameters, but because the event handlers that we are implementing for managing the mouse do not, we'll need to save a reference to the Silverlight control from within the *handleLoad* function. While processing in *handleLoad*, you might as well also get a reference to the *InkPresenter* by finding it based on its name (*inkEl*). This saves you from having to issue a *getHost* to get a reference to the parent UI element control to find the *Ink-Presenter* in each event handler invocation.

Now we're ready to learn more about the event handlers. First, let's look at what happens when the *MouseLeftButtonDown* event fires, in effect causing *inkMouseDown* to run. You'll want to capture the mouse movement in a fashion similar to the drag-and-drop processing you learned about in Chapter 6. After you have captured the mouse input, you will create a new *Stroke* that contains a *DrawingAttributes* object that defines the visual characteristics of this stroke. In the example presented here, *DrawingAttributes* for the stroke will provide it with a *Width* of 2, a *Height* of 2, a fill color of *White*, and an outline color of *White*. The *MouseEventArgs* type in Silverlight supports a *getStylusPoints* method, as you saw earlier in this chapter, that takes the *InkPresenter* as its sole parameter. This method returns a *StylusPointCollection* type that can be used with the stroke's *AddStylusPoints* method. You then add the stroke to the *InkPresenter*'s *StrokesCollection*. You can see the code here:

```
function inkMouseDown(sender,args)
    {
        // Capture the mouse.
        theInk.CaptureMouse();

        // Create a new stroke.
        newStroke = theControl.content.createFromXaml('<Stroke/>');

        // Assign a new drawing attributes element to the stroke.
        // This, as its name suggests, defines how the stroke will appear
        var da = theControl.content.CreateFromXaml('<DrawingAttributes/>');
        newStroke.DrawingAttributes = da;

        // Now that the stroke has drawing attributes,
        // let's define them...
        newStroke.DrawingAttributes.Width = 2;
        newStroke.DrawingAttributes.Height = 2;
        newStroke.DrawingAttributes.Color = "White";
        newStroke.DrawingAttributes.OutlineColor = "White";


        newStroke.StylusPoints.AddStylusPoints(args.GetStylusPoints(theInk));
        theInk.Strokes.Add(newStroke);
    }
```

Now, as you move the mouse over the canvas, if you are currently drawing a stroke (i.e., *newStroke* is not *null*), then you want to generate new points to add to this stroke, representing the track over which the mouse moved. Following is the code for this:

```
// Add the new points to the Stroke we're working with.
function inkMouseMove(sender,args)
{
    if (newStroke != null)
    {
        newStroke.StylusPoints.AddStylusPoints(args.GetStylusPoints(theInk));
    }
}
```

Finally, the *MouseLeftButtonUp* event will fire after you finish the stroke by releasing the mouse button (or by lifting the pen from the screen). Then, you want to clear the stroke and release the mouse capture. When the *newStroke* variable has been set to *null*, the mouse (or pen) movement across the screen will no longer collect points to add to the stroke, and stroke output will therefore not be drawn. Here's the code:

```
function inkMouseUp(sender,args)
{
    // Set the stroke to null
    newStroke = null;

    // Release the mouse
    theInk.releaseMouseCapture();
}
```

Figure 11-16 shows an example of an application before Ink annotation was added to it. Figure 11-17 shows the same application after Ink annotation has been added to it—the annotation was drawn on it using a mouse or pen.

FIGURE 11-16 Running the Silverlight Inked application.

FIGURE 11-17 Silverlight Inked application with Ink applied.

The previous example showed you how to program for Ink using Silverlight and JavaScript. The good news is that you can, of course, do the same with managed code. Here's the complete code-behind for C# to be able to build the same application:

```
using System;
using System.Collections.Generic;
using System.Linq;
using System.Windows;
using System.Windows.Controls;
using System.Windows.Documents;
using System.Windows.Input;
using System.Windows.Media;
using System.Windows.Media.Animation;
using System.Windows.Shapes;
using System.Windows.Ink;

namespace NetInkSample
{
    public partial class Page : UserControl
    {
        Stroke newStroke;
        public Page()
        {
            InitializeComponent();
        }

        private void inkEl_MouseLeftButtonDown(
          object sender, MouseButtonEventArgs e)
        {
            inkEl.CaptureMouse();
```

```
        // Create a new stroke.
        newStroke = new Stroke();
        DrawingAttributes da = new DrawingAttributes();
        newStroke.DrawingAttributes = da;
        newStroke.DrawingAttributes.Width=2;
        newStroke.DrawingAttributes.Height=2;
        newStroke.DrawingAttributes.Color=Colors.White;
        newStroke.DrawingAttributes.OutlineColor=Colors.White;
        // Beta 2

        newStroke.StylusPoints.Add(

            e.StylusDevice.GetStylusPoints(inkEl));

        // Beta 1

        //newStroke.StylusPoints.AddStylusPoints(

            e.GetStylusPoints(inkEl));

        inkEl.Strokes.Add(newStroke);
    }

    private void inkEl_MouseMove(object sender, MouseEventArgs e)
    {
        if (newStroke != null)
        {
            //Beta 1

            //newStroke.StylusPoints.AddStylusPoints(
              e.GetStylusPoints(inkEl));

            //Beta 2

            newStroke.StylusPoints.Add(
              e.StylusDevice.GetStylusPoints(inkEl));


        }

    }

    private void inkEl_MouseLeftButtonUp(
      object sender, MouseButtonEventArgs e)
    {
        newStroke = null;
        inkEl.ReleaseMouseCapture();
    }
  }
}
```

In addition to showing the flexibility of Silverlight, which allows you to develop applications in either parsed JavaScript or compiled .NET languages, this also demonstrates how straightforward it is to *migrate* from JavaScript to .NET, so if you have existing Silverlight applications in JavaScript, you can see that it is easy to upgrade it to Silverlight 2 with managed code.

Deep Zoom with the *MultiScaleImage* Control

Deep Zoom is a new technology that has been added to Silverlight 2, and it provides you with a new and unique way of managing images within your application. It is implemented by the *MultiScaleImage* element in XAML, which, as its name suggests, gives you the facility to control scale and zoom of your images, with Silverlight providing a huge virtual space on which these images can be drawn.

> **Important** The information in this book is based on the beta of Silverlight 2, and because Deep Zoom is a new technology, there have been many changes to it between betas. Be sure to check the companion Web site for this book to look for updated content on Deep Zoom if you are having any trouble with the code in this section!

The Deep Zoom feature is best described by example. Take a look at Figure 11-18, which shows an image of a kid's science project.

FIGURE 11-18 Looking at an image in Deep Zoom.

Now, this doesn't really look too fancy or even different from a normal photographic image. So, what's all the fuss about Deep Zoom, you might be wondering. Well, on this application, if you drag the mouse wheel, you can zoom in or out. So, if you look at Figure 11-19, you'll see another view of this image, but I've zoomed out so it no longer focuses on the orange, and now you can see this image relative to another image.

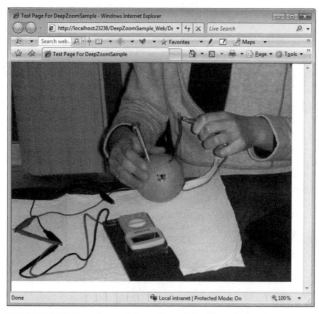

FIGURE 11-19 Zooming out from the original image.

If you look closely at the center of the orange in Figure 11-19, you'll see that the image from Figure 11-18 is embedded within the orange, right at its center. You can zoom out from this again to get the image shown in Figure 11-20.

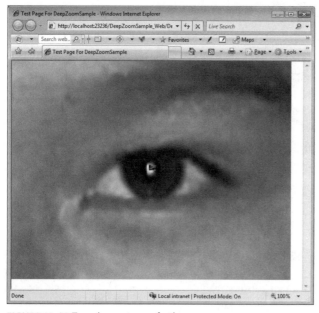

FIGURE 11-20 Zooming out even further.

As you can see, the entire second image is only a little larger than a pixel in the third image (it is within the pupil of the eye in Figure 11-20), and the entire first image is only a few pixels in size in the second image. It's hard to do the Deep Zoom feature justice by showing you these still images printed in a book—it really has to be seen to be believed—and when you play with it, you will see why the technology is called Deep Zoom . . . it allows you to arrange pictures so that you can zoom in and out of them very easily, painting them on a giant, scalable canvas.

Using the Deep Zoom Composer

But how do you build an application that will allow you to zoom in and out on images like this? It's fairly simple to create a basic application that will allow you to do this. You simply use the *MultiScaleImage* control and point it at a file that contains metadata about the images. You create this file using the Deep Zoom composer tool, which you can download from the Microsoft Download center. You can see the Deep Zoom composer tool in Figure 11-21.

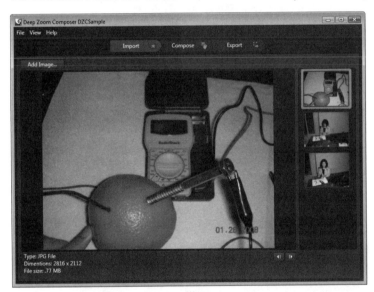

FIGURE 11-21 Deep Zoom composer tool.

This tool follows a simple workflow of *Import*, followed by *Compose*, followed by *Export*. So, first you select the Import tab, select Add Image to pick a picture to use, and then you repeat that step for each picture you want to use. You can see in Figure 11-21 that I've selected three images.

The next step is to *Compose*, which you will do with the options on the Compose tab. On this tab, you place an image on the design surface and then zoom in and out and place other images. For example, if you look at Figure 11-22, you'll see where I've placed one image and zoomed into the eye.

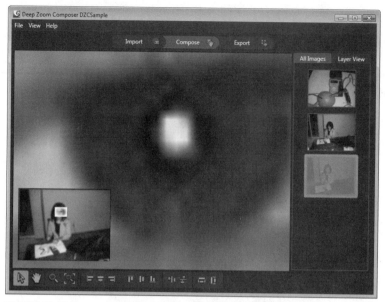

FIGURE 11-22 Composing an image for different zoom levels with the Deep Zoom composer tool.

Now, if we want to place a new image, it will be placed at its normal resolution after the Silverlight component is zoomed to the current level of the image in the composer. So, if you look at Figure 11-22, you'll see where the image has been placed within the eye. Later, when you run the application, you would have to zoom directly into the eye to see this image, and it will be tiny until you zoom further into it. In Figure 11-23, you'll see where the image has been placed.

FIGURE 11-23 Adding a new image to one that has been zoomed in on.

In this simple example, we've just added one image to appear when zoomed in on another. Deep Zoom allows you to build far more complex applications, but for the purposes of this sample, this example gives you a good idea of the feature's capabilities. We are now ready to go to the third step—exporting the details. You can see the Export tab of the composer tool that we will use to do this in Figure 11-24.

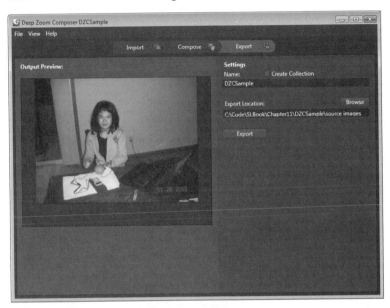

FIGURE 11-24 Exporting the Deep Zoom metadata.

To export the metadata for the images composed in Deep Zoom, you simply need to give the project a name and export it to a specified location. When you have done this, you'll see two files and a folder created in the output directory. The first file is the project file for the Deep Zoom composer. The second is named SparseImageSceneGraph.xml, and it is a configuration file that simply defines each image and the location of each image within the other at the different zoom levels. For example, you can see the scene graph for the two-picture XAML here:

```
<?xml version="1.0"?>
<SceneGraph version="1">
  <AspectRatio>1.33333333333334</AspectRatio>
  <SceneNode>
  <FileName>C:\Code\SLBook\Chapter11\DZCSample
     \source images\DSCN2961.JPG</FileName>
   <x>0</x>
   <y>0</y>
   <Width>1</Width>
   <Height>1</Height>
   <ZOrder>1</ZOrder>
  </SceneNode>
  <SceneNode>
  <FileName>C:\Code\SLBook\Chapter11\DZCSample
```

```
    \source images\DSCN2959.JPG</FileName>
    <x>0.451782754964542</x>
    <y>0.313488814592021</y>
    <Width>0.00099432659277551</Width>
    <Height>0.00099432659277551</Height>
    <ZOrder>2</ZOrder>
  </SceneNode>
</SceneGraph>
```

You can see that this is fairly straightforward XAML code. It contains the aspect ratio for the master image (derived from the dimensions of the first image), and then each image becomes a *SceneNode*. The first image is the first *SceneNode*. It is defined as being located at position (0,0), and it is a normalized image—that is, its width and height are set to 1. All other image sizes and locations are then set relative to the first image.

The second image, as you can see, is located at approximately 0.45 on the x-axis and at 0.31 on the y-axis, and it is sized at approximately 0.00099 on x and y relative to the first image. Thus, if you zoom into the first image to approximately 10,000 times the original size, you'll see the second image. Its Z-order is 2 (the Z-order of the first image is 1), meaning that it will be drawn on top of the first image.

In addition to this, the Deep Zoom composer slices the image into tiles so that you don't have to load every tile for every zoom level, giving you nice efficiency when you are dealing with large images. When you are zoomed out, you will have a small tile, indicating the apparent resolution for being zoomed out. When you zoom into the full resolution of the image (or beyond), you will only see a portion of the image, and thus you will only get the tiles representing the part of the image that you see, thus saving bandwidth and download time.

The other file to be exported will have the .dzi extension. This contains all the details of the tiles and where they are relative to the main image. You'll find it in the directory that the Deep Zoom composer made, along with a number of other numbered subdirectories containing the images. It's an XML file, so you can open it and inspect it!

Building Your First Deep Zoom Project

To use Deep Zoom in an application, create a new Silverlight application. Before doing anything else, you should compile the default application. This will create the *ClientBin* application in the Web application part of the solution. When this is done, close the solution.

Now, use Windows Explorer to copy the directory containing the Info.bin file and the subdirectories containing the fragmented images into the ClientBin directory of the Web application. When this is done, reopen the solution. Your project Solution Explorer will look something like the one shown in Figure 11-25.

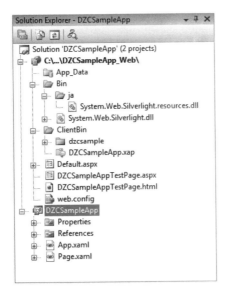

FIGURE 11-25 Adding the Deep Zoom data to your Web application.

Now, to render the Deep Zoom content, you simply add a *MultiScaleImage* to your Page.xaml and set its *Source* property to the location of the Info.bin file (in this case, it is located in /dzcsample/info.bin), as well as its desired width and height. Here's what your Page.xaml will look like:

```
<UserControl x:Class="DZCSampleApp.Page"
    xmlns="http://schemas.microsoft.com/client/2007"
    xmlns:x="http://schemas.microsoft.com/winfx/2006/xaml"
    Width="400" Height="300">
    <Canvas>
        <MultiScaleImage Source="dzcsample/info.dzi"
          Height="300" Width="400" />
    </Canvas>
</UserControl>
```

So, when you run this application, the *MultiScaleImage* control will render the top element in the *SceneGraph*, zooming into it from a 1 × 1 picture to the width and height specified (400 × 300, in this case).

You'll notice that there is no automatic mouse activity associated with the application, so you cannot pan or zoom the image. We'll look at how to do this in the next section.

Using the Mouse and Logical Coordinates in Deep Zoom

The *MultiScaleImage* is just like the other components in Silverlight in that it can declare the functions that should be used to handle events. For example, to pan around the image, you would use the typical mouse events, such as *MouseLeftButtonDown*, *MouseLeftButtonUp*, and

MouseMove, in a similar manner to drag and drop on any control. First, let's take a look at the XAML for the *MultiScaleImage* that defines these events:

```
<UserControl x:Class="DeepZoomSample.Page"
    xmlns="http://schemas.microsoft.com/client/2007"
    xmlns:x="http://schemas.microsoft.com/winfx/2006/xaml"
    Width="640" Height="480">
    <Canvas>
        <MultiScaleImage x:Name="dz" Source="dzcsample/info.dzi"
            MouseLeftButtonDown="MultiScaleImage_MouseLeftButtonDown"
            MouseLeftButtonUp="MultiScaleImage_MouseLeftButtonUp"
            MouseMove="MultiScaleImage_MouseMove"
            Height="480" Width="640"></MultiScaleImage>
    </Canvas>
</UserControl>
```

And now we'll look at each of these event handlers in more detail. First, there's some code that is shared across them all, and it is used for tracking the current state of the mouse and the currently viewed coordinates of the *MultiScaleImage*:

```
bool dragging = false;
double dx = 0;
double dy = 0;
Point p0;
Point p1;
Point pLast;
```

Now, let's examine what happens when the user clicks the mouse button on the image:

```
private void MultiScaleImage_MouseLeftButtonDown(
    object sender, MouseButtonEventArgs e)
        {
            dragging = true;
            p0 = dz.ElementToLogicalPoint(new Point(0, 0));
            p1 = dz.ElementToLogicalPoint(new Point(640, 480));
            dx = 0;
            dy = 0;
            double x = e.GetPosition(null).X;
            double y = e.GetPosition(null).Y;
            pLast = dz.ElementToLogicalPoint(new Point(x, y));

        }
```

We are going to assume that the user is dragging the mouse when he or she holds down the mouse button, so we will set the *dragging* Boolean to *true*. Then we want to get the *current* coordinates of the image that are visible. Remember that the top image is defined as being at (0,0), or x = 0 and y = 0, and that its width and height are both set to 1. These are the *logical* coordinates and the *logical* dimensions.

In Silverlight, if we want to derive the *logical* coordinates of the upper-left corner and the lower-right corner of the window, we can get them by using the *ElementToLogicalPoint* method. If you pass a *physical* coordinate to this, the *logical* result will be returned. So, if you can imagine that you are zoomed into a picture and you've panned around the image a little, then if you call this API for *physical* point (0,0)—that is, the upper left of *what you can see*—then the logical point representing that location on the *full* image will be returned. To get the lower right, you do the same for the point at the current width and height of the physical display (in this case, 640 × 480).

We want to track how much we're changing on x- and y-axes, so we will set the variables *dx* and *dy* to 0. We'll see more about why we've done this in a moment.

Finally, we'll also want to get the *logical* coordinates of the mouse pointer, and we do this with the *ElementToLogicalPoint* API call, passing the current mouse position (which can be derived from the *MouseEventArgs* object that is passed to this function) and then loading the results into the *pLast* variable.

Now that the mouse is down, what happens when the user starts dragging? We want to be able to pan around the image. Here's the code to achieve this:

```
private void MultiScaleImage_MouseMove(
    object sender, MouseEventArgs e)
{
  if (dragging)
  {
    if (e!=null)
    {
      double x = e.GetPosition(null).X;
      double y = e.GetPosition(null).Y;
      Point pCurrent = dz.ElementToLogicalPoint(new Point(x, y));
      if (pLast!=null)
      {
        dx += (pCurrent.X - pLast.X);
        dy += (pCurrent.Y - pLast.Y);
        Point origin = new Point(p0.X - dx, p0.Y - dy);
        dz.ViewportOrigin = origin;
      }
      pLast = pCurrent;
    }
  }
}
```

The *MouseMove* event will fire whether the button is held down or not, so we use the *dragging* variable to indicate whether or not the user is dragging. So, if the user is dragging and there are currently some event *args*, the rest of the code will execute.

In this case, we pull the current coordinates of the mouse and assign their logical equivalents (received using the *ElementToLogicalPoint* method of the control) to the *pCurrent* point. Now, if the *pLast* is not *null*, then the user is dragging, and the mouse has moved from its previous point. So, to get the change in logical coordinates that occurs from moving the mouse from the last point to the current point, we simply calculate them by finding the delta (the change) from the previous position to the current position on both the x- and y-axes. Then we set the *Origin* property of the *MultiScaleImage* to the initial position changed by the delta of both x and y. This will have the effect of "moving" the image as we drag the mouse, when we are in fact just changing the coordinates of the image origin (i.e., its upper-left corner). When we have finished this, all we need to do is set the *Last* position to the *Current* position, so that when the user moves the mouse again, we'll calculate relative to this new point and not the one where the user first held down the mouse button.

Finally, when the user releases the mouse button, you want everything to reset, which is fairly straightforward. Here's the code:

```
    private void MultiScaleImage_MouseLeftButtonUp(
object sender, MouseButtonEventArgs e)
{
  dragging = false;
  p0 = new Point();
  p1 = new Point();
  pLast = new Point();
  dx = 0;
  dy = 0;
}
```

With these three simple functions, you've now added the ability to let the user drag around the image, panning it regardless of its zoom level. In the next section, you'll see how to use the mouse wheel to zoom in and out of the image and thus reveal the images that were hidden when you were at the outer zoom levels.

Creating the Zoom Functionality with the Mouse Wheel

One problem with building Deep Zoom applications is that the de facto standard control for zooming in and out of an item is the mouse wheel, but Silverlight and .NET don't handle events using the mouse wheel. So what can we do? There are two options. The first is to use JavaScript rather than C# because the browser can capture the mouse wheel and fire an event upon rolling it. The second option is to use the browser bridge to Silverlight to have the browser capture the event and then inform .NET that it has done so, after which the code to handle it is implemented in .NET. This is a lot easier than it sounds!

First of all, you'll have to ensure that you are able to use the browser APIs in Silverlight, so be sure to have the following line to include them:

```
using System.Windows.Browser;
```

Then, within the *Page* constructor, make sure that you are registering the control to be scriptable. This exposes methods of the control that are attributed as *ScriptableMember* to JavaScript. Here's how you do this:

```
public Page()
{
  InitializeComponent();
  HtmlPage.RegisterScriptableObject("MySilverlightObject", this);
}
```

Next, on your page, you'll want to capture the mouse wheel events. Do this by first adding a *handleLoad* call to the <*Body*> tag to ensure that your JavaScript code will run when the page is rendered:

```
<body style="height:100%;margin:0;" onload="handleLoad();">
...
</body>
```

Then, within the *handleLoad* JavaScript function, you'll set up the event:

```
function handleLoad()
{
  window.onmousewheel = document.onmousewheel = onMouseWheel;
  if (window.addEventListener)
  {
    window.addEventListener('DOMMouseScroll', onMouseWheel, false);
  }
}
```

This defines the *onMouseWheel* JavaScript function to execute whenever you scroll the mouse wheel.

```
function onMouseWheel()
{
  if(!event)
  {
    event = window.event;
  }
  var slPlugin = $get("Xaml1");
  slPlugin.content.MySilverlightObject.dz_MouseWheel(
    event.clientX, event.clientY, event.wheelDelta);
}
```

This function simply gets a reference to the Silverlight component (in this case, it is called Xaml1 when it is created) and then calls a function within the code-behind for that. You call this by using the <*ComponentName*>.content.<*ObjectNameDefinition*>.<*FunctionName*> syntax.

The <*ComponentName*> is the variable that you defined in JavaScript to be a reference to the Silverlight object. The <*ObjectNameDefinition*> is the name you defined for the object when you registered it (take a look at the *Page()* constructor to see it). The <*FunctionName*> is the name of the function that you want to call. This function needs to be attributed correctly so that JavaScript can "see" it. In this case, you are calling the *dz_MouseWheel* function, so let's take a look at it:

```
[ScriptableMember]
public void dz_MouseWheel(double x, double y, int delta)
{
  double dZoomFactor=1.33;
  if (delta < 0)
    dZoomFactor= 1/1.33;
  Point pz = dz.ElementToLogicalPoint(new Point(x, y));
  dz.ZoomAboutLogicalPoint(dZoomFactor, pz.X, pz.Y);
}
```

First, as you can see, it is attributed as a *ScriptableMember*, meaning that JavaScript can see it and call it. The JavaScript function sends in the current mouse coordinates and the delta that came from the zoom. This should return a positive value if you are wheeling forward and a negative value if you are wheeling backward.

The zoom factor per wheel movement is defined as 33% (but you can define it to be whatever you want), so the *dZoomFactor* variable is set to 1.33 if you are zooming in and 1/1.33 if you are zooming out.

Next, you want to zoom around the current mouse coordinates, which is very simple to do by just converting the mouse coordinates to a logical point using the *ElementToLogicalPoint* method of the *MultiScaleImage* control. Now that you have the coordinates and the zoom factor, you simply call the *ZoomAboutLogicalPoint* method to cause the *MultiScaleImage* to zoom in and out.

Collections in Deep Zoom

In addition to being able to zoom in and zoom out on an image, you can also build *collections* of images and manipulate them in a zoomable environment.

You may have noticed that when you are exporting images from the Deep Zoom composer, there was an option to Create Collection. As its name suggests, this option creates a collection of images. Take a look at Figure 11-26, and you will see where I have placed many images on the design surface. Now, let's find out how we can export these as a collection.

When you export these images as a collection, instead of creating an Info.bin file, you will get a file with the extension .dzc, so make sure to point your *MultiScaleImage* XAML at this file (i.e., Items.dzc) to render it.

When using a collection, Silverlight will expose a *SubImages* collection that can be used to manipulate the images. Note that the full set of images will not be loaded on page render, so this collection will be empty at that point. Instead, make sure that you wire up the *ImageOpenSucceeded* event if you want to manipulate the collection. This event will fire upon the bin loading and rendering correctly.

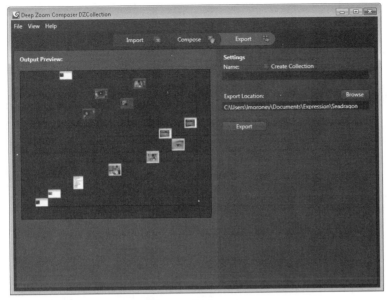

FIGURE 11-26 Creating a Deep Zoom collection.

Here's the XAML:

```
<MultiScaleImage x:Name="dz"
  Source="dzcoll/items.dzc"
  ImageOpenSucceeded="dz_ImageOpenSucceeded"
  Height="480" Width="640">
</MultiScaleImage>
```

At this point, the *SubImages* collection will be populated, and you can use it to manipulate individual images. Here's an example of changing the position of the images:

```
private void dz_ImageOpenSucceeded(object sender, RoutedEventArgs e)
{
  int nImages = dz.SubImages.Count;
  for (int lp = 0; lp < nImages; lp++)
  {
    dz.SubImages[lp].ViewportOrigin = new Point(lp*0.1, lp*0.1);
  }
}
```

As you can see, the process is exactly the same as the one we used earlier to manipulate a single image. In this case, each image is just manipulated by using the *SubImages[lp,]* where *lp* is a loop variable that counts from 0 up to the number of images. You can see the results of this in Figure 11-27. Note the difference between this and the original layout, as shown in the Deep Zoom composer in Figure 11-26.

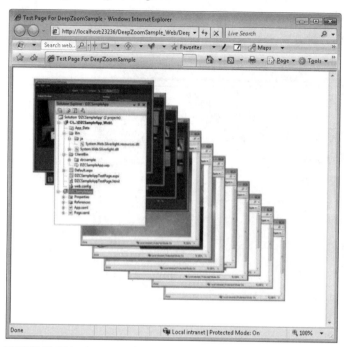

FIGURE 11-27 Laying out an image collection.

Summary

In this long chapter, you were introduced to three of the more powerful controls available in Silverlight 2. First, you took an in-depth look at the *MediaElement* control and how you can use Silverlight to render and transform video and/or audio content, including programming for opacity, markers, dynamic markers, and more. Then you looked at Ink annotation and the devices that support it, as well as how you can use Silverlight to provide Ink support on your Web pages. Finally, you looked at Deep Zoom and how this new control is implemented in Silverlight, and you learned how to create scenes and collections enhanced with deep zooming functionality.

Chapter 12

Styles and Templates in Silverlight 2

In the last few chapters, you've learned about many of the controls that are available in Silverlight, including a chapter that explained how to write your own controls. The Silverlight controls are designed to have a coherent, rich look and feel out of the box, but you may want to tweak the default appearance of the controls to fit your own particular design. Fortunately, Silverlight controls are very easy to customize, and Silverlight 2 offers you powerful styling and templating facilities that you can use to modify the look of your application.

Understanding Styling

To understand styling, let's take a look at a simple case in which we will use a button within a Silverlight application. Following is the XAML for a *Button* control:

```
<Canvas Background="LightBlue">
  <Button x:Name="btn" Content="Click Me!" Width="140"></Button>
</Canvas>
```

This will render a button in the default Silverlight style (which is silver and looks like it is lit from above), and the result will look like Figure 12-1.

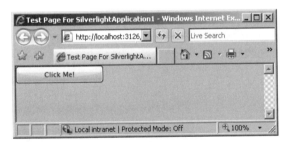

FIGURE 12-1 Basic Silverlight button.

As you saw in Chapter 7, "Silverlight Controls: Presentation and Layout," and Chapter 8, "Silverlight Controls: Advanced Controls," many Silverlight controls, including the *Button*, are what are called *Content* controls, meaning that they can render XAML content. In the case of a *Button*, this means that it can contain something much more interesting than just a string containing "Click Me!" and that you can add some features to it to give your user a richer experience when interacting with the control.

For example, if you want to create an image button—one that includes a graphic—you can do so by using an image as content. Here's an example:

```
<Canvas Background="LightBlue">
<Button Canvas.Left="40" Canvas.Top="40"
  x:Name="btn" Width="60" Height="80">
      <Button.Content>
        <StackPanel Orientation="Vertical">
          <Image Source="icon.jpg"
              Height="48" Width="48">
          </Image>
          <TextBlock Text="Click!"></TextBlock>
        </StackPanel>
      </Button.Content>
    </Button>
</Canvas>
```

You can see how this is rendered in Figure 12-2.

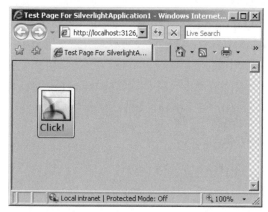

FIGURE 12-2 Button using XAML content.

Now, what if you are not happy with the default font and color used for the text on the button, and you want to alter the appearance of the button a bit more? This is quite straightforward in XAML. You can set properties that include the font family, size, weight, and so forth to customize the appearance of your button. For example, here's an updated *TextBlock*:

```
<TextBlock Text="Click!" FontFamily="Comic Sans Ms"
Foreground="MediumBlue" FontSize="20">
</TextBlock>
```

Let's also add a few other implementations of the button. This is fairly easy to do with XAML because you can just cut and paste the first button and then tweak the location properties. You can see an example of this in Figure 12-3.

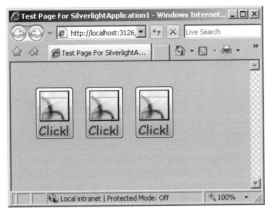

FIGURE 12-3 Multiple instances of the *Button* control.

This looks nice, and it is very easy to do, *but* when you do it this way, you end up having lots of XAML, and worse, lots of *repeated* XAML—and that makes your application harder to inspect, debug, manage, and update.

Consider the *TextBlock* controls alone—each one has its *FontFamily*, *Foreground*, and *FontSize* properties explicitly declared, even though they are all set to the same value. Consider what happens if you want to change some of this information—you'll have to go through each control one by one to update them all.

Here's where styles come in. Let's take a look at what is involved when you move some of this information into a style.

Creating a Style

You create a style within the *<Resources>* section of your container. Within this, you can create one or more styles to which you provide the target type for the style as well as a name for the style. For example, to target a *TextBlock* control with a style called *TextBlockStyle*, you would use XAML like this:

```
<Style TargetType="TextBlock" x:Key="TextBlockStyle">
</Style>
```

Note that although you specify the type of control that you want to use, you aren't limited to one style per type, so just because we're targeting the *TextBlock* with this style, it doesn't mean that all instances of the *TextBlock* control will use it. You have to configure the style to use on the control itself, and you point it at the *Key* of the style. Thus, you can have lots of different style definitions aimed at the *TextBlock* control, and each of them will have different *Key* settings. Then, you can pick the style you want by setting the *Style* property of each *TextBlock* to the particular named style you want. You'll see how to do this mapping in a moment, but first, let's see how you style properties on the *TextBlock*.

This is achieved using a *Setter*. A *Setter* is a XAML tag that defines the *Property* that you want to set and the *Value* that you want it to have.

Following is the XAML that you used earlier to set the *Text, FontFamily, Foreground,* and *FontSize* of the *TextBlock*:

```
<TextBlock Text="Click!" FontFamily="Comic Sans Ms"
Foreground="MediumBlue" FontSize="20">
</TextBlock>
```

Now, here is the style that does the same thing:

```
<Style TargetType="TextBlock" x:Key="TextBlockStyle">
  <Setter Property="FontFamily" Value="Comic Sans Ms"></Setter>
  <Setter Property="Text" Value="Click!"></Setter>
  <Setter Property="Foreground" Value="MediumBlue"></Setter>
  <Setter Property="FontSize" Value="20"></Setter>
</Style>
```

To use this style on the *TextBlock*, you use the *Style* property, and because the style itself is defined as a resource, this uses the *StaticResource* syntax to specify the name of the style:

```
<TextBlock Style="{StaticResource TextBlockStyle}">
</TextBlock>
```

And now you have a single place where you can specify the properties that you want for the *TextBlock* controls within the button, making maintenance much simpler and your XAML easier to read and understand.

You can override any of the properties that have been set by the style simply by setting them on the object itself. For example, if you want to override the *Foreground* property that was set by the style to *MediumBlue*, it's very easy to do, as shown in this example:

```
<TextBlock Style="{StaticResource TextBlockStyle}"
           Foreground="Black">
</TextBlock>
```

In this case, adding a *Foreground* property setting overrides the style, and the foreground of the *TextBlock* is now set to *Black*.

Also, do note that although our example *TextBlock* is within the image button that we've been using, the style isn't limited to these. You can put the style on any *TextBlock* on this *Canvas*.

Changing the Style Scope

In the example from the previous section, the style was created within the *Canvas* that contained the controls. This limits the scope of the style to this *Canvas* alone. So if you have multiple pages in your application, you would have to define the styles across each page, which is inefficient.

Fortunately, Silverlight allows you to define styles across the Application by setting them within *App.xaml*. Indeed, if you look at the default *App.xaml* file that is set up by the Visual Studio template, you'll see that the *Resources* section has already been defined!

```
<Application xmlns="http://schemas.microsoft.com/client/2007"
  xmlns:x="http://schemas.microsoft.com/winfx/2006/xaml"
  x:Class="SilverlightApplication1.App">
  <Application.Resources>

  </Application.Resources>

</Application>
```

So, now you can place your style definitions in this, and they'll be available throughout your application. Here's an example:

```
<Application xmlns="http://schemas.microsoft.com/client/2007"
  xmlns:x="http://schemas.microsoft.com/winfx/2006/xaml"
  x:Class="SilverlightApplication1.App">
  <Application.Resources>
    <Style TargetType="TextBlock" x:Key="TextBlockStyle">
      <Setter Property="FontFamily" Value="Comic Sans Ms"></Setter>
      <Setter Property="Text" Value="Click!"></Setter>
      <Setter Property="Foreground" Value="MediumBlue"></Setter>
      <Setter Property="FontSize" Value="20"></Setter>
    </Style>

  </Application.Resources>
</Application>
```

With this style, you can set the style of any *TextBlock* in your application using the same syntax. And in a similar manner, you also can override any of the *Style* properties by specifying them on the control.

Templates

In the previous section, you built an image button, taking advantage of the fact that the button is a *Content* control—and instead of having it only contain text, you had it contain XAML that defined a *StackPanel* containing an *Image* and a *TextBlock*. You then used styles to efficiently set the properties of the *TextBlock* to consistent settings.

The next logical step, of course, is to be able to set the style of the *entire* control, consisting of the *Button* and each of the subcontrols that make it up—that is, the *StackPanel*, *Image*, and *TextBlock*—all in one step. This is where templates become essential tools for customizing the look of your Silverlight applications!

Templates work in exactly the same way as styles—you place them in a *Resources* section and use a *Setter* to define your template. To create a *Template*, you apply the setter to the

Template property and then use *<Setter.Value>* to define the *ControlTemplate* for the specified target.

This is easier understood by looking at the code:

```
<Canvas.Resources>
    <Style TargetType="TextBlock" x:Key="TextBlockStyle">
      <Setter Property="FontFamily" Value="Comic Sans Ms"></Setter>
      <Setter Property="Text" Value="Click!"></Setter>
      <Setter Property="Foreground" Value="MediumBlue"></Setter>
      <Setter Property="FontSize" Value="20"></Setter>
    </Style>
    <Style x:Key="ImageButton" TargetType="Button">
      <Setter Property="Template">
        <Setter.Value>
          <ControlTemplate TargetType="Button">
            <Button>
              <Button.Content>
                <StackPanel Orientation="Vertical">
                  <Image Source="icon.jpg" Height="48" Width="48"></Image>
                  <TextBlock Style="{StaticResource TextBlockStyle}"
                             Foreground="Black">
                  </TextBlock>
                </StackPanel>
              </Button.Content>
            </Button>
          </ControlTemplate>
        </Setter.Value>
      </Setter>
    </Style>
</Canvas.Resources>
```

Here you can see that the style called *ImageButton* is created, and it contains a setter for the *Template* property. This contains a *ControlTemplate* that defines the *Button* we saw earlier that contains a *StackPanel* with an *Image* and a *TextBlock* within it.

Note that this can contain a style reference too because the *TextBlock* control within the template has its style set to the *TextBlockStyle* that we created earlier.

Now, to define our buttons, we simplify the XAML even further:

```
<Button x:Name="btn1" Style="{StaticResource ImageButton}"
        Canvas.Top="20" Canvas.Left="20"></Button>

<Button x:Name="btn2" Style="{StaticResource ImageButton}"
        Canvas.Top="20" Canvas.Left="120"></Button>

<Button x:Name="btn3" Style="{StaticResource ImageButton}"
        Canvas.Top="20" Canvas.Left="220"></Button>
```

Each of these buttons sets its *Style* to the *ImageButton* resource, which in turn defines the overall template for the control. Figure 12-4 shows the output of this XAML.

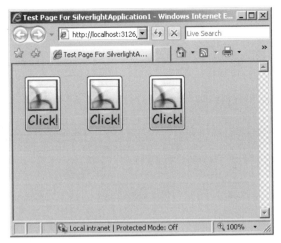

FIGURE 12-4 Templated buttons.

The really great thing about templates is that you don't necessarily have to have the type of control within the template that you are templating. That probably sounds a little confusing, so let's take a look at an example to clarify this. In the previous example, we define a template for a button that contains content that turns it into a simple image button. But, to create a button template, you don't actually need a *Button* control. So, if we want our image buttons to contain the image and the text only and not have the "standard" *Button* control behind them, we can do this very easily. Here's the template:

```
<Style x:Key="ImageButton" TargetType="Button">
    <Setter Property="Template">
      <Setter.Value>
        <ControlTemplate TargetType="Button">
          <StackPanel Orientation="Vertical">
            <Image Source="icon.jpg" Height="48" Width="48"></Image>
            <TextBlock Style="{StaticResource TextBlockStyle}"

                        Foreground="Black">

            </TextBlock>
          </StackPanel>
        </ControlTemplate>
      </Setter.Value>
    </Setter>
 </Style>
```

Now, you have a button template (specified by the *TargetType*) that doesn't include a button at all, but it will be treated as a button, including all relevant properties and events, by Silverlight. For example, if you've changed the template to this (buttonless) one, when you run the application, you'll see something like Figure 12-5.

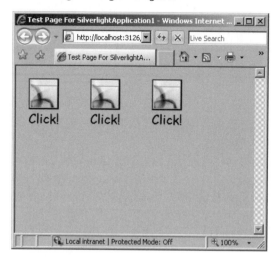

FIGURE 12-5 Buttonless buttons.

You can see that these are real buttons by writing code against them. For example, they support the full IntelliSense of a *Button* control within Microsoft Visual Studio, as you can see in Figure 12-6, where the *Click* event is being coded.

```
public Page()
{
    InitializeComponent();
    btn1.Click+=
}       new RoutedEventHandler(btn1_Click);   (Press TAB to insert)
```

FIGURE 12-6 Coding against your templated button.

Since templates are just special styles, you can also use them in *App.xaml* in the same manner as discussed earlier to allow your control templates to be used across multiple XAML pages.

Summary

This chapter provided an introduction to the use of styles and templates. These are very important features in Silverlight because they allow you to centralize and finely tune the look and feel of all your controls. You learned how to define a style and how to bind a control to that style as a *StaticResource*. You then saw how a style can be set to be used across your application using *App.xaml*.

Then you looked at how this could be extended with templates, which are similar to styles but provide the power to "skin" an entire control. You saw how you could create an *ImageButton* control without using a *Button* but that still had all the properties, methods, and events of a *Button* by defining a *ControlTemplate* for it.

In the next chapter, you will be introduced to yet another aspect of Silverlight 2 as you look in more depth into the ASP.NET controls that are provided in the Silverlight SDK.

Chapter 13
Silverlight ASP.NET Controls

The Software Development Kite (SDK) for Silverlight 2 contains two ASP.NET controls that can be used to deliver Silverlight applications from an ASP.NET–based server. Do note that these are not *necessary* to use Silverlight in ASP.NET, but they certainly make it much more *convenient* to help you manage and deliver your Silverlight content.

The first control is the *Silverlight* control. It provides the facility to use ASP.NET declaration on the server, which will emit the requisite *<OBJECT>* and *<PARAM>* tags to the browser, allowing you to use the server-side paradigm that you'll be familiar with if you are an ASP.NET developer.

The second is the *MediaPlayer* control, which similarly provides an ASP.NET declaration model—but instead of delivering a generic Silverlight control, it will actually deliver a full Silverlight media player application, complete with all controls and functionality.

In this chapter, you'll look at both of these controls and the properties, methods, and events that they offer you as a developer.

> **Tip** Before using the Silverlight ASP.NET controls on your Web form, you have to register the assembly that contains them. This is typically done with code like this at the top of your page markup:
>
> ```
> <%@ Register Assembly="System.Web.Silverlight"
> Namespace="System.Web.UI.SilverlightControls"
>     TagPrefix="asp" %>
> ```

The *Silverlight* Server Control

The *Silverlight* control lives in the *System.Web.UI.SilverlightControls.Silverlight* namespace. Note that in order to use this on your page, you will first need a *ScriptManager* control on the page.

When you create a Silverlight application using the Microsoft Visual Studio template, an ASPX page also will be created for you that hosts the Silverlight ASP.NET control. The tag should look something like this:

```
<asp:Silverlight ID="Xaml1" runat="server"
     Source="~/ClientBin/ASP1.xap" Version="2.0"
     Width="100%" Height="100%" />
```

As you can see, it follows the familiar ASP.NET attribute-based syntax, whereby the properties of the control are set using XML attributes.

Using the Frame Rate Counter

The *EnableFrameRateCounter* attribute will allow you to see the frame rate that Silverlight is presently giving you. This is a handy way to check your application's performance, particularly if you are running a lot of animations.

For example, consider the following XAML application that animates a line, rotating it through 360 degrees:

```
<UserControl x:Class="ASP1.Page"
 xmlns="http://schemas.microsoft.com/client/2007"
 xmlns:x="http://schemas.microsoft.com/winfx/2006/xaml"
 Width="400" Height="300"
 xmlns:d="http://schemas.microsoft.com/expression/blend/2008"
 xmlns:mc="http://schemas.openxmlformats.org/markup-compatibility/2006"
 mc:Ignorable="d">
 <UserControl.Resources>
  <Storyboard x:Name="Storyboard1" RepeatBehavior="Forever">
   <DoubleAnimationUsingKeyFrames Storyboard.TargetName="path"
     Storyboard.TargetProperty="(UIElement.RenderTransform).
       (TransformGroup.Children)[2].(RotateTransform.Angle)"
         BeginTime="00:00:00">
    <SplineDoubleKeyFrame KeyTime="00:00:00" Value="0"/>
    <SplineDoubleKeyFrame KeyTime="00:00:04" Value="359"/>
   </DoubleAnimationUsingKeyFrames>
  </Storyboard>
 </UserControl.Resources>
 <Grid x:Name="LayoutRoot" Background="White">
  <Ellipse HorizontalAlignment="Stretch"
        Margin="147,79,151,96"
        VerticalAlignment="Stretch"
        RenderTransformOrigin="0.5,0.48"
        Fill="#FF6A2020" Stroke="#FF000000"/>
  <Path Height="115" HorizontalAlignment="Stretch"
        Margin="199.564,30.436,194.436,0"
        x:Name="path" VerticalAlignment="Top"
        RenderTransformOrigin="0.891,0.983"
        Fill="#FFFFFFFF"
        Stretch="Fill" Stroke="#FF000000"
        StrokeThickness="6" Data="M196,137.15463 L196,35.15464">
   <Path.RenderTransform>
    <TransformGroup>
     <ScaleTransform/>
     <SkewTransform/>
     <RotateTransform Angle="0"/>
     <TranslateTransform/>
    </TransformGroup>
   </Path.RenderTransform>
  </Path>
  <Button Height="30" HorizontalAlignment="Left"
        Margin="30,19,0,0" VerticalAlignment="Top"
        Width="59" Content="Start" x:Name="btnStart"
        Click="btnStart_Click"/>
 </Grid>
</UserControl>
```

The *Button* has the *Click* event wired up. The code for the *Click* event simply starts the *Storyboard* animation like this:

```
private void btnStart_Click(object sender, RoutedEventArgs e)
{
  Storyboard1.Begin();
}
```

To see the frame rate, enable the frame rate counter on the ASP.NET *Silverlight* control like this:

```
<asp:Silverlight ID="Xaml1" runat="server"
  Source="~/ClientBin/ASP1.xap" Version="2.0"
  Width="100%" Height="100%"
EnableFrameRateCounter="true" />
```

When the application runs and the button is pressed, the animation will start, and the frame rate will display in the browser's status line. You can see this in Figure 13-1.

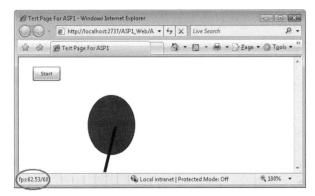

FIGURE 13-1 Using the frame rate on the *Silverlight* control.

It is recommended that you only use this while debugging; turn it off for your production applications.

Setting the Maximum Frame Rate

The Silverlight frame rate defaults to 60 frames per second. This means that all timeline animations are sliced into property changes where the property should change 60 times per second. For example, if you are rotating the line through 360 degrees in 1 second, it would be divided into 60 equal operations that rotate 6 degrees each. This can be computationally intensive, so you can improve performance overall by reducing this frame rate, or—if performance isn't an issue, and you want to increase the smoothness of your applications—you can *increase* the frame rate.

Here's an example that shows you how to change the frame rate to 10 frames per second:

```
<asp:Silverlight ID="Xaml1" runat="server"
    Source="~/ClientBin/ASP1.xap" Version="2.0"
    Width="100%" Height="100%" EnableFrameRateCounter="true"
MaxFrameRate="10" />
```

If you run the rotation animation mentioned earlier, you'll see that it doesn't sweep as smoothly as it did previously. You'll also see that the frames per second (fps) reading in the status bar has dropped to around 10 frames per second. Figure 13-2 demonstrates this.

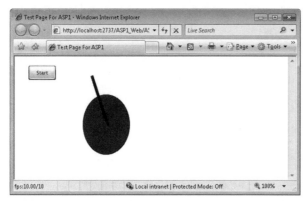

FIGURE 13-2 Reducing the frame rate.

Enabling Access to HTML

You can get or set your *Silverlight* control's access to the HTML DOM with the *EnableHtmlAccess* property. By default, this is set to *true*, which enables access to the DOM.

To manipulate the browser DOM, you'll use the *System.Windows.Browser* namespace in your application. This gives you access to classes such as *HtmlPage* that can be used to query metadata about the page that the *Silverlight* control is hosted on, as well as the ability to seek through the document to find a particular element. HTML elements can be represented in .NET with the *HtmlElement* class.

For example, if you have a *<DIV>* on your HTML called *testDiv*, you can access and change it from your Silverlight code like this:

```
HtmlElement testDiv = HtmlPage.Document.GetElementById("testDiv");
testDiv.SetAttribute("innerText", "This is the testDiv");
```

A very useful class is the *HtmlPage.BrowserInformation* class, which provides metadata such as the Browser Version, Sub Version, Name, Platform, User Agent, and whether cookies are enabled or not.

Here's an example of its contents at run time:

```
    ? HtmlPage.BrowserInformation
{System.Windows.Browser.BrowserInformation}
    BrowserVersion: {4.0}
    CookiesEnabled: true
    Name: "Microsoft Internet Explorer"
    Platform: "Win32"
UserAgent: "Mozilla/4.0 (compatible; MSIE 7.0; Windows NT 6.0;
SLCC1; .NET CLR 2.0.50727; Media Center PC 5.0;
.NET CLR 3.0.04506; InfoPath.2; .NET CLR 3.5.21022;
MS-RTC LM 8)"
? HtmlPage.BrowserInformation.BrowserVersion
{4.0}
    Build: -1
    Major: 4
    Minor: 0
Revision: -1
```

Using Redraw Regions

Another useful visual aid to help you understand how your Silverlight application is working is the concept of a *Redraw Region*. This is a visual indicator of which parts of the *Silverlight* control are being redrawn. You can turn it on using the *EnableRedrawRegions* attribute, which defaults to *false*; when set to *true*, it will turn on these markers. So, if you consider the rotating line example you looked at earlier and change the ASP.NET control markup as shown in the following code, you will see the redraw regions being turned on:

```
    <asp:Silverlight ID="Xaml1" runat="server"
    Source="~/ClientBin/ASP1.xap" Version="2.0"
    Width="100%" Height="100%" EnableFrameRateCounter="true"
EnableRedrawRegions="true" />
```

Figure 13-3 shows the effect of this; you can see that the redraw regions are highlighted.

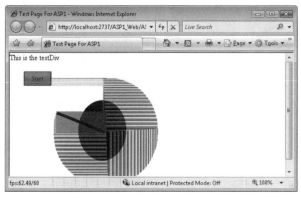

FIGURE 13-3 Using redraw regions.

As with the frame rate property, I would recommend that you only use this to debug your applications—turn it off when you go to production.

Setting the *PluginBackground* Property

The *PluginBackground* property allows you to set the plug-in background color. Remember that the ASP.NET control runs on the *server* and emits the markup, so this allows you to use *System.Color* properties, including the ability to use some of the system colors themselves (such as using the *Window* or *ActiveBorder*) as well as the named system colors.

Take a look at Figure 13-4, where you'll see that Visual Studio IntelliSense allows you to select system and named colors for the plug-in background.

FIGURE 13-4 Setting the plug-in background.

Figure 13-5 shows what the Silverlight content will look like when the *PluginBackground* property is set to *WindowFrame*. Do note that you will have to change the background of the *Grid* control in XAML, or it will overwrite this. You can simply delete this property if you want everything to have the plug-in's background property.

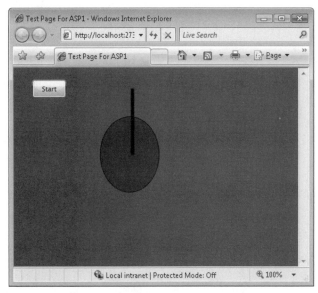

FIGURE 13-5 Setting the background of the plug-in to a system color.

At this point, if you look at the page source, you'll see that the *Background* parameter on the *Silverlight* object is set to a hard-coded color. The example in Figure 13-5 has the background plug-in color set to #FF646464.

Managing Plug-in Installation

If Silverlight is not installed on your client's system, then when the user browses to a page that contains Silverlight content, he or she will get the default Silverlight installation "badge," as shown in Figure 13-6.

FIGURE 13-6 Default installation badge.

You can override this behavior with a custom HTML template. This HTML will render *instead* of the badge, so you will need to have a link to the badge within it. Microsoft offers a handy URL that performs the appropriate browser and OS detection and provides you with the appropriate file to download. This URL is *http://www.microsoft.com/silverlight/handlers/getsilverlight.ashx?v=2.0.*

So, if you want to provide a simple replacement install experience for Silverlight, you can do so using the *<PluginNotInstalledTemplate>* child tag of the *Silverlight* ASP.NET control. Here's an example:

```
<asp:Silverlight ID="Xaml1" runat="server" Source="~/ClientBin/ASP1.xap"
Version="2.0" Width="100%" Height="100%"
    PluginBackground="WindowFrame">
    <PluginNotInstalledTemplate>
       <a href="http://www.microsoft.com/silverlight/handlers/
             getsilverlight.ashx?v=2.0">
       If you want to install the Silverlight control, you can click here!
       </a>
    </PluginNotInstalledTemplate>
</asp:Silverlight>
```

This uses a hyperlink (the *<a>* tag) to the aforementioned URI that hosts the *Silverlight* control and also provides some friendly text. You can, of course, provide something a lot more compelling to your end users, but this simple demonstration shows you what is possible. If a user without Silverlight comes to your page, they'll be presented with the content that shows them how to install Silverlight; otherwise, they'll go straight to the Silverlight content itself.

Using *Stretch* Mode

As the user manipulates the size of the browser, you may want to adjust your Silverlight content to fit. You can do this in code by capturing the various resize events, or you can do it automatically using the *ScaleMode* property.

This property can take three values:

- **None** This will leave your content as is, so even if the user changes the browser size, the content's dimensions will not change.

- **Stretch** This will stretch the Silverlight content when the browser is resized and will *change* the aspect ratio to fit.

- **Zoom** This will stretch the Silverlight content when the browser is resized but will *not* change the aspect ratio to fit.

Figures 13-7 and 13-8 show the use of *Stretch* and *Zoom*, respectively.

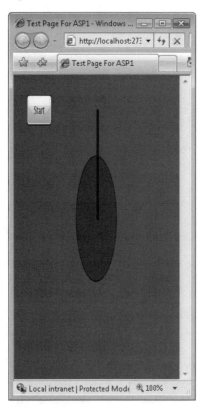

FIGURE 13-7 *Stretch* will change the aspect ratio.

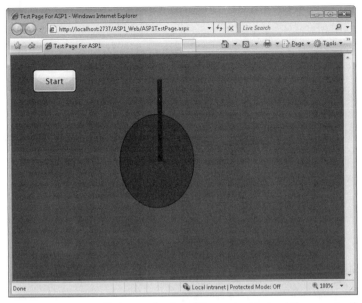

FIGURE 13-8 *Zoom* will change the size of the content but not the aspect ratio.

Using *Windowless* Mode

By default, Silverlight will overwrite all content in the same space within the HTML page. You can change this by using *Windowless* mode, which allows the opposite to occur—that is, the HTML content will be written on top of the Silverlight content. This is useful if you want to enhance existing applications with Silverlight. Your HTML controls (or the HTML emitted from ASP.NET, JSP, or other servers) can simply be written on top of the Silverlight content. For example, you may have controls that are available in HTML that aren't (yet) available in Silverlight, such as a Rich Text Box editor, or you may want to use a different Input Method Editor (IME) than the one provided with Silverlight. In these cases, if there are browser controls available that give you what you want, you can write their content over the Silverlight content.

Here's an example:

```
<asp:ScriptManager ID="ScriptManager1" runat="server"></asp:ScriptManager>
<div style="position: absolute; width: 600px; height: 100px; z-index: 1;
            left: 0px; top: 0px">
 <form action="">
   <textarea style="height:100px; width:300px; left:30px; top:30px"
            title="TextArea">
   </textarea>
 </form>
</div>
<div  style="position: absolute; height:100%;top:0px;">
<asp:Silverlight ID="Xaml1" runat="server"
    Source="~/ClientBin/ASP1.xap"
    Version="2.0" Width="100%" Height="100%"
```

```
    PluginBackground="WindowFrame"
    ScaleMode="Stretch" Windowless="true">
</asp:Silverlight>
</div>
```

Note that the *<DIV>* elements that contain the HTML *TextArea* control and the Silverlight content are both styled with absolute position at 0 pixels from the top. Thus, they will occupy the same space. If we were to render this without setting *Windowless* to *true*, then we would only see the Silverlight content. However, when *Windowless* is set to *true*, the HTML content will be written on top of it. See Figure 13-9 for details.

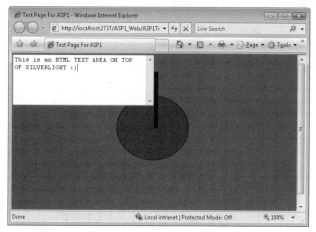

FIGURE 13-9 Using *Windowless* mode in Silverlight.

Take care only to use *Windowless* mode when you need it because it can have an impact on performance, particularly if you have a lot of animations.

Silverlight Server Control Events

The server control also exposes a number of events that can be captured by JavaScript event handlers. These are:

- **OnPluginError** This specifies a JavaScript function to call whenever an error is encountered in the Silverlight application. This is discussed in detail in Chapter 5, "XAML Transformation and Animation."

- **OnPluginFullScreenChanged** This specifies a JavaScript function to call whenever the user changes to full screen. There is no automatic way of going to full screen, but there is a property on the control (*isFullScreen*) that can be changed based on a user action. If you want to respond, perhaps to re-layout the screen, then you can do it within the event handler defined by *OnPluginFullScreeenChanged.*

- **OnPluginLoaded** This specifies a JavaScript function to call whenever the plug-in finishes loading. This is discussed in more detail in Chapter 5.

- **OnPluginResized** This specifies a JavaScript function that will be called whenever the plug-in is resized, which will typically happen if you set the stretch mode to *Stretch* or *Zoom* (discussed earlier in this chapter), and the user resizes the browser.

Thus, the ASP.NET control allows you to specify everything that the client-side object needs, so you can do everything that you can with the *<Object>* tag from the ASP.NET designer and programming model!

The Silverlight *MediaPlayer* ASP.NET Control

The *MediaPlayer* control will deliver a full Silverlight media player (video and/or audio) to your page. It comes with a number of skins that not only provide the *presentation* of a media player, but also the full functionality for managing play, stop, pause, markers, volume, full screen, and more. Note also that the *MediaPlayer* ASP.NET control has all the properties, methods, and events of the generic *Silverlight* control discussed in the first part of this chapter, so everything that you learned there, such as setting *Windowless* or other properties, you also can apply to *MediaPlayer*.

Using the *MediaPlayer* control is very straightforward—simply add an instance of it to the design surface of an ASP.NET Web form. At the upper right, there is a button that opens the MediaPlayer Tasks assistant, as you can see in Figure 13-10.

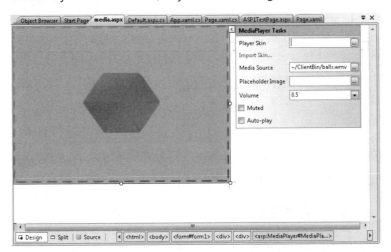

FIGURE 13-10 Using the *MediaPlayer* control.

MediaPlayer Tasks

The MediaPlayer Tasks assistant will help you set the main properties that you'll want in order to have a media player on your site:

- The Player Skin setting allows you to set the look and feel of your player. The Silverlight ASP.NET tools come with a set of skins, or you can create your own using Expression Blend. How to build them goes beyond the scope of this book, but there are tutorials available at *http://www.silverlight.net*.

  Click the Import Skin link to import one of the preset skins. By default, these are stored at C:\Program Files\Microsoft SDKs\Silverlight \v2.0 \Libraries \Server \MediaPlayerSkins.

- Media Source is the location of the media file that you want to play back.

- The Placeholder Image is an image that will display before you play back the media or after you are done. This has to be a JPG or PNG image.

- The Volume setting is a value between 0 and 1 that indicates the default volume at which to play back the media.

- When the Muted check box is checked, the media will play back, but the audio will not be heard, regardless of the volume setting.

- Auto-Play, when checked, will cause the media to play back as soon as it is available. The default setting for *Auto-Play* is *false* (unchecked).

If you look closely at Figure 13-11, you'll see that the volume is set at the halfway point on the slider because the default value for the volume in the MediaPlayer Tasks assistant (Figure 13-10) is 0.5. This setting shows just how flexible this control is, thus allowing you to fine-tune your media player to meet the precise needs of your application.

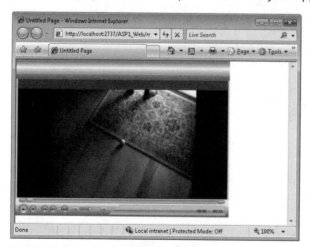

FIGURE 13-11 Media player delivered by the *MediaControl*.

There are a number of other properties that are available to you beyond those presented by the MediaPlayer Tasks assistant. For example, the *AutoLoad* property, when set to *true*, will automatically load the media into the underlying control, regardless of the user action. When set to *false*, it will not load until the user or program plays back the media.

The *EnableCaptions* property is used to turn on/off closed captions if they are encoded into the stream.

Interacting with Media

Before we go on, it's a good idea to have a media file available that has been encoded with markers. There is a nice example of how to do this with Expression encoder in Chapter 11, "Media, Ink, and Deep Zoom."

When you have markers in your video stream, you may want to write code that responds to these markers, and the Silverlight media element will fire events when it hits them. If you are delivering your media experience from the ASP.NET server control, you'll need a way of wiring up these markers, and you'll be pleased to learn that there are attributes available to do so. For example, *OnClientChapterStarted* defines a JavaScript function to call when you start a new chapter in the video. Chapters can be defined by Expression Encoder and encoded into the video, or they can be defined within your ASP.NET markup. Here's an example of the latter:

```
<asp:MediaPlayer ID="MediaPlayer1" ScaleMode="Stretch" runat="server"
    MediaSource="~/ClientBin/balls.wmv" Height="325px"
MediaSkinSource="~/Classic.xaml" Width="461px"
OnClientChapterStarted="doChapter" >
  <Chapters>
    <asp:MediaChapter Position="1.0" Title="Chapter1" />
    <asp:MediaChapter Position="2.0" Title="Chapter2" />
  </Chapters>
</asp:MediaPlayer>
```

When a chapter is reached, the JavaScript function defined within the *OnClientChapterStarted* attribute will fire.

You can track what is going on with your media using the *currentState* property of the *MediaElement* control. This is covered in detail in Chapter 11, and it is a value that represents the current state of your media playback, with states such as "playing," "buffering," "paused," and so on. If you want to set up an event handler that fires whenever the state changes, for example, you use the *OnCurrentStateChanged* attribute of the ASP.NET control to define the desired JavaScript handler.

Markers are similar to chapters in that they are pieces of metadata that are encoded into the video stream. By default, all markers are also defined as chapters. You can specify the Java-

Script function to fire when a marker is reached with the *OnMarkerReached* attribute of the ASP.NET control.

In addition, you can specify what to do upon opening, closing, and failing of the media using the *OnMediaOpened*, *OnMediaEnded*, and *OnMediaFailed* attributes, respectively.

Summary

In this chapter, you took a look at the two ASP.NET controls that come with the Silverlight SDK. The general *Silverlight* control is used to manage and deploy your Silverlight content using a server-side programming paradigm. The *MediaPlayer* control is used to deliver skinned media content to your clients. These are particularly useful productivity tools if you are using ASP.NET to deliver your Silverlight site, and it is well worth your time to check them out and learn more about them. In the next chapter, you will look at a new and exciting addition to Silverlight 2—support for dynamic languages.

Chapter 14
Using Dynamic Languages in Silverlight 2

Silverlight 2 adds support for the use of *dynamic* languages, which are defined as programming languages that execute many features at *run time* that other languages, such as C#, execute at *compile* time. Such behaviors include things such as extending objects and definitions, modifying the type system, and more. This approach is designed to give dynamic languages a simple approach for learning through a run-evaluate-print loop with lots of trial and error as you develop.

Silverlight 2 supports three of the more popular dynamic languages: Ruby, Python, and Dynamic JavaScript. This book is written to the Silverlight beta 2 specification, which does not include a Microsoft Visual Studio 2008 project template, but the SDK does provide a tool, Chiron.exe, that allows you to work with dynamic languages.

The dynamic language initiative from Microsoft is open source and is available on the CodePlex Web site located at *http://www.codeplex.com/sdlsdk*. In this chapter, you will explore building some basic applications for Silverlight 2 with dynamic languages. It isn't intended to be a learning tool for the languages themselves, but the programs are fairly straightforward, so you'll be able to figure out what they're doing even if you aren't an expert in the particular language.

This chapter is intended solely as a primer in dynamic languages and how to use them in Silverlight. You'll spend most of your time in this chapter touring Visual Studio and learning how you can use it to create IronPython, IronRuby, and managed JavaScript applications in Silverlight, as well as how to integrate Chiron.exe into Visual Studio. Later on, you'll tour the famous Silverlight clock sample and find out how it was implemented in Ruby.

Your First Silverlight IronPython Application

The Chiron tool is easiest to use if you have a specific application directory structure set up for your application. In this section, we'll go through how to do this step by step.

First, launch Visual Studio, and create an *empty* Web site by selecting New Web Site from the File menu. You'll see Empty Web Site as an option on the New Web Site dialog box, as shown in Figure 14-1.

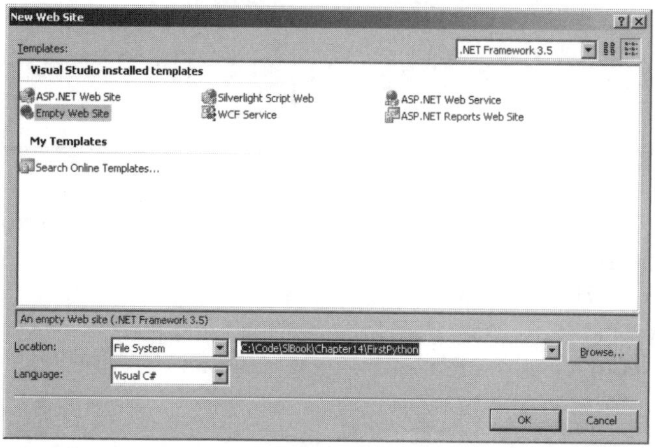

FIGURE 14-1 New Web Site dialog box.

This will create an empty directory that Visual Studio can access as a Web site. You will be using Chiron to run the site, but you will find that creating the pages, code, and so on is easier in Visual Studio.

From the Solution, right-click the project folder, and select Add New Item—this will open the Add New Item dialog box that you can use to create a new HTML page. Select the HTML page option, and give it the name Default.html. See Figure 14-2.

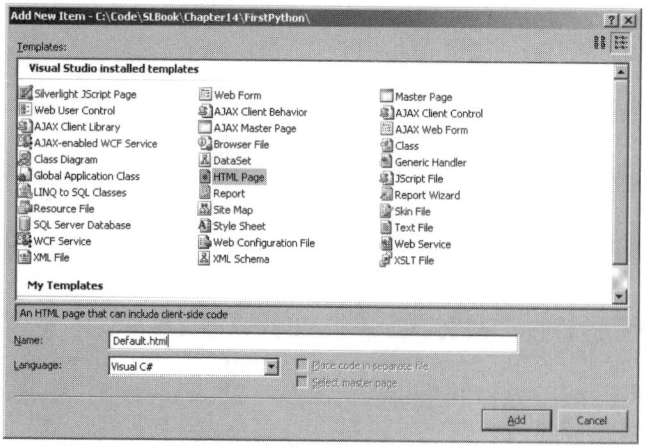

FIGURE 14-2 Add a new item to your site.

This will give you a basic HTML page, which you will need to edit to turn it into a page that will host the Silverlight application. Following is the code for such a page:

```
<html xmlns="http://www.w3.org/1999/xhtml" >
<head>
  <title>Dynamic Silverlight Test Page </title>
  <style type="text/css">
```

```
    html, body {
      height: 100%;
      overflow: auto;
    }
    body {
      padding: 0;
      margin: 0;
    }
    #silverlightControlHost {
      height: 100%;
    }
  </style>
</head>
<body>
  <div id="silverlightControlHost">
   <object data="data:application/x-silverlight,"
    type="application/x-silverlight-2-b1"
    width="100%" height="100%">
      <param name="source" value="app.xap"/>
      <param name="background" value="white" />
      <param name="windowless" value="true" />
    </object>
    <iframe style='visibility:hidden;height:0;width:0;border:0px'></iframe>
  </div>
</body>
```

This uses the *<object>* tag approach to host Silverlight in the page. This is a very simplified example, so it doesn't include the code to provide an install experience if Silverlight isn't present on the system. For more details on how to do this, refer to Chapter 6, "The Silverlight Browser Control."

Note the *source* parameter, which is set to *app.xap*. Chiron will build this for you, as you'll see in a moment. In order for it to have this name, your code file will need to be called app. First, you'll look at how to build your application with IronPython and an app.py file, and later you'll see how to create the same functionality with IronRuby and Dynamic JavaScript.

Next, create a directory within your Web site called app. Within this, select Add New Item, and then select the XML File template and call the file app.xaml.

Here's some simple XAML that you can put into this file:

```
<UserControl
        xmlns="http://schemas.microsoft.com/client/2007"
        xmlns:x="http://schemas.microsoft.com/winfx/2006/xaml"
        x:Class="System.Windows.Controls.UserControl"
        x:Name="Page"
        >
  <TextBlock
      x:Name="txtMessage" TextWrapping="Wrap"
      Foreground="Black" Text="Hello World," >
  </TextBlock>
</UserControl>
```

This defines a simple *UserControl* object that contains a *TextBlock* called *txtMessage*. This *TextBlock* contains the text "Hello World,"—note that it ends with a comma. You'll see why in a moment.

Now let's add the IronPython code file. Again, right-click the app folder within your Web site, and select Add New Item. In the dialog box, select Text File and call it app.py (py is the extension for Python).

As a quick check, Figure 14-3 shows what your solution should look like at this point.

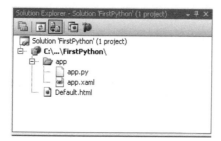

FIGURE 14-3 Your solution structure.

Now you can edit your Python code file to make it do something more interesting. Here's the code:

```python
from System.Windows import Application
from System.Windows.Controls import UserControl

def handleClick(sender, eventArgs):
    sender.Text = sender.Text + " from Python!"

class App:
    def __init__(self):
        self.scene = \
          Application.Current.LoadRootVisual(UserControl(),
                                             "app.xaml")

    def start(self):
        self.scene.txtMessage.MouseLeftButtonUp += handleClick

App().start()
```

If you've been writing Silverlight applications in C# or VB, the syntax will be somewhat familiar to you. For example, the line

```python
from System.Windows import Application
```

is equivalent to the C#

```csharp
using System.Windows;
```

and then a reference to the *Application* class in code.

The code then defines a Python class called *App* and sets the *scene* object for this *App* by loading the XAML file that you defined earlier. As part of this class definition, it defines the startup event hander with

```
def start(self):
```

and specifies the code to execute within this handler. This code defines the event handler for the *MouseLeftButtonUp* event on the *TextBlock* control called *txtMessage* that you defined earlier. The event hander is called *handleClick*.

The event handler code itself is as follows:

```
def handleClick(sender, eventArgs):
    sender.Text = sender.Text + " from Python!"
```

This adds the text "from Python!" to the end of the *Text* property of its sender (which in this case is the *TextBlock*) upon being called.

To run this application, you'll use Chiron. You can configure Visual Studio to launch Chiron by right-clicking the project file in Solution Explorer (note that you must use the Project file and not the Solution file—the Project file is usually the first child of the Solution) and selecting Property Pages from the shortcut menu.

From the Property pages, select Start Options, and then select Start External Program. Use the ellipsis button to browse to the location of Chiron.exe, which should be found in C:\Program Files\Microsoft SDKs\Silverlight\v2.0\Tools\Chiron\Chiron.exe.

Enter **/b** in the Command Line Arguments setting, and then enter the location of the Web site in the Working Directory setting. Figure 14-4 shows an example of this.

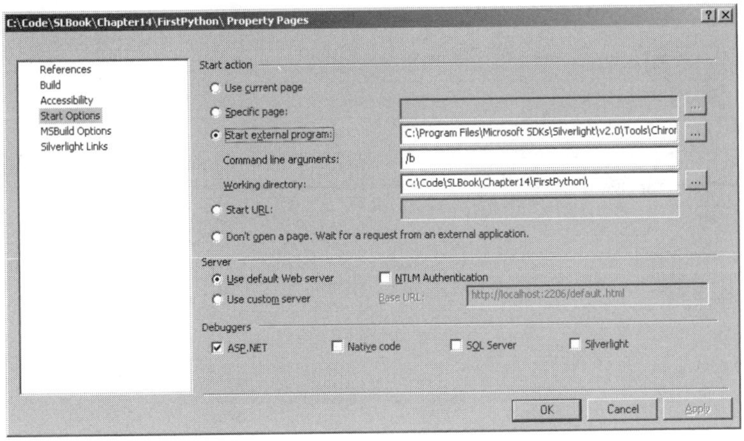

FIGURE 14-4 Configuring Visual Studio to use Chiron.

Now you can execute your dynamic Silverlight application by pressing F5 in Visual Studio. Chiron will launch, and you'll see evidence of this in a command prompt window that looks like Figure 14-5.

FIGURE 14-5 Chiron being executed by Visual Studio.

This shows you that the application is accessed via *http://localhost:2060*. Visual Studio will also launch a browser at this address, which gives you a listing of the files within the Web directory, as you can see in Figure 14-6.

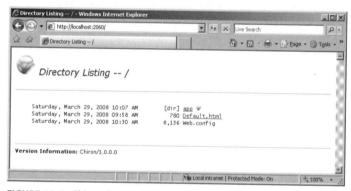

FIGURE 14-6 Chiron directory listing.

Select Default.html to see your dynamic Silverlight application. The "Hello World," message will display in the browser, as shown in Figure 14-7.

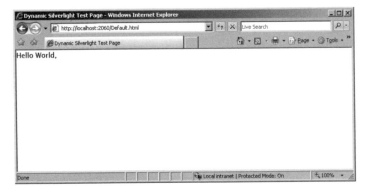

FIGURE 14-7 Your first Silverlight Python application.

Now, if you click the "Hello World," text, the additional message "from Python!" will be added to the block, as shown in Figure 14-8.

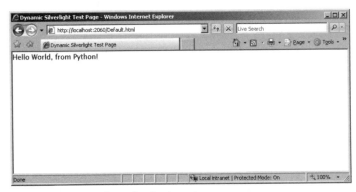

FIGURE 14-8 Dynamic application in action.

Although this is an extremely simple application, it demonstrates how the Dynamic Language Runtime works in Silverlight and how you can configure Visual Studio to use dynamic languages. In the next section, you'll learn about how you can use IronRuby and managed JavaScript in the same application.

Using Ruby and JavaScript

In the previous section, you stepped through the process used to configure Visual Studio to build dynamic language applications in IronPython. Because the Dynamic Language Runtime also supports Ruby and Dynamic JavaScript, we'll look at how you can use them in the same application in this section.

Using Ruby

To begin the process using Ruby, first you need to create a similar project structure, including an HTML file and an XAML file, to the one you created for IronPython in the previous section. In this case, within the app folder, you don't create an app.py file, but instead create an app.rb file for your Ruby code. Also make sure that you set up the project settings to launch Chiron the same way as you did in the previous example. (Look back at Figure 14-4 for details on how to do this.)

Edit the app.rb so that it contains this IronRuby code:

```ruby
include System::Windows
include System::Windows::Controls

def handleClick(sender, eventArgs)
  sender.text = "Hello World, from Ruby!"
end

class App
  def initialize
      @scene = Application.Current.LoadRootVisual(UserControl.new(),
                                                 "app.xaml")
  end

  def start
      @scene.find_name('txtMessage').mouse_left_button_up
      { |sender, args| handleClick(sender, args) }
  end
end
App.new.start
```

As you can see, it is very similar to the example in IronPython. This includes the *System.Windows* and *System.Windows.Controls* namespaces. It then defines a *handleClick* event handler to change the text whenever it is called.

Then the class, called *App*, is defined. The class constructor loads the XAML and uses it to initialize the class, and the *Start* event wires up the event handler to the *TextBlock* defined in the XAML and named *txtMessage*.

Now, when you run the application, you'll get the same results—the *TextBlock* renders "Hello World," and when the user clicks the text, it adds "from Ruby!"

Using Dynamic JavaScript

To use JavaScript, follow the same routine as you did in the previous two examples; that is, create a Web site in Visual Studio, and then add the HTML and XAML files to it. Remember that you also need to configure the project to use Chiron. You can see how to do this by referring to Figure 14-4.

This time, instead of app.py or app.rb files, you will add an app.jsx file to the app directory. Edit the contents of the app.jsx file so that it contains the following JavaScript code:

```
Import("System.Windows.Application")
Import("System.Windows.Controls.UserControl")

function handleClick(sender, eventArgs) {
    sender.Text = sender.Text + " from Dynamic JavaScript";
}

function App() {
    this.scene =
      Application.Current.LoadRootVisual(new UserControl(),
                                "app.xaml")
}

App.prototype.start = function() {
    this.scene.txtMessage.MouseLeftButtonUp += handleClick
}


app = new App
app.start()
```

As you can see, the code is still very familiar. Managed JavaScript uses the *Import* statement to add a reference to the *SystemWindows.Application* and *System.Windows.Controls.UserControl* classes. In JavaScript, the application itself is a function to which you add properties, so the *scene* is a member of the *App* function, and it is defined by loading the XAML. The *MouseLeftButtonUp* event is handled by the *handleClick* function, and this is defined in the *start* function for the application.

The *handleClick*, as in the earlier examples, adds specific text, in this case, "from Dynamic JavaScript", to the string in the *txtMessage TextBlock* that is defined in the XAML.

The results are essentially the same as those for the two previous examples. The application displays a "Hello World" message, and then it is amended with additional text when the user clicks on the message.

A More Complex Example

The first Silverlight sample to see the light of day (back when Silverlight was called WPF/E) is the clock example. You can see what it looks like in Figure 14-9.

This is a great sample of a Silverlight application, because it demonstrates many of the principles of programming in Silverlight. The clock itself requires no programming to operate—it is all managed by Silverlight animations, and all you need to do is initialize the clock hands to the starting position based on the system time.

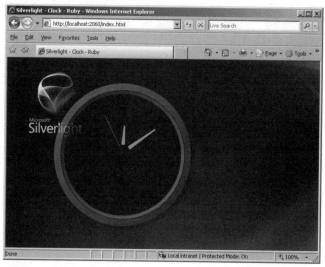

FIGURE 14-9 Silverlight clock.

Let's first look at the XAML for the clock. Note that this XAML is abbreviated just to show the three clock hands and their animations:

```
<Canvas x:Class="System.Windows.Controls.Canvas"
    xmlns="http://schemas.microsoft.com/client/2007"
    xmlns:x="http://schemas.microsoft.com/winfx/2006/xaml"
    Opacity="0" x:Name="parentCanvas">

  <Canvas.Triggers>
    <EventTrigger RoutedEvent="Canvas.Loaded">
      <EventTrigger.Actions>
        <BeginStoryboard>
          <Storyboard>
            <DoubleAnimation x:Name="hour_animation"
                Storyboard.TargetName="hourHandTransform"
                Storyboard.TargetProperty="Angle"
                From="180" To="540"
                Duration="12:0:0"
                RepeatBehavior="Forever"/>
            <DoubleAnimation x:Name="minute_animation"
                Storyboard.TargetName="minuteHandTransform"
                Storyboard.TargetProperty="Angle"
                From="180" To="540"
                Duration="1:0:0"
                RepeatBehavior="Forever"/>
            <DoubleAnimation x:Name="second_animation"
                Storyboard.TargetName="secondHandTransform"
                Storyboard.TargetProperty="Angle"
                From="180" To="540"
                Duration="0:1:0"
                RepeatBehavior="Forever"/>
          </Storyboard>
```

```
            </BeginStoryboard>
          </EventTrigger.Actions>
        </EventTrigger>
      </Canvas.Triggers>

      <!-- Hour hand -->
      <Path Data="M -4, 16 1 3 40 3 0 2 -40 z" Fill="white">
        <Path.RenderTransform>
          <TransformGroup>
            <RotateTransform x:Name="hourHandTransform"
                    Angle="180"/>
            <TranslateTransform X="150.5" Y="145"/>
          </TransformGroup>
        </Path.RenderTransform>
      </Path>

      <!-- Minute hand -->
      <Path Data="M -4, 16 1 3 70 3 0 2 -70 z" Fill="white">
        <Path.RenderTransform>
          <TransformGroup>
            <RotateTransform x:Name="minuteHandTransform"
                    Angle="180"/>
            <TranslateTransform X="150.5" Y="145"/>
          </TransformGroup>
        </Path.RenderTransform>
      </Path>

      <!-- Second hand -->
      <Path Data="M -1, 16 1 0 70 2 0 0 -70 z" Fill="red">
        <Path.RenderTransform>
          <TransformGroup>
            <RotateTransform x:Name="secondHandTransform"
                    Angle="180"/>
            <TranslateTransform X="150.5" Y="145"/>
          </TransformGroup>
        </Path.RenderTransform>
      </Path>

    </Canvas>
```

The XAML begins with the three animations stored within their storyboards. Because you can think of the hands of the clock as lines that rotate, you can see that these are *DoubleAnimation* types that are affecting the angle of the rotation. For more about animation and how it works in XAML, see Chapter 5, "XAML Transformation and Animation."

The thing to take note of in the animations is their names. They are called *hour_animation*, *minute_animation*, and *second_animation*, respectively. Remember these when you look at the code. Each animation targets a named transform where the hour, minute, and second target the transforms called *hourHandTransform, minuteHandTransform,* and *secondHandTransform*, respectively. You can see these transforms farther down in the XAML. Each of the hands is implemented as a *Path*, and these paths have transforms associated with them that are called by the names that you saw targeted previously.

So, the animations will begin on *Canvas.Loaded* and will repeat forever, moving the hands through the 360 degrees of the clock over the appropriate length of time. But how can they be initialized to represent the current time on the clock? That's where your code comes in.

The code for the clock is in two Ruby modules; the first is a helper class that was built by the Silverlight Dynamic Languages team to share across all your Ruby-based applications. It's listed here:

```
include System::Windows
include System::Windows::Controls
include System::Windows::Media

class SilverlightApplication
  def application
    Application.current
  end

  def self.use_xaml(options = {})
    options = {:type => UserControl, :name => "app"}.merge(options)
      Application.current.load_root_visual(
        options[:type].new, "#{options[:name]}.xaml")
  end

  def root
    application.root_visual
  end

  def method_missing(m)
    root.send(m)
  end
end

class FrameworkElement
  def method_missing(m)
    find_name(m.to_s.to_clr_string)
  end
end
```

This defines a number of helper functions and objects, including the following:

- **application**   Points to the current application (simply abbreviating *Application.current*)

- **root**   Points to the root visual, namely the top-level element within the XAML

- **method_missing**   Handles the translation of a method name into a *clr* string format to aid in programming

- **use_xaml**   Manages the loading of the XAML into the Visual Tree

The code for the clock application uses the *root* and *use_xaml* helper functions, so let's take a look at it:

```
require 'Silverlight'

class Clock < SilverlightApplication
  use_xaml :type => Canvas

  def start
    d = Time.now()
    root.hour_animation.from    = from_angle d.hour, 1, d.minute/2
    root.hour_animation.to      = to_angle   d.hour
    root.minute_animation.from  = from_angle d.minute
    root.minute_animation.to    = to_angle   d.minute
    root.second_animation.from  = from_angle d.second
    root.second_animation.to    = to_angle   d.second
  end

  def from_angle(time, divisor = 5, offset = 0)
    ((time / (12.0 * divisor)) * 360) + offset + 180
  end

  def to_angle(time)
    from_angle(time) + 360
  end
end

Clock.new.start
```

Note that the first line of this code is

```
require 'Silverlight'
```

which means that the Silverlight.rb file must be included because we are going to be deriving our application class from it.

Then we define a *Clock* class that derives from *SilverlightApplication* (defined in Silverlight.rb) like this:

```
class Clock < SilverlightApplication
```

The *use_xaml* function from *SilverlightApplication* is called, and we specify that the type of XAML we are using is *<Canvas>* based. This is a throwback to Silverlight 1, when all XAML had *<Canvas>* as its root.

Next comes the *start* function, which will be called by this function after the initialization is completed. It gets the current time using the *Time.now* function and then uses this to figure out the *from* and *to* values for the three animations. Remember when we looked at the animations and they were called *hour_animation*, *minute_animation*, and *second_animation*? Now you can see how they are used. In Ruby, you call a function with its name, followed by a space, followed by a comma-separated list of parameters, so the angle representing the current *hour* is derived by calling the *from_angle* and passing it the appropriate parameters, which in this case are the current hour, 1, and the current minute divided by 2. The reason for dividing the minute by two is that the 0-degree case for the transform is actually pointing downward, so we want to offset it by180 degrees and thus divide the current minute by 2 to "flip" the angle that the *minute* value will give.

You can see the function here:

```
def from_angle(time, divisor = 5, offset = 0)
    ((time / (12.0 * divisor)) * 360) + offset + 180
End
```

Looking back at the code, you'll see that the start condition simply uses this function to calculate what the appropriate transformation angles to start animating from are and then assigns those to the *from* property of the animation. Similarly, the value that you are animating *to* is 360 degrees plus the current *from* value. Thus, the transformation will sweep the hand through 360 degrees from the starting value over the appropriate time frame (24 hours for the hour hand, 1 hour for the minute hand, and 1 minute for the second hand).

Finally, the application is started by creating a new instance of the *Clock* class and starting it:

```
Clock.new.start
```

Thus, using Ruby, you've now created a functional Silverlight application—a working animated clock.

Summary

In this chapter, you were introduced to dynamic languages and saw how to build a simple *Hello World* application using IronPython, IronRuby, and managed JavaScript. You saw how to configure Visual Studio to work with the Chiron tool that is used to build and manage the running of dynamic applications.

This is just a simple illustration of what is possible, however—enough to get you going and then inspire you to keep experimenting with dynamic languages for yourself.

And with that, this book comes to an end. Before you picked up this book, you might have been curious about Silverlight and what can be done with it. When I wrote this book, I did not want to take the approach of creating an exhaustive and encyclopedic reference, but instead I wanted to present all the great features of Silverlight 2 in an approachable way so that you could pick it up, select any chapter, work your way through it, and by the end understand what is involved in the technology—and have the confidence to go even further with what you have learned.

I hope you have had as much fun working through these chapters as I had writing them!

Index

Z

What do you think of this book?

We want to hear from you!

Do you have a few minutes to participate in a brief online survey?

Microsoft is interested in hearing your feedback so we can continually improve our books and learning resources for you.

To participate in our survey, please visit:

www.microsoft.com/learning/booksurvey/

...and enter this book's ISBN-10 or ISBN-13 number (located above barcode on back cover*). As a thank-you to survey participants in the United States and Canada, each month we'll randomly select five respondents to win one of five $100 gift certificates from a leading online merchant. At the conclusion of the survey, you can enter the drawing by providing your e-mail address, which will be used for prize notification only.

Thanks in advance for your input. Your opinion counts!

* Where to find the ISBN on back cover

ISBN-13: 000-0-0000-0000-0
ISBN-10: 0-0000-0000-0

Example only. Each book has unique ISBN.